WOODBURY

A VIEW FROM THE BEACON

Ursula W. Brighouse

To

the pupils of Woodbury Primary School, past and present, and that includes my son, Henry, who drew many of the illustrations for this book.

First edition 1981
Second edition 1998

Published by Ursula W. Brighouse
Woodbury, Devon

ISBN 0 9533160 0 9

Typeset & Printed in Great Britain by Penwell Ltd., Callington, Cornwall.

Contents

List of Illustrations

Front Cover: A view from the Beacon, drawn by Henry W. Brighouse.

(see page 13)

(see page 13)

Introduction

A View from the Beacon

Stand on Woodbury Beacon on a clear, sunny day and you will be rewarded with one of the finest views in England. Here, 580 ft. above sea level, is the highest point in the parish and the oldest man-made feature of its landscape. Before you is spread out half of Devon and Woodbury's place in it is immediately known.

The eye, sweeping round clockwise from the mouth of the Exe estuary, takes in the red cliffs of Dawlish and Teignmouth, the highest points of Dartmoor sticking up in blue peaks above the straight line of the Haldon Hills, the great green basin of the Exe valley hemmed in by the red hills of mid-Devon; to the north-east, framed by the Honiton Gap in the Blackdown Ridge, is the familiar and favourite silhouette of Dumpdon — a prehistoric hill-fort crowned with beech trees; to the east rises Pinn Beacon with the sea beyond and in the distance Portland Bill, looking like an elongated island, sixty miles away in Dorset. This is the grand setting in which the village of Woodbury finds itself.

But it is the great prehistoric earthwork known as Woodbury Castle which dominates the immediate scene. Brooding darkly over the village in a way which sometimes seems positively sinister, it is easy to see why it imparted its name to the first English settlement. Though most early spellings of Woodbury give "Wodeberi", or something like it, there are some variations which give "Wodnesberi". Is it just possible that our early ancestors imagined that the pagan god Woden lived in that dark and fearful place, built by giants long ago?

From our vantage-point on the Beacon most of the 6790-odd acres that comprise the parish of Woodbury can be seen. The southern boundary is the River Exe itself and one can pick out the fine trees that surround Nutwell Court, the tall buildings of the Royal Marine Infantry Training Centre and the white houses of Exton, all within the southern perimeter of the parish. At the opposite end of the parish the northern boundary follows for some distance the Exeter-Sidmouth A3052 (a Roman road) identifiable from here by the glint of the sun on passing traffic.

The east and west boundaries are less obvious today. In the west Woodbury was once divided from Clyst St. George by a no-man's-land of wild, wet scrubby heathlands which eventually gave their names to Postlake, Heathfield and Moor Lane on the Woodbury side of the boundary, and Bushhayes and Mariannepool on the Clyst St. George side. Even today, after centuries of cultivation, bracken and gorse flourish in the hedgebanks of this area and would soon take over again if allowed to do so.

The eastern boundary is even more nebulous for much of what is known as Woodbury Common is in reality made up of the commons of many parishes of which Woodbury is only one. Close scrutiny of the 2½ ins. Ordnance Survey map is here required to trace the parish boundary. There is a point of great interest where the boundary crosses the Otterton road (B3179), for astride the boundary are two pairs of round barrows, one pair on either side of the road, and the boundary has given its name to Boundridge Wood. The road here is prehistoric, as are the barrows which no doubt formed a handy and indisputable landmark when the bounds were originally being drawn.

For most of its long recorded life Woodbury Common has been an important grazing ground but no animals graze the Common nowadays. It is a huge playground for the work-weary folk from a wide area of East Devon and Exeter — as well as countless holiday-makers in the summer. It is an area beloved of naturalists, horse-riders, picnickers and kite-fliers, and remembered with nostalgia by a whole generation of soldiers and marines, both British and American, who camped and trained here in the Second World War.

The Beacon has seen life come and go. Every age has left a mark that can be seen from here. The hill where we stand was man-made at least 3500 years ago. How did they make it, with what tools and for what purpose? Does it house the last remains of a local chieftain and his family? Little is known of these ancient people and very few excavations have been carried out on the Common. But that people lived here before Woodbury existed is certain. Besides the great earthworks and the small barrows they have left us flint arrow-heads, bronze axe-heads and fragments of pottery.

Prehistoric man looked down on a great sea of trees which stretched from the edges of the Common to the bank of the Exe. Vestiges of the forest can still be seen clinging to the deep ravines which have never been worth clearing. Ancient, well-worn trackways criss-crossed the forest where now the Otterton Road (B3179) and Woodbury Castle road (B3180) carry modern traffic.

By the time the first English settlers arrived soon after 600 AD and started clearing the land at the north end of the parish there may have been nobody left on the Common to see the blue smoke rise and the little islands of cultivation appear in the forest. Those early settlers embanked their first fields on the lower slopes of the Common in the Hogsbrook area and their banks are probably there to this day. If the number of different species of shrubs in the hedgerow is anything to go by, some of those hedgebanks may well go back to Celtic times.

When the Domesday Book was compiled in 1086 A.D. the manor of Woodbury consisted of some 3200 acres of which roughly half was under the plough. Much of the ploughland lay in huge fields devoid of hedgebanks, punctuated here and there by pockets of uncleared woodland and pasture enclosures and still wrapped around by the forest.

By 1300 Exton and Ebford has been opened up and it was not long before watchers from the Beacon could make out the shapes of many little fishing boats pushing and bobbing their way out of Exton to fish in the waters of the estuary and the open sea beyond. From here also could be obtained a good view of the tower of St. Swithin's church as it rose up out of its scaffolding in 1409. With a west wind the sound of the bells would have carried as far as the Beacon.

Woodbury Wood, that great green band that divided the Common from the farmland, was slowly whittled away until by 1526 only 160 acres of it remained. The common itself presented a very different view from the one we know so well, for it was the grazing ground for thousands of sheep who cropped it closely and inhibited the growth of bracken, heather and gorse.

The Woodbury men who manned the Beacon to watch for the Spanish Armada in 1588 saw an agricultural pattern not so vastly different from that with which we are familiar. The common ploughland had given way to the patchwork of small fields bounded by hedgbanks and many more farms had appeared away from the village.

The next two hundred years saw the building or rebuilding of most of the cob farmhouses, both in the village streets and in the farmland around. Many of these houses have now disappeared for good, like Sparkeshayes, Scorches, Scotsmore and Dagworthy's, all visible from here. And the turnpiking of the roads brought a regular coach, with four in hand, within 20 yards of the Beacon as it rumbled over the now-lost London road.

By the beginning of the nineteenth century the scene was beginning to be sprinkled with the first red brick, and the arrival of leisured, well-to-do people brought white stuccoed "gentlemen's residences", such as Oakhayes, which added a touch of elegance and sophistication to the village. During the troubled times of the Napoleonic and the First World Wars, the Common provided a vast camping and training area for the army. And the 1930s saw the start of Blackhill sand and gravel quarries which have ripped apart the Common and provided 50 people with their livelihoods.

Agriculture is still the main industry as it always has been, though it now employs fewer men. The pattern has changed here, as elsewhere. Farms have been amalgamated into larger units and while some redundant farmhouses have disappeared, others have been done up by newcomers: mechanization has replaced both the horse and the farm labourer, whose tied cottage now houses university students or summer visitors. Many farm animals spend their lives in large sheds instead of in fields or farm-yards — though in the last few years sheep have made a welcome return to the landscape, thanks to European Common Market policy.

The saddest physical change that Woodbury has seen in many centuries of change has been the loss of elm trees from the hedgerows through the calamitous spread of Dutch Elm Disease. Woodbury is fortunate to have other trees (oak, beech and birch for example) but there is no substitute for the tall elm and the landscape has been diminished and trivialized by their loss.

There has been much building in recent years — more especially in Woodbury itself. Some of the old Saxon strips are now covered by estates of bungalows and a stream of cars takes many of their owners to work daily in Exeter seven miles away. The newcomers have brought their own ideas and enthusiasms with them and have injected new life into the shrinking agricultural population. They are a part of Woodbury's history, as are those whose surnames stride through the pages of the parish registers. The pattern changes: life goes on.

Despite development, mechanization and pollution it is still a green and pleasant land. One can still find a brook babbling over the pebbles, or pick primroses to the sound of the lark overhead. It is a good place to live. The climate is soft; the soil is fertile; recreational possibilities abound. More than anything, perhaps, one senses here the feeling of continuity, of being on the conveyor belt of time – and the stability that comes from it. A country without a past is like a man without a memory. All of the past has gone into making the present what it is.

1.
The Mists of Time

A man is walking over a freshly-ploughed field just north of Oakhayes Lane. It is late afternoon and the slanting autumn sunshine creates a rainbow over the Common where the recent rain is still falling. But our man is not looking at the rainbow: he walks slowly, looking at the ground immediately in front of his feet.

He pauses: the sun glances on a stone washed clean by the shower. He stoops and picks it up and examines it intently. To the inexperienced eye it looks much like any other piece of local flint (or 'chert' as it is known)

but a closer inspection reveals that the sides have been expertly knapped to remove flakes from which small, sharp tools can be made. As the flint core lies there in the palm of his hand he experiences a strange sensation: he is the first person to have handled it since the Stone Age man, squatting on his heels on this very spot, maybe six thousand years ago, worked it to make barbs, scrapers, knives and arrowheads.

It was somewhere about that time, 4000 BC, that these Neolithic people from across the Channel began arriving on these shores in search of pastures new. Here in the land we call Woodbury they found dense broadleaf woodland in which could be found most of the wildlife we know today, together with a great many creatures no longer here, such as wolves, bears, boar and auroch (wild cattle). It was sparsely populated with nomadic people who roamed wildly, hunting the abundant wild game with bows and arrows. With stone hammers they would crack the bones to extract the marrow. Women and children gathered edible leaves, roots and fungi and harvested nuts, fruits and seeds in the autumn. Winter living must have been very frugal indeed and, without agriculture, the land could not have supported a very large population. They left little behind them here in Woodbury to tell us of their daily lives.

The newcomers brought with them a very different way of life, for they were the first farmers. Not only could they clear the land by chopping down trees with stone axes but they brought with them domestic animals

– mainly cattle and sheep – which further helped to clear the land by grazing and trampling. On the cleared areas they planted the seed-corn they had brought with them. This was a wild form of wheat called Spelt (Triticum spelta), still widely grown in the Middle East and containing a higher protein content than modern wheats. It was sown on a surface barely scratched with the digging stick – as it still done in many primitive societies.

The Neolithic people lived in settled communities and built themselves houses of wood, wattle and turf. Some huts had pits in them for winter storage of corn and such things as crab-apples and hazel nuts. In the centre of the house was a hearth and the smoke made its way out through the thatch. Cooking was mainly done on flat, hot stones, though small pits containing hot charcoal were also probably used, and maybe coarse cooking-pots. The fire meant that meat, fish and fungi could be hung in the roof and cured by smoking, adding greatly to the diet available in winter. Community effort, too, could provide many amenities, such as coppicing hazel to build compounds in which livestock and people alike could be protected from the depredations of wild animals.

One of the crafts that came with the domestic animals was the spinning and weaving of sheep's wool. Sheep were the most numerous of the animals found here and it is likely that the Neolithic farmers had trained dogs to help them. Stones, thought to be spinning whorls and loom weights, sometimes turn up in the locality.

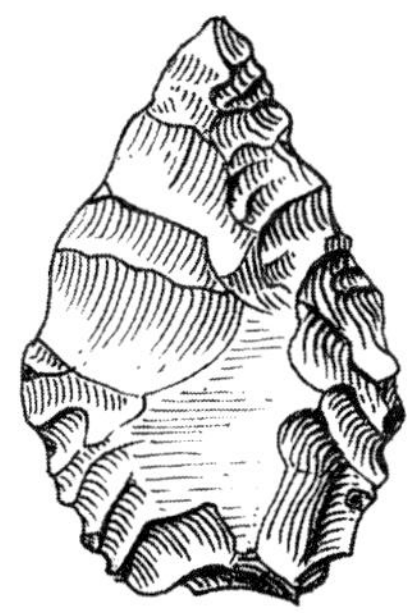

The weaving of cloth would give the local inhabitants a form of "currency" to exchange for articles imported from other areas. Not content with the poor quality of the local chert, they imported the very superior flints from Beer (some ten miles Eastward along the coast). Beer flints went far and wide but whether they were worked in Beer by experts and exported as finished goods (most likely) or whether our locals worked them from the raw flint is not known: but some of those found on Woodbury Common look like specialist work rather than "do-it-yourself" jobs.

Flints were not the only goods to come into the area. The occasional stone quern (for grinding corn) made of Dartmoor granite has been found, and coarse pottery not made in this area. Trade on this scale could only be carried on with a well-developed network of trackways. Two of these very ancient routes crossed each other at Four Firs, the present B3179 leading via Yettington to Beer while the B3180 ran along the ridge of the Common to link up with a countryside system of trackways.

In the course of the next two thousand years the impetus these Neolithic people had brought with them slowed down and Southwest Britain became something of a backwater of civilization. During those centuries the Mediterranean regions were seeing the wonders of Tutankhamen's Tomb in Egypt and the building of Solomon's temple in Jerusalem, with all its elaborate metalwork so graphically described in the Bible. Metal working was unknown here. It was time for another wave of colonizers with new skills.

The new people from the Continent started to arrive in Britain about 2000 BC. They did not constitute an invasion. The first few were likely to have been skilled metal prospectors who knew how to make bronze by smelting together the ores of copper and tin. They settled in the areas where these ores naturally occurred, the nearest sites to Woodbury being the Devon-Cornwall border and South Wales. But for most people the old way of life went on unchanged and stone implements continued in general use for many centuries. The new bronze implements were obviously something of a luxury, for most of the ores had to be obtained by deep mining.

As time went by more and more people crossed the Channel bringing with them improved methods of farming which led to a considerable increase in population. A new social order was emerging. Distinct tribes developed in the regions, each having its own aristocracy at the top and its slave-labourers at the bottom, who could be employed in constructing protective earthworks and elaborate burial mounds. Woodbury Common has a dozen or so of these round barrows, most notably the Beacon itself and two others near it, four barrows astride the Yettington Road (B3179) at Boundbridge Wood, and possibly (but doubtfully) the four mounds at Four Firs. One mound excavated in the Yettington area revealed grave goods, including a battle-axe made in Shropshire, while another, South of the Castle, contained the remains of pottery thought to be the urn in which the cremated bones were buried, together with a bronze dagger and a stone battle-axe.

The people buried in these barrows were the V.I.P.s of the tribe, an indication that religious beliefs and rituals were becoming important – at least for those who could afford them! The earlier tradition of burying the dead was replaced by cremation (which sadly destroyed much evidence) but the ceremonies must have been impressive. The body was burnt on a funeral pyre which lit up the night sky and could be seen for many miles. Watchers on the other hill-tops would know what had happened.

Religious ritual is also underlined by the discovery in recent years of woodhenges. Everyone is familiar with Stonehenge, the finest Bronze Age ritual monument in Europe, but woodhenges are being identified by aerial photography and represent an exciting leap forward in our knowledge of the period. The most recently discovered woodhenge is in Somerset – an extraordinary complex made of huge tree trunks, rivalling Stonehenge itself in size – but a woodhenge has been identified near Crediton, in that cluster of places with the name Nymet ('Nemeton' is Celtic for 'sacred grove') – Nothing now remains but the darkened earth where the timber posts have rotted and the shadow of the outer ditch, but its sheer size (60 x 70m) must mean that it was used for special occasions and designed to cater for people from a wide area. Such an occasion might have been mourning for a dead chieftain or electing his successor: or for religious ceremonies such as the Summer Solstice, combined with, perhaps, a trade fair together with feasting and dancing – in fact much like the medieval fairs based on saints days. There may be other woodhenges nearer home waiting to be discovered.[1]

The Woodbury area abounds in artifacts from the Bronze Age, not all of them bronze but all of them interesting. In 1986 three gold bracelets were found near Colaton Raleigh. Of fairly plain design, they lay one inside another, as though they had been in a bag hidden temporarily and forgotten, a goldsmith's hoard, perhaps, but not local. A stone arm-guard, or bracer, found in 1983 within 200 metres of the Castle, is a rare item (Beaker) and was worn with a leather strap to protect the forearm from the bow string. And the finely crafted, well-preserved bronze axe-head found by Mr Harry Stokes while ploughing just below the Common in 1960 was probably made in South Wales.[2] These items would have been

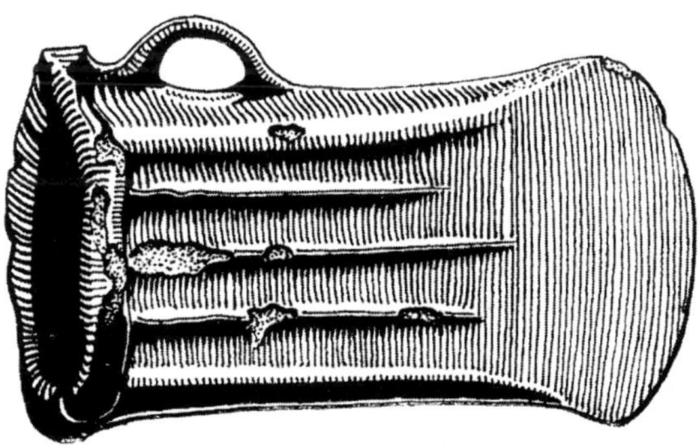

Late Bronze Age Socketed Axehead
made c.700 B.C., ploughed up near Common in 1960.

treasured possessions and, although general goods flowed along the trade routes of the known world, it is now thought that many special items, such as these, arrived here as gifts from travellers to their hosts.

But most Bronze Age finds in this area are more warlike. Bronze swords and rapiers, and the carved stone moulds in which they were cast, together with an impressive collection of weapons to be seen in the Royal Albert Museum in Exeter, suggest that the people of that period were warriors who lived in troubled times. This is further borne out by the discovery that the earliest earthwork of Woodbury Castle dates from the late Bronze Age (800 - 600 BC). Limited excavations carried out in 1971, in advance of road-widening, established that the South Outwork (see diagram) was of an earlier date than the huge banks and ditches we know so well. An analysis of pollen from the old ground level beneath the bank revealed that at the time it was constructed the ground supported mature oak trees in association with ivy, underlaid with hazel, alder, holly, bracken and grass – typical of forest being opened up by some felling and grazing. This early earthwork is something of a mystery as it appears not to have been finished, though it is obviously part of a defensive system.[3]

Maybe the warlike preparations were designed to fend off the next influx of invaders who began arriving around 600 BC. Population explosions in Southern and Eastern Europe were driving people to seek space further afield and large groups of Celtic people were constantly on the move: "Go west young man" is no new idea! They had already colonized most of France, Spain, Central Europe and southern Germany. The Celts were a virile and warlike nation whose characteristics were well-described by Greek and Roman writers. They were great horsemen and had horse-drawn vehicles (most notably war chariots), which presupposes that at least some trackways had become roads. They gloried in war and in stories of heroes and brave deeds, many of their stories told in song, for they were accomplished musicians. Their high-priests, the Druids, were men of power and influence in whom was lodged the history, law and religion of the tribe, committed to memory and handed on, word for word: there was no written language. Human sacrifice was an accepted practice and there was a deep knowledge of the medical properties of plants, and of magic.

Most importantly the Celts brought with them the knowledge of iron smelting. Iron ore was more widely distributed than other metals and could be obtained by open-cast mining. The Celts had solved the problem of smelting by the use of bellows to generate the greater heat required. Iron could be made into ingots to be traded on and made into implements by local smiths.[4]

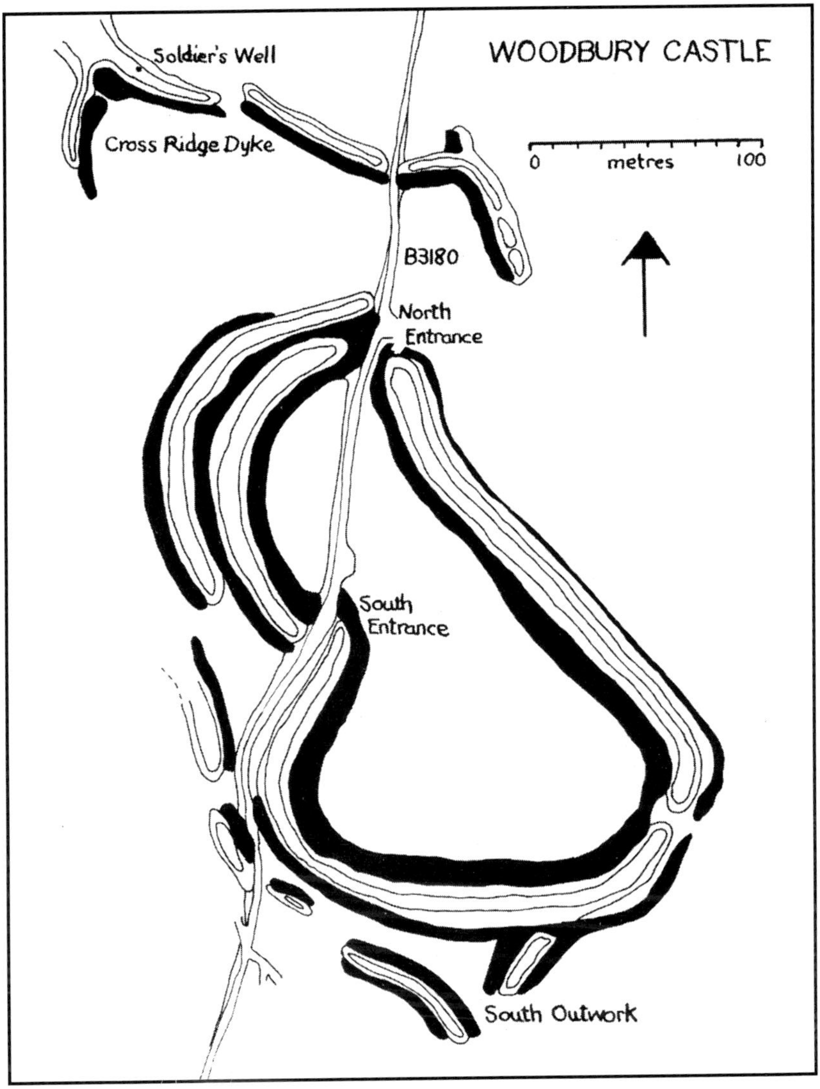

But for the moment the new-comers still found it necessary to live in hill-forts and it is these impressive structures that we associate with the Iron Age. In East Devon Woodbury Castle, Hembury, Peak Hill, Blackbury Castle, Dumpton and many more were all constructed at about this time. The excavation of 1971, already referred to, revealed that the first defensive structure of this new phase was a simple wooden palisade – the post-holes being found on either side of the north entrance. The inhabitants had lived in round wooden houses and a clay oven was found. A small piece of pottery dated it to 600-500 BC.

Then, inexplicably, the inhabitants dismantled their palisade and departed. Slowly a layer of soil formed over the deserted site before the builders of the Castle itself arrived, maybe more than 100 years later. The Castle went through several phases of building, altering and adding, and there were probably several periods when it was not occupied at all. Reasons are hard to come by: it might be some disaster like war or disease, or it may be that the surrounding land became worked out, necessitating a move to allow it to recover.

The site as we now see it occupies five acres and is surrounded by banks and ditches which even today measure some twenty feet from top to bottom. The strange shape of the structure is dictated by the contour of the western escarpment which it follows closely. Curiously, there is a double bank and ditch on this steep side, while the flat and more vulnerable east side has only single defences. A little further to the north is a cross-ridge dyke, presumably to offer some protection to the well which served the fort. Through the centre runs the ancient trackway, controlled by north and south entrances. The entrances themselves would be closed by double gates and the gateways surmounted by massive timber towers (the post-holes have been excavated). These were linked to a wooden walkway, or fighting platform on top of the banks. Pollen analysis of the soil below the entrances indicated that the large trees and much of scrub had disappeared since the building of the South Outwork, and been replaced almost entirely by grasses and associated plants. This all points to a change in agriculture which had affected the landscape. Within the enclosure evidence of square wooden buildings was found which might have been granaries. They were dated to around 400 BC.

For all the hard work that went into its making Woodbury Castle does not seem to have been inhabited for very long. The site yielded no evidence of occupation after 300 BC. Most of the East Devon hillforts were abandoned before the arrival of the Romans in the first century AD. As the Roman armies marched westward in AD 46-48 they met with determined resistance from the Durotriges Tribe in Dorset where over twenty hillforts had to be reduced by force, some of them more than once. No such resistance met them in Devon: there is not a single reference to a battle, nor to the capture of a hillfort. The Second Augusta Legion under Vespasian built a fort at Seaton and garrisoned Hembury briefly (to guard their back against the Durotriges, no doubt) until Exeter was established as a permanent base about AD 50-60; but Hembury, like Woodbury, had already been abandoned.[5]

It seems probable that the Dumnonii Tribe of Devon and Cornwall, unlike their neighbours in Dorset, posed no threat. Peaceful, small-time trading between Rome and the Westcountry had been going on for some time to their mutual benefit and Rome probably saw neither military necessity nor commercial expectations to warrant a heavy occupation. Exports of copper and tin continued – though whether the Westcountry participated in the glamorous export of trained hunting dogs ('clever dogs' Tacitus called them) or the fine, smart woollen cloaks so much prized by wealthy Romans, is not known.

The west seems to have remained the backwater it had always been and although Exeter was a garrison town and a cantonal capital it lacked the refinement and sophistication of such centres elsewhere. There was a forum with public buildings and small shops, barracks and baths, but no amphitheatre. It had been thought that the native population was sparse, which accounted for the lack of Roman artifacts (especially coins) in the country districts around Exeter. It now seems more likely that farming was going on in the lowland areas and that the locals preferred to stick to their old bartering methods, walking into Exeter with their cattle, skins and farm produce and returning with clothes, footwear, metalwork and pottery.

As far as Woodbury is concerned it is of great significance that the Roman coin, the pottery shard and part of a bronze "trumpet" brooch found by Mr Nigel Tucker in 1996 came from the village area, not from the common. One site that might reward further investigation is Pilehayes. The name, though Saxon, probably relates to a pillar or post that was enough of a landmark to give its name to the farm and adjacent land called Piledown. In Saxon times, Pilehayes found itself an island in the middle of the Great Field and surely it must have been there first. An aerial photo suggests the outlines of small fields around the farm.[6] Pilehayes may well have been there hundreds of years before the Saxons came, as indeed may Hogsbrook and others just below the Common such as Greendale. The Roman armies marched along the northern edge of Greendale (the A3053) and left a memento of their stay in the form of a milestone. It was still there in 1240.[7]

Nowadays, in the age of fieldwalking, metal-detecting and aerial photography, much of Woodbury's prehistory is still waiting to be discovered.

2.
The First English Settlement

The Roman legions finally departed in the early years of the 5th century A.D. and the extraordinary civilization which had created towns with shops, theatres, public baths, drains and running water, and houses with mosaic floors and central-heating slowly stumbled to a halt.

Before the century was out a new wave of invaders, the Anglo-Saxons, had arrived from Germany. At first the landings in south-east Britain were at the invitation of the Britons who needed their help but soon the invaders were sweeping the Britons back and occupying the land. While the Angles colonized East Anglia and the Midlands, the Saxons settled in the south and west, giving their name to Wessex — the land of the West Saxons. But whether Angle or Saxon, the people became known as Englishmen and spoke a language from which our mother-tongue has descended.

For some reason not fully understood, the Saxon drive westward slowed down before it reached Devon's borders and Devon continued to be a British province long after the rest of England had been overrun. If Prof. Hoskins' theory is right, the first battle of the Saxon thrust into Devon was fought at Bindon, above Axmouth, in 614 A.D.[1] Striking out along the line of the old Roman road from Dorchester to Exeter, the invaders pushed towards the fertile lands of the Exe valley, an advance remembered, perhaps, in the name Harpford — Herepathford, literally the Saxon Army's river-crossing. And, while East Devon could not be considered secure until after the battle of Peonan (which Hoskins equates with Pinhoe) in 658 A.D., the more adventurous settlers would have been establishing themselves on the land west of the River Axe before that date.

The first Saxon settlers in East Devon probably came from the villages of Dorset and Somerset founded during the previous hundred years — restless younger sons, maybe, unlikely to inherit their fathers' farms and fired by the pioneering instinct of the Anglo-

Saxon race. The mere 30 or 40 miles which separated the old settlement from the new meant that several journeys could be made to move their modest households; axe, spade and pick; cow, sheep and pigs; wife and children and a bare minimum of domestic necessities. Perhaps not even a plough and ox-team, though these would not be very fare behind. The Saxons were looking for good ploughland on which to grow corn and could recognize it by the type of vegetation it supported. They were quite undeterred by the huge oak trees and tangled undergrowth of holly and hazel that had to be removed before ploughing could begin. What did they find here? How much of the land had been farmed by Britons? Did the Saxons oust them and take over their farms or did they start from scratch and carve clearings for themselves out of the forest?

Probably both. The Anglo-Saxon Chronicle tells us that over 2,000 Britons were slain at Bindon. If those killed amounted to 20% of the total it would mean that Devon could muster an army of some 10,000 men to oppose the Saxon advance. Such an army seems to represent a larger British population in East Devon than the few place-names they left behind them suggest. Branscombe is a British name. Otterton has Breadon Lane and Pinn Farm and Clyst Hydon has Aunk. Pinhoe itself is British, as might be expected.

Yet in Woodbury there is not one place-name of known British origin and very little evidence that they were here – unless some significance attaches to a farm called Blacklands from early times.[2] Blackland, like Oldland (or Yelland) was a name sometimes given by early settlers to land which had been anciently cultivated over a long period.

Recent excavations in advance of the A30 road improvement between Honiton and Exeter have shown that lowland farms were well established before and throughout the Roman occupation. We have already seen that at least some of Woodbury's lowland areas were probably cultivated, though exact locations have not been identified. Nevertheless, the British population in relation to the total land available was almost certainly sparse and the cultivated areas patchy rather than continuous. There was plenty of forest, heathland, moor and marsh awaiting the newcomers.

Out of these daunting beginnings the early Saxon settlers, their sons and grandsons, laid the foundations of Woodbury as we know it today. They gave it its name – the Fortress in (or towering over?) the forest. 'Wood' is by far the commonest element in Devon place-names and the fact that woodland dominated the name clearly implies that it very much dominated the scene in Woodbury.

The first settlements may have been in the area of Greendale Barton, with the Grindle Brook and its tributaries supplying the vital water and the Saxon army patrolling the Roman road along its northern edge. Here these few brave men – related to each other perhaps, or friends from the same Dorset village – cleared their first little farms, building their lonely single-roomed farmhouses where they had felled the trees, burning the ground to produce a workable tilth and embanking their tiny fields with the stones and roots cleared from the site. In the early stages these farms were probably pastoral, with only as much arable land as a man could dig with a spade.

The name Grindle is something of a mystery. It is easy to assume that it means "green valley" but there are two good reasons for thinking otherwise. Firstly, valleys usually take their names from their rivers, not *vice versa* (Wharfedale is the valley of the River Wharfe). Secondly, the word dale for valley is Scandinavian and is otherwise unknown in the South West. So "the Place-Names of Devon" suggests that Grindle stems from a Saxon word meaning gravel, which suits the nature of the stream perfectly well.

Greendale Barton took its name from the stream; nearby Winkley, now in Colaton Raleigh parish, was probably the clearing made by a 7th or 8th century farmer called Winca and later became the freehold property of the de Winkleigh family; Hogsbrook — Hocga's farm on the brook, home of Robert de Hoggesbroc in 1240; Cannonwalls, known as Camma Hilla in 1240 and Wotton (now incorporated in Cannonwalls) — the farm cleared from the wood, later the home of Michael de Wotton. Bridge Farm was also known at an early date and was the 13th century home of a family variously known as de Ponte or Atte Brugge. [3]

These early, isolated farms are a special feature of Salterton. They did not constitute a village. The village of Woodbury, when it came, was sited some two miles further south, over the rising ground and down into the next river valley. Perhaps as the area became more secure, and the trickle of pioneers swelled to a steady stream of settlers, the best land within reach of the Grindle Brook was already occupied and they had to look further afield.

And they found the perfect site. Sheltered from the north and east by the high ridge of Woodbury Common, open to the south, watered by the Gillbrook and its sparkling tributaries and with an abundance of rich, red ploughland there for the clearing — the choice of Woodbury as an important settlement was no accident. It must have seemed like paradise. Here they could spread themselves out, grouping their farmhouses round a central green, dominated by a church, sharing their open strip-fields in common — a pattern repeated all over Saxon England.

The name Gillbrook poses another question for the word seems to be compounded from two words, one Scandinavian and the other Saxon, simply meaning 'stream-stream'. This time the 'Place-Names' has nothing to say and the question remains unanswered.

The first land to be broken for the cultivation of corn was in all probability a small area north-west of the village between Parsonage and the Exeter road. With so much land to choose from they were obviously going to start with the best. And as their needs increased there was plenty of room to spread out towards Salterton, until eventually the hundreds of strips in "the Great Field", as it was called, extended to some 1000 acres.

Between the ploughland and the stream is the red sandstone bluff on which the church stands. The site may have been a sacred spot from the beginning. It sloped steeply down to the edge of a clear stream rising half a mile to the north (at Parsonage). Just across this stream from the churchyard lay not only the Green, where animals could be safely impounded at night, but also a farm known as Thorn Barton (now Nos. 1 & 2 The Green).

The name Thorn Barton is highly significant for Barton was the name given almost exclusively to the chief farm of a village or hamlet, e.g. Exton Barton, Ebford Barton and Greendale Barton. One would therefore suspect that a farm called 'Barton' in Woodbury's Church Village would turn out to be the home-farm of the original manor. The name 'Thorn' is also of special interest. The hawthorn tree was considered sacred by the early Saxons and was frequently used to mark a holy place, a meeting-place or a boundary. (see p. 40). The two names together therefore suggest the original manor-farm near a sacred spot or meeting-place.

For the first four hundred years after its foundation — i.e. roughly 650—1050 A.D. — Woodbury was in the personal ownership of the kings of Wessex. It was one of several manors hereabouts that became known as "the ancient demesne-lands of the King".[4] Numbered amongst our landlords were those kings who first called themselves "Kings of all the English". Alfred the Great, Edward the Elder and Athelstan — "lord of warriors, ring-giver of men" as the Anglo-Saxon Chronicle describes him.

The manor was presided over by the King's Reeve who would have lived at Thorn Barton and was a person of considerable status and authority. The families who lived in Woodbury were bound to one another and to their lord by strong ties of mutual loyalty which were the greatest strength of Saxon society: a man gave his lord unswerving allegience and part of his labour and in return he could expect land and protection for his property, person and family. Each manor was to some extent self-governing and the making and keeping of "the customs of the manor" was the responsiblilty of every farmer, who guarded them with jealous pride.

From their wooden houses clustered round the Green farmers went out daily to their work in the communal ploughland, to the hay-fields by the Gillbrook, grazing grounds on the Common or the forest. For these purposes a network of tracks came into being, tramped out by thousands of feet over the centuries and radiating out from the village like a star. Exeter Road and Broadway; Gillbrook and Ham Lane; Watery Lane, Town Lane and Deepway; Castle Lane and Cottles are all part of the beginnings of Woodbury and laid down a structure plan that has shaped all its subsequent development. South west of the village lay the as yet unconquered wet clays that separated Woodbury from the independent Saxon manor of Nutwell. Exton and Ebford were not to make their appearances for several centuries and the names of still later farms, Venmore (fen) and Bagmores (bog), testify clearly enough to the nature of the ground there.

These were not, unfortunately, all years of peaceful development. They were punctuated from 851 A.D. onward by a series of devastating raids by the Danes, sometimes overland, sometimes by the dreaded long-boats sneaking into the Exe estuary. They laid waste, burned, plundered and killed wherever villages and farmsteads were to be found. With the king and his army dealing with trouble elsewhere, it seems unlikely that Woodbury altogether escaped the attentions of the Danes and there must have been times when the terrified inhabitants grabbed their children and ran for the forest.

It was in those dangerous days that the Beacon acquired the name of Virbecna — Fire Beacon.[5] It was used, in all probability, to warn Exeter and the surrounding countryside of the approach of the Danes by sea and it shows that there was some overall scheme of defence for the whole neighbourhood in which Woodbury had an important part to play.

During King Alfred's reign the Danes occupied Exeter and held it all one winter. In 1001 A.D. they returned and the Anglo-Saxon Chronicle for that year records:-

> "They went....to the mouth of the Exe and in one continuous drive penetrated inland as far as Pinhoe where they were opposed by Kola, the King's high-reeve, and Eadsige, the King's reeve, with such levies as could be mobilized; but they were put to flight and many of them slain, and the Danes had possession of the place of slaughter. Next morning they burnt down the manors of Pinhoe and Broadclyst and many other goodly manors of which we do not know the names."[6]

Were Woodbury men included in the levy? And was Woodbury one of the manors of which the chronicler did not know the name? We shall never know: but for certain the Danes were too close for comfort and everyone must have heard spine-chilling first-hand accounts of "the place of slaughter" — still called Danes Wood to this day.

Before leaving the subject of Woodbury's early beginnings and the 'double village' of Woodbury and Salterton we should, perhaps, discuss the unsolved mystery of the name Salterton. How did Woodbury Salterton get its name?

Salt was a vital commodity in the days when people had to live on salt-meat during the winter months. From Roman times salt was evaporated from numerous 'salterns', or salt-pans, round the coast. Most Devon estuaries had salterns before 1066 and Domesday Book lists 33 salt-workers at nearby Otterton. An elaborate and far-reaching system of distribution developed, the salt being transported by carts or pack-horses along routes marked by white crosses.

Woodbury Salterton had neither salt mines nor salt-pans yet the word 'salt' seems to crop up too frequently to be coincidental. The name 'Salterton' itself is first recorded in 1306.[7]. In 1433 there is a mention of a field called 'Saltmede'[8] and the Tithe Map (1839) shows a 'Salt Pit Field' (though Mr. Jeffrey Dagworthy, whose field it is, says it is called 'Saw Pit Field'). Salters Farm, now lost, but formerly in Shop Lane, was of unknown age. It may have been called after its owner, for Salter is a common enough name in Devon: or was it called after salt-workers or salt-sellers engaged in some sort of storing and distributing business connected with the salt trade?

Another factor that fits into the distribution theory is 'White Cross' on the Exeter-Sidmouth road at the very corner of the parish. It seems fairly obvious that a white cross did, in fact, once stand there. (It is the greatest pity that the White Cross Hotel has been renamed the White Horse. Thus can significant historical clues be obliterated). Yet it is hard to see, looking at the map, how Woodbury Salterton could have been on a direct route leading from any of the known saltpans to an inland market. And if the trade had flourished in the post-Domesday period there would surely have been references to tolls and taxes on the traffic. But none has come to light and the name remains a mystery.

3.
The Saxon Guild and Church Land

Before turning to the coming of the Normans and the compiling of the Domesday Book, this is perhaps the moment to consider a rare and important survival which forms a link between Saxon and Norman life in Woodbury.

By a happy chance a document has survived that throws a ray of light on a period about which very little is known for certain. It concerns a guild run by the canons of St. Peter's in Exeter of which Woodbury householders were members. It is known that Saxon society had many guilds, though few details have come down to us. People with similar interests gathered together in associations for the protection of their members, for religious or trade purposes, or for mutual benefits of other kinds. Most were of a semi-religious, semi-social character whose function was to look after sick members and their families, bury the dead and support widows and orphans, "for we know not which of us shall soonest depart hence" as one such guild charter poignantly puts it. Five guild statutes from the late Saxon period, written in Anglo-Saxon, have survived — from Abbotsbury, Bedwyn, Cambridge, Exeter and Woodbury.[1] The Woodbury document owes its survival to the fact that it became bound, at some date unknown, into the Exeter Book of Poetry — Bishop Leofric's personal gift to Exeter Cathedral Library which he founded. (Leofric's episcopate was 1050-1072).

There are three entries for Woodbury. The first one reads:-[2]

> "In the name of Christ and St. Peter the apostle, a guildship is gathered at Woodbury land; and the bishop Osbern and the canons within St. Peter's monastery at Exeter have adopted the same society in fellowship along with the other brethren. They will now, as an acknowledgement, pay to the canons yearly, for every hearth *(i.e. household)*, one penny at Easter; and also for every departed guild-brother, for every hearth, one penny as soul-shot *(burial fee)*, be it a man be it a woman who

belongs to the guildship. And the canons are to have the soul-shot, and perform such service for them as they ought to perform. And these are the names of those who are in the guildship. Brihtwi, Wilnoth, Ealdwine, Leofric, Brihtmaer, Alfric, Eadmaer, Edwine, Algar, Edwi, Wlword, Alword, Edwine, Godwi, Osgod, Atheleone, Brihtmaer, Godric.''

The second entry reads:-

''In Woodbury land there is also another guildship gathered to Christ and St. Peter; and they pay at Martinmas, from every hearth, one penny to St. Peter's monastery, for the canons, and also every soul-shot, for every hearth one penny. And these are the names of the men: Kytel, Theodric, Durrurd, Ailnoth, Ailmer, Yulmer, Ailric, Alfgaer, Saewine, Alwine, Edric.... Alwi, Alword, Hierding, Edmaer, Godwine, Colswein, Britric, Edwine, Aelward, p. Saemor.''

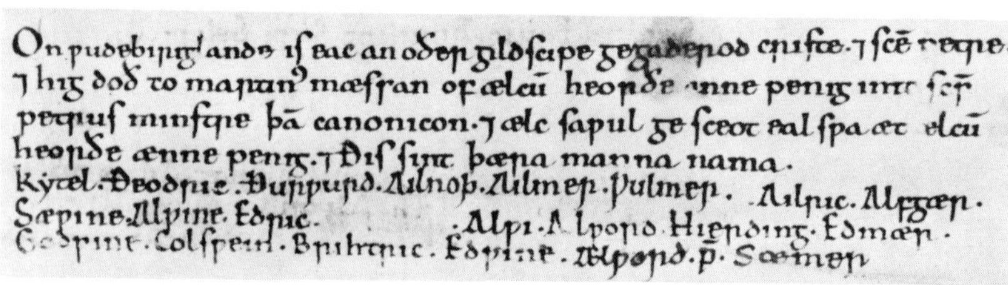

The Saxon Guild: (second list) written in Anglo-Saxon.
(Note the end of the fourth line ''manna nama'' — men's names.)

A brief third entry contains nine names.

Reading between the lines of the first entry it becomes clear that although it must have been written during Bishop Osbern's episcopate (1072-1102) his name was in fact being added as a new member of an old guild. By Bishop Osbern's time St. Peter's had been the cathedral of the diocese for over twenty years, yet the list still uses the old word 'minstre' (here translated as 'monastery') as though it were being copied from an older document, and even the rules of the guild are not clearly set out as they must originally have been. What, for instance, does ''perform such service for them as they ought to perform'' mean? *We* do not know but obviously *they* did and there was no need to spell it out again.

The names are a fascinating study in themselves. Colswein, Kytel and Algar are Danish or Viking names. Had they settled here peacefully in Canute's time and married Woodbury girls? Atheleone may have been a woman — a householder in her own right. Hierding, meaning literally "son of a shepherd", is the forerunner of the Devonian surname Harding, though among simple village folk surnames were not yet in use and one name was enough.[3] But in another sense the names have an even greater interest. In the next chapter we shall discover the Domesday Book, written in 1086 when Osbern was Bishop of Exeter. It shows that Woodbury had some 52 householders, while we already know that the number of Woodbury members in the three guild-lists totalled 50. It seems highly possible therefore that Woodbury has the almost unique distinction of knowing the actual names of at least some, if not most, of its farmers in 1086. The 'villeins' and 'bordars', lumped together in Domesday Book like so many head of cattle, become householders whose names we know and with insurance policies to protect them from some of the harshest winds that blew in those uncertain times.

How did it come about that St. Peter's in Exeter looked after the needs of Woodbury people a thousand years ago? What was the tie between them? There are no means of knowing for sure but it might have had something to do with an unexplained mystery that shrouds the Saxon beginnings of Woodbury Church and a small estate that belonged to it.

We first hear of Woodbury church land in the Domesday Book which tells us that in Saxon times it amounted to more or less a 'hide' (two versions are given) — or some 300 acres — and that it had belonged to "the priest". This is an irritatingly vague term for 300 acres is much larger than a normal glebe and hardly likely to have been the personal possession of the incumbent of Woodbury. So we must look for a more likely interpretation of the word "sacerdos".

If we now turn the pages of history back 150 years , to the time when King Athelstan owned Woodbury (926-940), we come across a charter in which Athelstan made a gift of "26 cotliffs" to St. Peter's monastery in Exeter. The word "cotliff" is not fully understood but is thought to mean a parcel of land large enough to support one family — a farm or a 'hide'. Of the 26 cotliffs only four have been identified: one was in Topsham but there is no knowledge of one at Woodbury. Could Woodbury church and land have belonged to St. Peter's since Athelstan's time? The area is just about one-tenth of Woodbury's ten 'hides' and sounds very much like the sort of gift a king might make to a religious foundation.[4] When in 1066 King William helped himself to the manor of Woodbury he did not lay his hands on the church estate but gave it intact to the Abbot of St. Michael's Mount in Normandy. Surely William, a religious man, was respecting an ancient link between this estate and a religious foundation.

One hundred and twenty years after Domesday Book was written a later Bishop of Exeter retrieved Woodbury church estate from St. Michael's Mount and gave it to the Vicars Choral of Exeter Cathedral as an endowment. Was his act an isolated one, out of the blue? Or was he restoring something which had previously been associated with St. Peter's in Exeter? Was it King Athelstan who made the original gift and is that why St. Peter's ran a guild for the benefit of the king's subjects in Woodbury? Even as late as the 15th century Athelstan was still being remembered by name in special prayers for benefactors in Woodbury Church.[5]

4.
The Arrival of the Normans

Every school-child knows "the Battle of Hastings 1066". In it Harold, the last Saxon King, was slain and William of Normandy became King of England in his place. England fell to William at a single blow and only a few pockets of resistance gave him serious trouble thereafter.

One such was Exeter. Harold and his family had acquired vast estates in Devon. He himself had fourteen manors, including Topsham and Colaton Raleigh, while his mother, Gytha (or Guitda) had eight manors of which Woodbury was one. It is thought that Gytha was living in Exeter at the time of the Conquest and it is not surprising that anti-Norman feelings were running high in the regions so long associated with the royal house of Wessex. William came in person at the head of his army and besieged Exeter for eighteen days. Gytha and her daughter fled overseas, never to return.[1]

William ruled with an iron hand and the people groaned under the oppression. Saxon landlords were dispossessed and their lands given to William's Norman friends and relations. In these parts only the Saxon named Donne, the owner of Nutwell, still owned it by 1086. Punishments were harsh and mutilations such as the amputation of hands and putting out of eyes were common for crimes of theft and poaching game from the forests. Norman-French became the language of the court and people and masters could no longer communicate in a common tongue. The Anglo-Saxon Chronicle leaves us in no doubt about the horror and misery of the times.

Taxes increased greatly. To help him extort the maximum levies on the land William devised a survey of the whole country. The Domesday Book was the result. It was an extraordinary undertaking, carried through in 18 months and completed in 1086. As can be seen from Geld Tax returns, Woodbury's contribution rose from 18 pounds by weight (of silver) to 23 pounds annually.

Two copies of the Devon Domesday were made. The Exchequer Book went to Winchester. The Exeter Book stayed in Exeter where it can still be seen. The entry for Woodbury in the Exeter version, translated from the Latin, reads:

"The King has a manor called Wodeberia which Guitda held on the day that King Edward was alive and dead and it paid geld for 10 hides. These 35 ploughs can till. Thereof the king has 5 hides and two ploughs in demesne and the villeins 5 hides and 20 ploughs. There the king has 30 villeins, 22 bordars, 6 serfs, 2 pack-horses, 15 head of cattle, 4 swine, 60 sheep, one mill paying 7 shillings and 6 pence, woodland 1 league in length by ½ in breadth, 30 acres of meadow and 300 acres of pasture. It pays 23 pounds by weight; when Baldwin received it 18 pounds. Thereof the abbot of St. Michael of the Mount holds the church and the land which the priest held on the day that King Edward was alive and dead, that is ½ hide (Exchequer version gives 1 hide) and 1 virgate and ½ ferlong. Worth 20 shillings with common pasture."

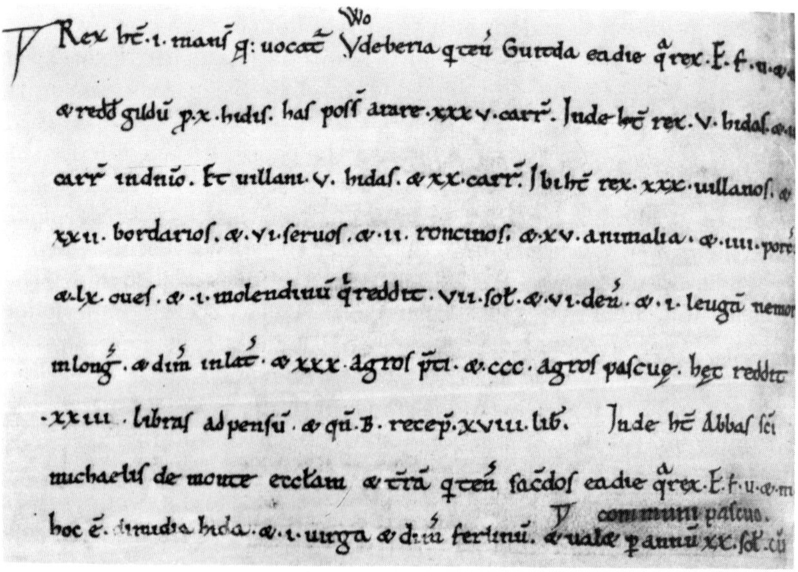

Woodbury's entry in the Exeter Domesday Book.

With this entry Woodbury leaps out of the haze of guess-work into the light of recorded history and, despite possible errors and omissions, not to mention the extreme difficulty of interpreting the information, it presents a factual account of what was here and how it worked. We cannot be sure how big the manor was for the size of a 'hide' was variable. Often it is reckoned at 160 acres but Reichel writes of Woodbury's 10 hides as being 3,200 acres[2] — or nearly half the size of the present parish. The most likely area was from the Roman road north of Greendale Barton to Ham Lane south of Woodbury village, and from the present boundary on Woodbury Common to a line crossing the Exeter road near Postlake. To the South-west of this area lay Nutwell, a separate Domesday estate, while Exton and Ebford were still a long way in the future.

The word 'demesne' means the landlord's own farm — probably, as we have seen, Thorn Barton. Domesday Book tells us that the home farm had two ploughs. A ploughland is another imprecise measurement, usually taken to be about 64 acres, or as much land as one plough-team could cultivate in a season. If so, the arable land of Thorn Barton amounted to some 128 acres. Later documents make it clear that the landlord's acres lay not in separate fields belonging to the farm but in strips in the common fields. The same documents suggest that the amount of ploughland was not always constant — that new land was taken in from the 'waste' from time to time, cultivated for a few years and then allowed to go back to waste again[3] — a practice which almost certainly gave us Heathfield, an area that reverted to heathland after having been a part of the adjacent common fields. This, and the more regular practice of fallowing fields for a season, may account for the statement in Domesday that Woodbury had enough land for 35 ploughs but only 22 ploughs in actual use.

The livestock mentioned in the survey all belonged to the home farm, together with possibly 16 oxen for the two ploughs, not mentioned.[4] These animals give us some idea of the size of the farm and the buildings, yards and labourers required to run it. Almost certainly the 6 serfs were employed there — one of them, perhaps, tending the 60 sheep on the Common — and there was also work to be done in the dairy, making butter and cheese from the milk of the '15 head of cattle'.

The 30 villeins were mostly, if not all, farmers and although several no doubt had their own farms at Salterton (included in the manor of Woodbury) the majority would be living in Woodbury and sharing the common fields. In a later century we hear of 24 Woodbury villeins farming 20 acres of arable land apiece and the Domesday villeins would have done much the same.[5] If Reichel is right, Woodbury's communal ploughland probably amounted to almost 1,000 acres, even allowing for a considerable acreage of arable on the farms at Salterton. The farmhouses with their little yards, orchards and paddocks occupied sites in the village where Woodbury's old farms have always stood, particularly on the side of the village street facing the Green, where their 'back-door fields' can still be seen. The Priory and the Beals are obvious examples.

The arable land carried with it grazing rights for livestock on the communal stubble, pasture, the Common, and at Heathfield, and hay from the precious meadows by the side of Ham Lane and the Gillbrook. In return for their tenancies the farmers gave various sorts of service to their landlord.

Bordars were lower down the social scale than villeins, though they too were fairly independent. They can be described as cottagers or smallholders, partly supporting themselves on their garden plots and single acres, partly by hiring out their labour. The 6 serfs were the lowest grade, landless and entirely dependent on their master. They had few rights and could be bought and sold like cattle.

The mill was something of a bonus for Woodbury. Water-mills were relatively modern in 1086 and less than 10% of Devon manors had them (others, presumably, still using the old hand-quern). It is unlikely that the Domesday mill was at Rydon Mill. Rydon depended on a long and complicated leat system not developed in Norman times and there is no evidence of any activity in that heavy land before the 16th century. Besides, there was no need to go so far afield when there was an adequate supply of water nearer at hand. The most likely place was on the Gilbrook, either in the vicinity of Gilbrook House or, more likely perhaps, on the other side of the road near Brookside, after the Gilbrook had been joined by the additional water of the Pollybrook. The mill-wheel would be placed directly in the stream — a simple wooden paddle depending on the natural flow of the water to turn it.

The woodland of Domesday Book is of particular interest because part of it is still there. Identified today by its ancient and important name of Woodbury Wood, it stretched in 1086, so we are told, 1 league in length by ½ league in breadth, i.e. 1½ x ¾ miles or, say, from Woodmanton to Castle Brake and from the lower edge of the Common to the upper edge of Town Lane — possibly some 600 acres. Indeed, part of Town Lane may have been the boundary of the wood at that time, the huge oak trees casting their dark, morning shadows across to the village side of it.

The wood was an important part of village economy and was properly managed. From two inventories already mentioned we get a brief glimpse of this management at work. The 1289 document describes 20 acres of "barren woodland of which the underwood is worth 12d" — a policy of organised coppicing after felling — while the 1321 document tells us that 40 acres of young oak trees had been newly planted. Nothing in the woodland was wasted. After the valuable timber came the bark for tanning, the branches for fencing, the brushwood for fuel — even the acorns were gathered as fodder for pigs. Householders in Woodbury had certain rights to take such wood as was considered necessary for life and to cut peat from the turbary, on the slopes of Woodbury Common.

In all the Exeter Domesday Book's 1,200 entries only seven places are mentioned as having churches: Woodbury was one of them. The previous chapter dealt with the church and its 'manor within a manor' based on Parsonage, which William the Conqueror gave to the Abbot of Mont St. Michel in Normandy. Besides the enclosed fields grouped round the farm buildings, Parsonage also had arable strips in the common fields and, as Domesday tells us, common pasture (i.e. grazing rights on fallow land and on the Common) included in the 20 shilling assessment. By 1225 we know that their grazing rights covered 16 oxen, 10 cows, 200 sheep with their lambs, as well as goats, horses and other livestock.[6] It was undoubtedly for this purpose that Cottles Lane came into existence — to drive livestock from Parsonage to graze on the Common. Woodbury village had its own drove road for the same purpose — Castle Lane — and the two lanes converged before they reached the Common.

And so, through Domesday Book, there emerges some kind of a picture of what life was like in Woodbury at the time of William's conquest of England; but it gives no idea of how heavily the Norman hand oppressed the land and the free spirit of the Saxon people. It was not long before Woodbury began to feel the burden. The Geld Tax paid to the Crown, as we have seen, increased by almost a third and the expansion of farm land by the clearing of forest, which had gone on throughout the Saxon period, came to an abrupt end with William's earmarking of all forests for royal hunting. The Forest Laws were among the harshest and most deeply resented of all William's innovations. The Saxon farmer, who had benefitted from the abundance of wild game, now risked losing a hand if he so much as snared a rabbit. For Woodbury folk it meant no more hunting and no more clearance.

As time went by farmers, both Norman and Saxon, were crying out for more farm-land. But it was not until 1204 that the men of Devon wrested a charter of disafforestation from King John for 5,000 marks (a mark was 13s.4d. or 66p) and it was another 38 years before it was finally put into effect in 1242. Ford Farm, first mentioned in that year, must have been the first new farm to be cleared from the forest of Woodbury for nearly 200 years.[7] The sound of the axe was again ringing as the woodland was rolled back from the edge of Town Lane and the clearance did not stop until it reached its present line, near the upper reaches of the Gilbrook at Ford Water.

That same year saw the emergence of Exton, probably closely linked with the necessity for a really adequate water-mill and developed by an enterprising villein encouraged by his landlord. The de Exton family soon had the place humming with activity, with a farm (Exton Barton), a mill and a fishery.[8] Exton was closely followed by Postlake (Pottslake in early spellings), first noted in 1249, and the next 80 years were to see the arrival of Ebford, Gulliford, Coombe and Heathfield — all pushing out the edges of cultivation. Gulliford was first spelt Goldeford and is one of four old Woodbury place-names in which 'golden' or 'yellow' were associated with water, the others being Yellowford on the Grindle, Golden Spring near Greendale and Golden Well on the Common. Could these places have been carpeted with yellow flowers — kingcups, perhaps, wild daffodils or golden saxifrage?

The Domesday Book has been used as a guideline for calculating population, since the number of working men is given. Historians differ widely in their estimates and the results can never be more than approximate. But with 58 people mentioned in the Woodbury survey, plus the tenants of Thorn Barton and Parsonage, it is likely that Woodbury's population in 1086 was more than 200 but less than 300. We have already seen that members of the Saxon Guild at that time had names like Brihtwi, Wilnoth, Ealdwine and Alfric. One hundred and twenty years later there had been a complete shift from Saxon to Norman names. The Greendale Charters (see next chapter) show that farmers' names in Salterton c.1200 were Robert, Geoffrey, Richard, Ralph, Walter, Michael, Roger and William — Norman names, every one of them, though not all of them would have been Normans. Most would have been of Saxon descent with fashionable Norman names.

5.
A Resident Landlord

William the Conqueror gave the manor of Woodbury to Baldwin of Brionne. Baldwin, related to William by marriage, held 177 manors in Devon and was made Sheriff of the county and Seneschal of William's new castle at Exeter.

Baldwin did not live in Woodbury, neither did his son who inherited it, nor subsequent landlords the Mandevilles and Carbonells. All these owners came and went in less than a hundred years and Woodbury folk knew little more about them than the annual rents they extorted. But in 1174 an event took place which was to make a considerable impact on Woodbury's everyday life.

In that year the last of the Carbonells, a daughter Avelina or Alice, inherited the manor and by her marriage to her cousin Reginald de Albemarle brought Woodbury to the Albemarle family.[1] It is likely that Reginald was a younger son for he does not seem to have inherited any of the major Albemarle properties in West Devon (although Lympstone came into his hands when his half-sister died childless).[2] What is virtually certain is that Reginald and Alice had made their home in Woodbury by 1175 and that it remained the principal family home for almost 200 years — eight generations, father to son. So for the first time Woodbury had a resident landlord.

Reginald was soon busying himself in the running of his manor and from that date onward there exists a small mountain of documentary evidence recording the family's actions — their marriages, debts, squabbles, and generosity: even their call-up for military service. The Albemarles held Woodbury from the king for a 'knight's fee' — that means their ownership of Woodbury depended on their providing an armed horseman for forty days in any one year at their own expense whenever the king required to raise an army. Twice during the 13th century members of the family were called up to serve in this way — once in Wales and once in France.[3] One can imagine the preparations and the goodbyes from family and villagers alike as their young lord set off with his retinue for the king's wars, bearing on his arm a shield with three crescents – symbols of the crusades. This was the age of chivalry in which horsemanship and the martial arts were of supreme importance. So we find that when Reginald II's wife's uncle, Fulk Montgomery, became tenant of Hogsbrook in 1256 he had to render "therefor yearly 1 pair of gilt spurs or 6d. at Easter and rendering therefor the foreign service which to the said land belongs for all service, custom and exaction".[4]

Within a few years of his arrival in Woodbury Reginald de Albemarle "with the consent of Avelina his wife and Geoffrey his son" gave the farm of Greendale Barton in Woodbury Salterton (some 160 acres) to his sister's son, Lord William Brewer, for "one twentieth of a knight's fee" (i.e. an armed horseman for two days). In exchange William gave Reginald a gold ring and a horse and to the young lad Geoffrey gave a hunter. The document was signed at Greendale in 1181 and it must have been a cheerful family party that rode home to Woodbury in high spirits after the signing and handing over of Greendale to its new owner.[5]

Greendale remained the property of Lord William Brewer until in 1197 he founded Torre Abbey (at Torquay) and gave Greendale as an endowment. It is listed in the Foundation Charter, to which both Reginald and Geoffrey de Albemarle added their signatures as witnesses. Though William Brewer does not enter Woodbury's story again it is worth noting that he was at that time Sheriff of Devon and rose to become an eminent judge and close friend and confidant of four successive kings of England – Henry II, Richard I, John and Henry III. The Albemarles themselves were directly descended from William the Conqueror's sister Adeliza and the relationships remained close.

It should be remembered that there were never monks at Greendale. It was a farm occupied by a tenant farmer for the benefit of the Abbey. But there was a manorial court there and the Abbot of Torre visited Greendale twice a year to receive his rents and tithes, hear complaints and administer justice.

Over the next sixty years or so after the founding of the Abbey successive generations of Albemarles continued to benefit the Abbot's manor of Greendale by giving rights of enclosure and embankment and grazing on the Common. The remarkable series of charters, twenty-five in all, most, if not all, signed at Greendale and witnessed by Woodbury farmers, have a homely ring to them. Hogsbrook, Wotton, Winkley and Bridge Farm are mentioned and fields, woods and hills which are still identifiable after 750 years. With Albemarle's permission the Abbot caused a mill to be built at Greendale Bridge and, when the water supply proved inadequate, borrowed an additional supply from a spring at Winkley Farm.

All the charters are worth studying in detail but perhaps Charter 98 has the greatest interest here and so is quoted in full.

> "This is the final agreement made between the Abbot and Convent of Thorre of the one part and Reynald (Reginald II) de Albamara of the other: namely the said Reynald granted etc., for ever to the same Abbot etc., common pasture in the manor of Woodbury which extends by these boundaries: that is to say from the way from Grendel which extends between the land of the Abbot and the house of Geoffrey de Hogsbrook and leads to the hill towards *virbecna* as far as to the Thorn-tree which stands above the fosse called Blachedic and thus ascending by that fosse as far as the main road *(magna via)* which lies near by on the east side under the *virbecna*; and just as that way stretches as far as to chastiller: and thus extends by the fosse of chastiller on the east side as far as the way which comes out of chastiller on the south side and leads to the cross which stands on the main road between Wodebire and Otteritun and thus by that way as much as his land extends to the east. That they may have free entrance and egress with their cattle throughout the whole of his land which is on the east side of the said bounds, excepting wood, meadow and growing corn. (Clause of damages, to be assessed by four law-abiding men). For this grant the Abbot gave him five marcs. Whoever transgresses this agreement shall pay one barrel of wine or forty shillings".

There is no difficulty in following these boundaries. The 'way' from Greendale to Hogsbrook is the cart-track (formerly a public right-of-way) which in another charter is referred to as 'Warkedunsweye' and the field through which it passes was still called Walkidons in 1839. From there an old lane goes on up to the Common and joins the 'main road' somewhere near the Beacon. The fact that a single hawthorn tree could serve as a landmark in what is now a jungle of trees and undergrowth shows how complete the clearance of the area was at that time: and as at Thorn Barton, the thorn tree here had a special significance.

The 'virbecna' must be the Beacon and it is from this charter that we know it was already called Fire-Beacon as early as the first half of the 13th century — the earliest known firebeacon in Devon. The boundary then follows the existing road to the Castle and, following the eastern line of the ditch, joins the road again on the south side of the Castle and so on to Four Firs. Here again the charter sheds light, for it is the only known reference to a cross which then stood at the cross-roads (does its shaft still form a gatepost in the vicinity — unrecoginsed for what it is?). The boundary then followed the Otterton road until it came to the point where the parish boundary crosses it at Boundridge Wood. Then, by turning left and following the parish boundary all the way back to Grindle Bridge, the line of the grazing land is completed.

Torre Abbey was not the only religious foundation to benefit from the Albemarles' personal interest. It will be remembered that from 1086 onward Woodbury church and the Parsonage land (in company with the Priory in neighbouring Otterton) belonged to the Abbey of Mont St. Michel in Normandy. When the Albemarles first arrived in Woodbury Reginald seems to have exercised his right to appoint a priest to Woodbury church. But in the year 1200 he decided to grant this right to Abbot Jordan of Mont St. Michel. It was intended as a generous gesture, but the arrangements left Woodbury in a vulnerable position, for communications across the Channel were slow and hazardous and Woodbury might have been left without an incumbent for many months at a time. So it was arranged that the Prior of Otterton should be responsible for providing proper services in Woodbury church at all times.

This led to complications, for within five years the Bishop of Exeter was negotiating with Abbot Jordan in Normandy for the release of Woodbury church estate, which he wanted for another purpose. Reginald de Albemarle was now dead and his son Geoffrey had to appear in court before King John to retrieve the incumbency of the church from the Prior of Otterton — for which he gave the Prior 33 marks of silver.[6] The matter was satisfactorily resolved and the way was clear for the estate to be properly transferred to Bishop Marshall and this was done in 1205 or 6.

The Bishop now gave the estate to the Vicars Choral of Exeter

Cathedral as an endowment and from that date onwards the Vicars provided one of their number to be the priest at Woodbury. Soon Woodbury church was being rebuilt by the Vicars and, although there is no documentary evidence, it is likely that the Albemarles substantially financed the new building. Landlords all over the country were busy building or rebuilding churches in their manors as the Gothic style of architecture blossomed and gripped England in a marvellous burst of creative energy.

In about 1225 Geoffrey de Albemarle gave further help to the Vicars Choral by extending the Parsonage grazing rights for "the animals of the men of the Sanctuary-land of Woodbury church to be able to pasture wherever Albemarle's men pasture with rights of carriage of crops through their lands."[7]

Of all the Albemarles of Woodbury it was probably Sir William (the first of three) who has the greatest claim to a place in Woodbury's history. It was he who obtained from King Edward I a charter for an annual three-day fair at St. Swithinstide and a weekly Tuesday market.

It so happened that King Edward and Queen Eleanor, accompanied by a glittering court, spent Christmas 1285 at Rougemont Castle in Exeter. It was customary at these festivals for the king to receive petitions from his subjects and no doubt Sir William availed himself of the opportunity to ride over to Exeter and present his request to the king in person. Woodbury's Fair and Market Charter was signed and dated at Exeter on New Year's Day and William must have been a happy man as he returned to Woodbury with the charter tucked under his belt.[8] The charter ran …

> "…Granted and confirmed to my brother William de Aubemarle he and his heirs in perpetuity shall have a market weekly on Tuesdays at his manor of Wodebuir in Devon and one fair there annually to last three days; that is on the vigil and the day and on the morrow of St. Swithin. But this market and fair is not to be to the harm of neighbouring markets and fairs and we wish the said William and his heirs shall have the said market and fair at his manor with all liberties and free customs belonging to the said market and fair."

Witnesses included the Bishop of Bath and Wells, Edmund, Earl of Cornwall, Gilbert de Clare, Earl of Gloucester, John de Warenna, Earl of Surrey, Peter de Chanpernent and others.

It was a time when markets and fairs were springing up all over Devon, especially in the prosperous Vale of Exeter,[9] and the intention was to foster trade and encourage a town to grow that would warrant the granting of a borough charter. Just why it didn't happen in Woodbury we do not know. Tiverton had received a borough charter almost a century earlier, yet in 1332 Woodbury had a taxable population of 34 paying 49s. while Tiverton's 30 paid only 35s. 10d.[10]

Nevertheless, the weekly market continued for several centuries and the fair survived into modern times. Originally Woodbury's fair was for serious trade purposes. But such a big annual event was regarded as an exciting relief from the hard routine of daily life. The fair brought strangers to Woodbury and where there was money to be spent there was also a wide variety of enterprising individuals on the fringe of the fair — strolling players and morris men, tinkers, tricksters, fortune-tellers, pie-men and sellers of everything imaginable. Gradually the trade side of these fairs dwindled until nothing was left but the fringe activities which survived as fun-fairs. Many people still remember a fair of this sort on Woodbury's Village Green, though latterly the date shifted from July to May.

One cannot help but admire the ingenuity and enthusiasm for new ideas by which William sought to raise the status of Woodbury. Prosperity brought a population explosion and soon the growing needs for more corn-milling outstripped the capacity of the old Domesday mill at Gillbrook which suffered from an inadequate water supply. The problem was solved by a series of new measures. Part of Salterton's milling needs were hived off by the building of the Abbot of Torre's mill at Greendale and Woodbury's own solution took the novel form of a windmill behind Parsonage. But this does not seem to have been a great success for by 1289 it was already broken — "from which no profits can be levied until the grain-intakes are mended."[11] Perhaps they never were. With the opening up of Exton and the development there of a larger mill, with a leat and an ample supply of water, first the windmill and finally the Domesday mill became redundant. Both Woodbury and Exton mills were working in 1289 but by 1321 only one is mentioned and that must be Exton.[12] The decline of Woodbury mill and the rise of Exton necessitated the making of a road to take the corn from the Great Field to Exton and Rydon Lane was the result. The antiquity of the lane no doubt explains why its hedgebanks have such an extraordinary variety of shrub-plants. For were the lane only as old as Rydon Farm (c.1525) one would not expect to find so many.

William de Albemarle died in 1289, after a colourful and highly successful life, and was succeeded by his son Geoffrey II about whom little is known — and nothing to his credit. He seems to have been something of a scamp who was married off by his scheming father at the age of fifteen to an heiress (thereby causing a family row), owed money and kept peacocks in his 4-acre garden at Woodbury — for he held the hamlet of Lympstone from the King "by bringing to the King when he will hunt in Dertemore an oaten loaf worth half a farthing, and 3 barbed arrows feathered with peacock's feathers placed upon the loaf".[13] Apart from these bizarre details he seems to have been involved as defendent in a number of dubious court cases.

In the summer of 1301 a ship carrying a cargo of wine from France to Exeter was wrecked off Teignmouth and 10 casks, each holding 240 gallons, were washed ashore at Lympstone where they came into Geoffrey's hands. The crew of the vessel survived to report the loss to the owners in Exeter and Geoffrey was asked to hand them back. One may suppose that by this time the casks were no longer intact. At any rate Geoffrey had no intention of handing them over and in September of that year, after the owners had failed to get any compensation, the King ordered the Sheriff to distrain on Geoffrey's goods without delay to satisfy the merchants for the price of the ten casks — valued at 4 marks each —" so that the King may not hear renewed complaints for lack of justice".[14]

During the 14th century the family sold off large tracts of their manor (to pay their debts?). Instead of the "knight's fee" of his ancestors, Geoffrey died possessed of "three-quarters of a knight's fee" and his successor reduced it to half a fee. It is possible that Ebford was sold to the Haydons and Salterton to a family named Okebeare.

The last years of the Albemarles' lordship of Woodbury were clouded by the horrors of the Black Death from which possibly one third of the entire population of Devon died. The Black Death (bubonic plague) spread from the East across Europe, carried by the black rat and transmitted to humans by fleas. It laid waste the populations everywhere. It arrived in England in 1348 and between 1349 and 1352 changed the face of this country. Farms went back to waste for want of tenants, cows wandered at will in the corn, hungry survivors roamed in dangerous gangs in search of food and there was none to stop them. There were barely enough people left to bury the dead who shared a common grave of quick-lime.

We know little of how the Black Death affected Woodbury except that here, as in so many other places, its presence is underlined by a total absence of new farms between 1350 and 1426. The previous century had seen enormous expansion, both on the edges of the manor and at Salterton, where a 'village street' seems to have been emerging. Clayhill Farm (now Pigeons), Bass Farm (Trevannin) and Browns were all there by 1333.[15] Suddenly the expansion stopped and it is probable that so many people died and so much farmland went back to waste for want of farmers that it was over half a century before the population increased enough to get the old land back into cultivation. The next new farm to appear was Woodmanton, first noted in 1426,[16] though it is possible that Sparkshayes just preceeded it. Sparkshayes, now gone, lay between Woodbury village and Woodmanton and it seems sensible to suppose that the nearer land was developed first. It may have been the farm of Richard Sparke who received a bequest of 10 marks from Woodbury's landlord in 1407.[17]

Did the Albemarle family feel the chill hand of the Black Death? A strange silence falls upon their activities. Geoffrey's son William Albemarle II, created Knight Banneret in 1326, was still here in 1346 but when the next reference emerges it concerns the death of his son, William Albemarle III, on 15th November 1361. An inventory made then is a very sketchy affair compared with that made when Geoffrey died in 1321. There is no mention of the 24 villeins farming 20 acres apiece and even the Albemarles' house and 4-acre garden, previously worth 6s. 8d. was now worth nothing. Only the mill at Exton shows increased profit — not, one suspects, because of more milling but because of rampant inflation in the face of great calamity.[18]

This William left a son and heir, also William, 12 years old, but he only survived his father by about two years and when he died the manor of Woodbury passed to his sisters Margaret and Elizabeth. Margaret married Sir William Bonville of Shute, near Axminster, and Woodbury came at length to the great Bonville family. Margaret Albemarle and William Bonville had no doubt known each other since childhood for the Bonvilles previously had a house at Otterton and the Albemarles had, by 1332, a second home at

LORDS OF THE MANOR OF WOODBURY

WILLIAM CARBONELL (died c.1160)

William? (2)m. Mabel m.(1) Geoffrey de Albermarle

WILLIAM CARBONELL

Muriel m.
Rbt of Bickleigh

Daughter
m. Henry Brewer

REGINALD
de Albemarle
d.1201?

m. ALICE CARBONELL

Lord Wm. Brewer
founded Torre
Abbey 1197
d.1226

Engelesia

GEOFFREY de Albemarle

Lord Wm. Brewer
d.1232
Buried at Torre Abbey

REGINALD de Albemarle II
m. Joan Montgomery
(Called for foreign service 1230)

WILLIAM de Albemarle
m. Margery?
d.1289
(Fair and Market Charter 1285)

GEOFFREY de Albemarle II
b.1267 d.1320
(Called for service against Welsh 1294)

WILLIAM de Albemarle II
b.1296 d.1346?
(Knight Banneret 1326)

Sir Nicholas Bonville

WILLIAM de Albemarle III
d.1362

SIR WM. BONVILLE
of Shute d.1406

m. MARGARET
d.1399

Elizabeth
m. John Maltravers

William
b.1349
(died
young)

John Bonville m. Eliz. FitzRoger
d.1396

LORD WILLIAM
BONVILLE
b.1393 beheaded 1460
(after B. of St. Albans)

Sir. W. Bonville
(m. Eliz. Courtnay)
Killed B. of Wakefield 1460

William Bonville
Killed B. of Wakefield 1460

Henry Grey (1). m. Elizabeth Woodville m.(2) King Ed. IV
Duke of Suffolk
Killed B. of Towton
1461

CECILIA BONVILLE m. (1474) Thomas Grey
b.1460 d.1530 Marquis of Dorset
Earl of Huntingdon

Elizabeth m.
King Hy. VII

THOMAS GREY
Marquis of Dorset

Frances m. HENRY GREY
d. Chas. Brandon Duke of Suffolk
Duke of Suffolk beheaded 1554

Lady Jane Grey
beheaded 1554

Colyton, near Axminster. It was only a small estate but one can imagine them riding over from Woodbury to Colyton from time to time and entertaining their neighbours the Bonvilles.[19]

Nevertheless, the departure of the resident landlord struck a blow at the hearts of Woodbury people. The manor-house stood empty and gradually subsided into ruin. The manor court moved to Shute. Though the Bonvilles continued to take a very personal interest in Woodbury it could not be the same. In eight generations of Albemarles it is unlikely that all of them had been good landlords or pleasant people. When they first came they came as Norman overlords of a vanquished English people. But in 200 years Woodbury had absorbed them and made good Englishmen of them. They had been heads of the family, known to everyone and knowing everyone by name, riding the lanes of Woodbury to see things for themselves, attending St. Swithin's church on Sundays and carrying their infants to the font to be baptized.

Where did they live, these eight generations of Albemarles? It is one of the most baffling mysteries for anyone studying the story of Woodbury. Nearly every village knows where its manor house was — even if there is nothing left but a name — but Woodbury's manor house disappeared so long ago that all traces of it have been lost.

Well, not quite! There are clues for the observant. Take a trip to the churchyard and find a comfortable seat on a tombstone at the north-east corner. What do you see? Some twelve feet below is a deep sunk lane skirting the churchyard and beyond it rises a strange embankment – high and precise and man-made – partly enclosing a property now called Fairfield, though the name is not old. Such a site, close to the village, the church and the home farm, and with its own supply of well-water, is too obvious not to have been inhabited since the early days. Yet the purposeful embankments represent a physical labour and importance one would not associate with a modest village farmhouse. Here is a site singled out and set apart. But it is one thing to trust your intuition and say 'yes, this must have been the site' and quite another to find documentary proof. This turned up purely by chance in a survey of Woodbury made in 1525. The inventories already referred to in this chapter describe the Albemarles' manor house as the "capital messuage with 4 acres of fruit garden with pasturage." In the survey of 1525 we discover that "Richard Hopping holds there...the capital messuage (i.e. the manor house) *entirely in decay* excepting one tenement built thereon."[20] Richard Hopping later changed his name to Holwell and the Holwell family lived at a house rebuilt on the site. In his will of 1565 "John Hopping alias Holwell" had several properties in Woodbury but his main residence he left to his wife, together with two fields immediately opposite Fairfield.[21] Later the property became known as Culvery – a dove-cote: only lords of the manor could possess dove-cotes in mediæval times. Its stated two acres in the will are consistent with the site as far as the stream – a natural boundary – and the "one tenement", Culvery Cottage, is still to be seen on the 1906 O.S. map. For the two other acres of orchard mentioned in the 14th C. inventories, one would have to include the adjacent site of Webbers Farm and all the land between Bonfire Lane and Miry Lane. In 1839 nearly the whole area was orchard and Webbers Farm was on the other side of the village street. It seems possible that it was the Albemarles' orchard.

We do not know what sort of house it was that lay in ruins in 1525. Certainly not a castle. As the Albemarles were the first landlords to live in Woodbury, they presumably built themselves a house when they first arrived towards the end of the 12th century. Houses being built then often consisted of a large living hall for the main activities of the household – cooking, banqueting and the sleeping quarters for the men-at-arms – and numerous smaller rooms of a more private nature, often standing apart from the hall and protected by a wall or embankment and a gatehouse. There would be stables for the horses and other functional buildings: a simple pattern of life common enough in the days of the Albemarles.

A clue to their modest life-style is to be found in the Lay Subsidy Tax for 1332 in which Sir William Albemarle's taxable goods were assessed at only 3 shillings, while a certain Peter Shalleforde (possibly the tenant of Greendale) was assessed at 4s. But for all their simplicity the Albemarles' household would have given important employment in Woodbury. Every such household had men-at-arms, grooms, maids-in-waiting and a host of more menial servants some of whom, descendants of those six Domesday serfs, were born in bondage with little prospect of ever becoming free-men. On August 25th 1280 William Albermarle sold one of his serfs, John le Breghe, to Elias de Cirencester, Succentor of Exeter Cathedral, for two marks.[22]

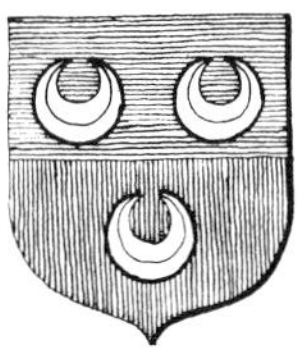

ALBEMARLE

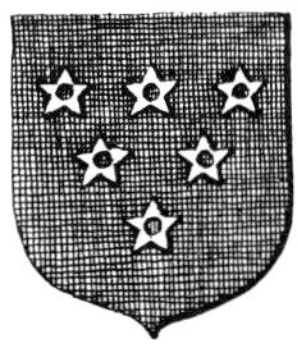

BONVILLE

The Albemarles' coat of arms bears the three crescents of the crusades. Stephen distinguished himself with gallantry at Antioch (1st Crusade 1097) and William was Commander of the Fleet at Cyprus, under Richard I (3rd Crusade 1191). Neither were from the Woodbury branch of the family.[23]

6.
Church Affairs and the Fifteenth Century

As we bid goodbye to the Albemarles the story of Woodbury is taken up by the College of Vicars Choral of Exeter Cathedral, many of whose documents have fortunately survived. They provide a great deal of information about the day-to-day running of Woodbury in the 15th century.

The Vicars Choral, as the name implies, were a body of priests concerned with the music of the services in the Cathedral. They had been founded by Bishop Marshall before 1200 and in 1205 he gave them Woodbury church and church land as an endowment. The grant, a handsome document in an unusually large, round hand can still be seen in Exeter Cathedral Library.

A translation of Henry Marshall's deed reads as follows:-

"To all to whom the present writing shall come, Henry by the grace of God Bishop of Exeter, health in the true Health Giver. It is fitting that they who labour abundantly in the offices of the Church should rejoice in remuneration from that Church. Wherefore we desiring to provide with fatherly care for the advantage of the Vicars of our Church at Exeter who, day and night devote themselves to the night and day offices, according to their ability, do grant and confirm to the said Vicars the Church of Woodbury, with all the appurtenances thereof, reserving a maintainence for a yearly Chaplain and Clerk serving the said Church; which Chaplain, indeed, shall receive forty shillings only and the Clerk ten shillings every year, by way of maintainence.... It is our will, also, that the said Church of Woodbury, with its ministers and parishioners, be quit and free from all Archidiaconal customs and exactions, in like manner as are the Chaplains of the Church of the Blessed Peter in Exeter. These witnesses; Anselm the Treasurer, Henry the Precentor, William of Swindon, Master Henry of Warwick, Master Hugh of Wilton, Master Milo,

Master Roger of Didesham, canons of Exeter, Master William Pace, Maurice and Geoffrey, Chaplains, Gilbert the Notary".

As a result of Bishop Marshall's gift, Woodbury church became what is termed a "peculiar". It has meant that the administration of St. Swithin's has differed in certain ways from normal custom. Though the church was free from the "visitation" of the Archdeacon, the Vicars themselves made an annual visit to inspect their buildings and the parish books to satisfy themselves that all was in order.[1] The only difference now remaining is that "according to ancient custom" the parishioners elect both their church-wardens (Woodbury has no vicar's warden) — a fact discovered by two recent vicars who tried unsuccessfully to overturn the custom and make their own appointments!

Did the yearly curate live with his brethren in the little bachelor chambers of their College in Kalendarhay, Exeter or did he live at Parsonage? Common-sense dictates that he lived at Parsonage. The drawing (see below) shows two houses, presumably the smaller one for the priest and the larger one for the tenant farmer who managed the sanctuary land. Yet the accounts have many items for the

vicars' expenses to and from Exeter and it is known that from a later date the vicars did not have the use of their vicarage.[2]

After the Reformation, when priests could marry, they lived in

Woodbury with their families and found their own accommodation. The association continued until the College went out of existence in 1933. Prebendary Llewellyn was the last Custos and the Reverend R.H. Neely the last vicar presented to the living by the College. Woodbury is now in the gift of the Dean and Chapter of Exeter.

The parish clerk referred to in the document lived in the village and kept the books and accounts for the vicars. At first he may have been a young man studying for the priesthood, for few but priests could write, but later he was certainly a layman who lived with his family in the house specially provided for him and built on church land. It was known variously as the Clerk's House, the Parish House or latterly Haydon's – because the land had been given to the church by the Haydons of Ebford. It is first mentioned in 1403 when 10d. rent "was received from the house which the clerk holds."[3] All that now survives is the Church Room, probably the single-storeyed hall of the original house. (See p.166)

The "appurtenances" of Woodbury church mentioned in the grant were the estate lands based upon Parsonage, first detailed in the Domesday Book. The earliest document of this estate now surviving is an indenture of a lease dated 25th October 1391 between the Vicars and their lessees Robert Rigge and John Lake, for the lifetime of John Lake, at a rent of 48 marks. The lease mentioned the land, buildings, garden and fishponds. Robert and John must not sell or otherwise part with any neifs (serfs, bondmen) and they must pay for the repairs of the church chancel and the expenses of the Vicars' annual visitation.[4]

Maybe John did not survive to enjoy his lease for very long. Ten years later there is no mention of him but the records of the letting of the fields suggests that the Vicars were running the farm themselves with the aid of their steward, Thomas Stokes.

Parsonage lay less than half a mile north of the church and comprised houses and a group of farm buildings in the shadow of a vast tithe barn. None of them now remains but most of those that appear on the Tithe Map of 1839 can be identified from the 15th C. accounts. (See opposite). There were two entrances to Parsonage; one, opposite the bottom of Cottles Lane, crossed the bright little stream that overflowed from the fishponds and the other, known as "the north gate", led between the tithe barn and the "little barn" into Windmill Lane.

Some of the land was gathered around the farm in small enclosed

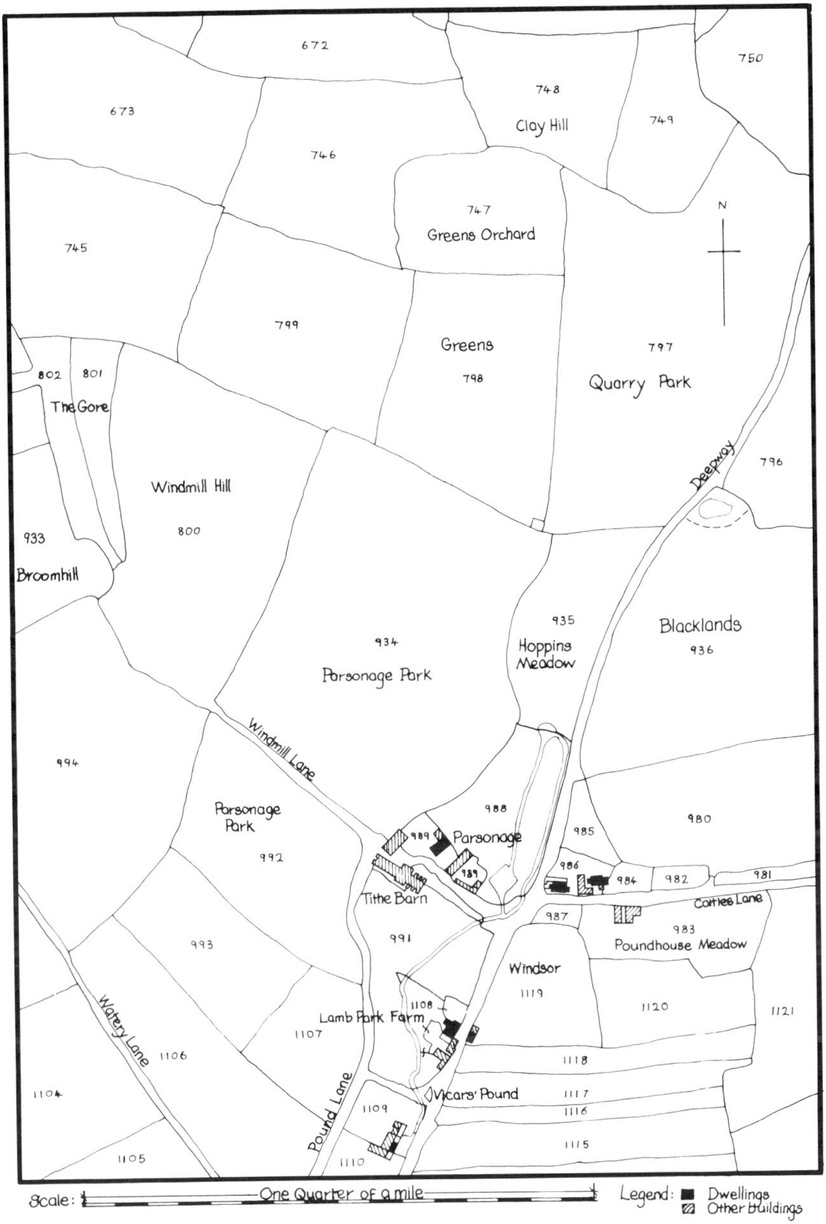

Parsonage in 1839

fields, while most of the arable was in strips in the Common Fields. Those fields to the south of Parsonage were allocated for the tithing lambs and gave their name, Lamb Park, to a small farmhouse built there in 1445.[5] Many people still remember the ruins of Lamb Park Farm, last inhabited by Mr. Walter Knott at the beginning of this century.

The giant tithe barn towered over Parsonage Farm. It had the rare distinction of a name, St. Theobald's Barn, or Tybbotsbarn as it came to be known. It was 153 ft. in length, 30 ft. longer than the church. The addition of two graceful, transept-like bays across the centre made it cruciform in shape. It is not known when it was built but it was being re-thatched in 1408 and again in 1441. This makes the life of the thatch more than thirty years and so it is fair to assume it was there in 1370 and probably very much earlier. The amount of work being done and the number of labourers employed in 1407 suggests that it may have been enlarged then. The ground plan of the Tithe Map shows that the two ends of the barn were differently constructed — one being buttressed, the other plain. It is possible that part of the barn is contemporary with the building of the church (c.1220), while an enlargement took place when the tower was built (1406-9) — the same stone and workmen being used.

Tybbotsbarn had a dovecote in it — "the colvyrhaye within the barn" — probably housed in the north gable for it is elsewhere described as "the culvyrhaye by the north gate". The barn was the scene of constant comings and goings as tenants and freeholders alike brought a tenth of their produce to the Vicars' steward. The two bays had huge doors in them so that a laden ox-cart could be driven right into the barn for loading and unloading.

In summer-time the precious hay was stored against the meagre days of winter and at sheep-shearing several hundred rolled fleeces found their way into the barn en route for the Exeter Wool Market. Autumn brought in the corn and the straw, the apples waiting for the cider press and the hides of animals slaughtered because of insufficient winter feed. At Michaelmas and Christmas even the lowliest small-holder had an offering of goose feathers to bring.

During the dark days of winter and early spring the process would be reversed and Woodbury folk bought back the tithe commodities from the Vicars. And pigeons from the dovecot helped to eke out a winter diet that almost excluded fresh meat. This distribution system not only ensured income for the College but also helped to hedge against crop-failure, famine and starvation — the real bogies of mediaeval England. Such a calamity may well have befallen Woodbury in 1473/4 when the accounts show a sudden drastic drop in rents of up to a third.

The Vicars were efficient administrators and their manor prospered. At the beginning of the 15th century they embarked upon further work to the parish church. Reading the transcript of the accounts one cannot help but catch their spirit of enthusiasm and the love they obviously had for Woodbury. Everything must be of the best. In 1403 two of the Vicars personally paid for new woodwork in the church — John Frak 12d. for a new door, and Frak and Roger Burnard 20d. each "for making a lectern and interclose there".[6] Neither of them was parish priest at the time.

But plans were already in hand for a major new building project — the addition of the church tower. Money had to be raised from many sources and the Lord of the Manor's continuing concern is shown by the legacy of 20 marks (£13.66p) "for the Tower of Wodbury" left by Sir Wm. Bonville in 1406.[7] The following year the parishioners of Woodbury had a whip-round amongst themselves and were able to hand over £2 to the Vicars.[8]

By the summer of 1409 their masterpeice was finished — in size a monumental 84 ft. high, in design and workmanship splendid. It ranks amongst the finest in the county. Then came the unforgetable day, 23rd September, when the inhabitants of Woodbury put on their best clothes and crowded the churchyard to see Bishop Stafford arrive in state to consecrate and dedicate the new tower.[9] The morning light fell on mitre and cope, silks and velvets, jewels and precious metals as the Bishop and his retinue, preceded by the Vicars, made their way slowly up the path to the south door. One can picture the people kneeling along the route to receive the Bishop's blessing, or lifting small children up to shoulder height that they should miss nothing. It was a day they would always remember.

The purpose of the tower, needless to say, was to house a peal of bells and the records fail to tell us if they were installed in time to give the Bishop a good send-off. But, no doubt, the one bell needed to toll for quite another kind of occasion was muffled one day in 1435 when a sad family party from Nutwell Court climbed the steep path to lay the infant son of Sir John Dinham in his grave. The entry comes immediately after one referring to "the purification of

Lady Dinham" after childbirth.[10]

Sir John had sought and been granted a licence from the Vicars for his son to be "entombed in the middle of the chancel". The high costs of such licences kept burials in the church to a minimum but the granting of them augmented the income of the church. There were other ways too, in which the Vicars could line their pockets while rendering real and valuable service to their flock. In an age of widespread illiteracy, the clergy enjoyed a highly profitable monopoly and the Vicars were kept busy writing letters, making wills and inventories and proving probate.

Typical entries are:-

"1407 To John Coscombe for a copy of a writ brought at suit of Richard Skynner.

1426 Expenses of John Foulere (curate) when executor of the wife of John Mote.

1440 2/- for the will of William Faryingdon and 18d. for the will of William Lucas and 14d. for will of John Towning junior and 2/- for the will of Robert Hethfyld.

1473 Profits of jurisdiction for the Will of Rich'd Milward."

A particularly unusual reference to Woodbury at this time is to be found in Exeter Cathedral Fabric Rolls for 1415, where the Cathedral received 3s. 2d. "*in* Galyhapens *de Ecclesia Parochiali de* Woodbury". Galyhapens is believed to be a form of "girl-ha'pence", a fee paid by young girls on marriage,[11] though why the Cathedral Fabric should have it is less easy to explain.

It is in the Vicars Choral accounts that we first discover that Woodbury had a thriving fishing fleet in the Exe. The early manor did not extend to the estuary but before the 14th century the existing manor of Nutwell and its neighbour Exton had been drawn into Woodbury. This gave Woodbury a very substantial area of foreshore and no doubt Exton was soon being exploited as a fishing port to rival Topsham, Lympstone and Exminster.

Judging by the number of names, Woodbury had quite a sizeable fleet of boats — some small single-handed craft ("Thomas Scutte by himself") and others requiring several crew-members and probably fishing in the open sea off Exmouth. The Livermores and Yerneways of Gulliford were obviously fishing families for their names appear over several generations. Often a father was in partnership with one or more of his sons. Entries detail payments to fishermen for their "winter craft" — presumably boat repairs — and one item in 1480 reads "pd for pycchyn and Lawying", while another mentions payments to John Aysche for "dradgyn". One can imagine the little channel where the Gilbrook runs into the Exe at Exton becoming silted up and requiring to be dredged, and the busy winter repair work being done on the boats pulled up on the shore that existed until the coming of the railway many centuries later.

Even these fishermen were to some extent farmers and aimed to be as independent and self-supporting as possible. It is hard nowadays to imagine a diet without tea or coffee, potatoes or sugar. But a great deal of meat, fish, bread and dairy produce was eaten, peas and beans were extensively grown and apples were plentiful in a good year. The church owned its own orchard, part of Haydon's gift, from which John Chamberlayn bought the entire apple crop in 1440.[12]

As honey was the only sweetener known, bees were greatly prized. Many people kept hives, as we know by the purchase of wax for church candles. The church-wardens' accounts in the 16th century also make it clear that there were "Church Bees", kept, presumably, in the Parish Orchard. But the biggest bee-keeper in Woodbury was the Abbot of Torre's tenant at Greendale Barton and it was no

The 15th century seal of the College of Vicars Choral of Exeter Cathedral.

doubt his bees that gave Honey Lane its name. From 1540 onward we find the church buying large quantities of bees' wax from the tenant of Greendale, Thomas Younge.

More than a hundred surnames appear in the Vicars Choral accounts and a large proportion have a familiar ring to them. The Jarmans, Lees, and Halls (originally the "Att Halles" and a family of some consequence) had been here at the time of the Lay Subsidy Tax of 1332. In the fifteenth century they were joined by the names of Stokes, Skinner and Hayman; Lake, Livermore and Ridler; Pyne, Pile and Pope. Others who laid their bones in Woodbury churchyard are now remembered only by the names of the places where they lived — Webbers, Bonds, Browns, Cadhayes and Ballymans to mention but a few.

In this category also comes the family of de Huntebeare (various spellings) who were already well-established by 1230.[13] Their small manor of Great Houndbeare, now in Aylesbeare but until 1884 part of the parish of Woodbury, is thought to have been a Domesday manor called Landshers. A thousand years of history is waiting to be discovered at Houndbeare.

7.
The Story of John Scorche

Very occasionally one is allowed brief but vivid glimpses of dramatic events long ago. Such an event happened in Woodbury in 1425/26 and, thanks to the records of the College of Vicars Choral of Exeter Cathedral,[1] we can piece together most of what happened.

It concerns John Scorche. His family gave their name to a small farm on the edge of the Common which disappeared during the last century. Most of the land now forms part of Hogsbrook and nothing remains of Scorche's farmhouse but the man-made terrace in the corner of the sloping field above the stream where it stood and a gap in the hedge embankment along its frontage onto the lane. Though the banks that enclosed John Scorche's small fields have gone and the ford has been replaced by a culvert and bridge there is still much that he would recognise after 550 years — the silence and remoteness, the hawthorn-shaded stream on its way to join the Grindle Brook and the Common always at hand to snatch back the land if work fell behind. In this north-facing valley where spring comes late, life must always have been a struggle and the Scorche family must have been poor. Certainly they were never prolific. Their names are thinly dotted about the parish register and they finally disappeared in 1664. What then could they possibly have done to create such a rumpus in 1425?

In that year John Scorche was excommunicated by the Consistory Court of the Bishop of Exeter. Excommunication was not uncommon at that time and was usually a means of putting pressure on those who did not pay their tithes or who obstructed the tithe collector. The accounts do not tell us what Scorche had done but he evidently felt aggrieved and was sufficently sure of his rights to accuse James Carsleigh, president of the Consistory Court, of "unfairness to him in the cause between them". Scorche appealed to the Archbishop of Canterbury (the great Henry Chichele) to be heard in the Court of the Arches. This was the highest court of ecclesiastical law (short of the Pope himself) and the equivalent of the House of Lords in civil law. The Court got its picturesque name because it took place in the arched crypt of St. Mary-le-Bow in London. Unfortunately the court records were destroyed in the Great Fire of London in 1666.

There must have been much to-ing and fro-ing between Exeter and London. A mandate from the Archbishop, dated at Lambeth on 28th July 1425, was read out in Exeter Cathedral on 30th August and the parties concerned were summoned to appear before the Archbishop in the Court of Arches. What happened next is not clear but presumably the Court found for Carsleigh against Scorche — who took to his heels and fled.

On 20th May 1426 William Palton, Sheriff of Devon, issued a writ commanding fifteen named persons to seize John Scorche "who has gone to foreign parts" and throw him into the gaol of Exeter Castle. Fifteen people seem quite a crowd to arrest one man. Did he have the support of friends and was he armed to resist arrest? We know for sure that they did catch him, brought him back and threw him into the gaol. The register of Bishop Edmund Lacy has this entry:- "17th Sept. 1426 Commission for the relaxing of the excommunication imposed.....on John Scorche.....for his violation of ecclesiastical liberties. He has now submitted and is to be sworn to obey the law of the church and not so to offend again; and, having confessed to his priest, to receive the sacrament of the Eucharist publicly in his parish church next Sunday, which he has not yet done this year".[2]

This time Scorche did as he was told. These three entries appear in the Vicars Choral accounts:-

"20d. for wax for John Scorche who did his penance".

"Expenses in connection with the visit of the Dean and Precentor (and others).....when they came to see that John Scorche carried out his penance imposed on him in due form".

"Expenses of Robert Colyn and John Fowlere when they came to absolve Scorche".

Thus ends the official account of an extraordinary affair. We shall never know what he did. The specific reference to his "violation of ecclesiastical liberties" makes it probable that his offence was connected with tithe. Yet the vigour with which the case was pursued suggests a more serious offence than simply witholding payment and the likelihood is that he used violence against the tithe collectors. At any rate John Scorche, having given them a run for their money and paid his penalty in full, lived to appear in the College accounts for many more years. And among the uncertainties one thing is surely certain. The little drama must have kept Woodbury buzzing with gossip for eighteen months.

Site of John Scorche's Farm

8.
Into a New Age

The latter half of the 15th century was a time of confusion and violence. The Wars of the Roses toppled thrones and wiped out or ruined a large part of the old feudal barony. Many of those who survived the bloody battles were executed afterwards for treason or stripped of their lands by succeeding kings.

Woodbury saw nothing of the battles that tore England apart but Woodbury's landlords, the Bonvilles of Shute and the Dinhams of Nutwell, were both deeply involved in the Yorkist cause and there is no doubt that Woodbury men fought alongside their Lords in some of the major battles.

The Yorkists received a set-back in a skirmish at Ludford (1459) which sent the Duke of York himself scurrying to Ireland, while his 17-year-old son Edward Earl of March, with his friends the Earls of Salisbury and Warwick, fled southwards for the safety of Woodbury, where Sir John Dinham hid them at Nutwell. They were able to purchase a ship at Exmouth for 110 marks in which they made their way first to Guernsey and then to Calais — still an English possession.[1]

The Earls were soon back in England, however, and joined in battle against the Lancastrians at Northampton (July 1460) where they won a victory. But on December 30th the same year their fortunes were reversed and at the battle of Wakefield the Duke of York was taken prisoner and beheaded, while two generations of Bonvilles, father and newly-wedded son, fell by the sword on the battlefield. Six weeks later old Lord William Bonville, head of his house, veteran of Agincourt, white-haired and nearing seventy, was captured at St. Albans — defending, it is said, the person of Edward Earl of March and was hurried to the headsman's block. So perished the great house of Bonville. Back home at Shute the dreadful news came to the waiting wives and little Cecily Bonville inherited the manors of Shute and Woodbury, and vast estates in Devon and Somerset, before her first birthday.

Yet the tide had turned for the Yorkists and on 26th February 1461 the Earl of March was acclaimed King Edward IV. He was nineteen. A grateful monarch now remembered his debt to John Dinham of Nutwell, creating him Lord Dinham and showering upon him many honours. He became Privy Councillor, a position he continued to hold under King Henry VII, who also appointed him Lord High Treasurer of England.

The battle of Towton which finally secured the throne for Edward claimed the life of Henry Grey, Duke of Suffolk, and three years later King Edward married Grey's widow Elizabeth. Elizabeth and Henry Grey had had a son, Thomas, later Marquis of Dorset, and in 1474 Thomas Grey married Cicely Bonville, at thirteen years of age the richest heiress in England,[2] and Woodbury passed to the Greys of Leicestershire. The Wars of the Roses ended in 1485 with the victory of Bosworth Field which put Henry Tudor on the throne of England. A Lancastrian, he healed the breach by marrying King Edward's daughter Elizabeth, "the White rose of York" and Cecily's sister-in-law. England settled down to a period of peace and stability.

It was time for long-overdue changes. The barons had fought themselves to a standstill and the old fendal system, which had served England well since 1066, lay in ruins — the manor courts in decay. Woodbury's Manor Court, which may have been held in a special ground-floor room at Thorn Barton, moved to Shute with the Bonvilles, and representatives of the Vicars Choral sometimes had to ride over there to see to their Woodbury affairs in the Bonvilles' Court. The chief officer of the Manor Court had been the Reeve and although Woodbury still had a Reeve until at least 1554 he had probably lost most of his old powers, with the exception of organizing the Constables. That, too, was soon to go, for a new kind of 'parochial government' was beginning to emerge — a body known as the Vestry. Exactly what the Vestry was is hard to define, as those eligible to serve on it and the manner of their election differed from place to place. But as the name implies, the Vestry was under the authority of the church, not the landlord, and broadly speaking all 'rate-payers' had a duty to attend meetings to elect officers. Church-wardens, Ale-Wardens, Way-Wardens, Overseers and Constables found themselves responsible for fund-raising, road maintenance, the care of the poor, control of vermin and public health, law and order, the training and equipping of militiamen and a hundred and one other things[3].

Woodbury has the good fortune to have preserved detailed accounts of the Vestry's affairs from 1536 and from these we know how they raised and spent the money. The earliest ledger is called the Malt Book and on its first page it describes how the householders agreed amongst themselves to tax their estates in proportion to their value by a voluntary gift of malt — or a money equivalent. The sum thus raised was for the maintenance of the church. Their method of raising it was to dine together twice a year, bringing their own food with them and paying for their ale with the malt or the money they owed. It is worth quoting.[4]

> "March 12, 1536, the 27th King Henry VIII
> The hole pisshens of the Pishe (parish) of Woodbury by there hole assent and consent hath agreid to gyff ev'y yere yerely to the Alle Wardyns of the Psshe Church of Wodbury....so much Malt or Monye the valew of the Malt for the mayntenaunce of the Church as apperyth upon ev'y of ther names hereafter following, and also the seide Pisshens hath ferder agreid....to dyne together the Tuysday yn the Whitsonwcke and the later Seynt Swythyns Dey at the Church House of Wodbury and....to brynge there Meyte & Brede with them and to paye....for there Drynke at there Dyners — for a Man and his Wyff the sum or sumes set ont ther names hereafter following. And also the seide Pishns hath ferder agreid that if thei do not come to Dyn....that thei so paye....for their Dyns....notwtstandyng to the Church Wardyns for the tyme beying, and also that no wedow man or wedow woman to paye for a Place but 2 pence...."

The raters signed their names or, in most instances, made their marks while the clerk wrote their names. In many cases the marks show just how unaccustomed the hand was to holding a pen. But the two Trapnells at Exton not only signed for themselves but Walter drew a little boat and Richard a large anchor; they were fishermen.

The assessement varied from 4 bushels of malt from the Haydons at Ebford to half a peck from John Roundell of Exton, the most usual amount being a bushel. Eighty-two names appear (though the final page of the list is missing) and the final assessment was 137 bushels and three quarters of a peck valued at £9.2.11d.

In the Malt Rate list we discover Rydon Farm, Higher and Lower Venmore, Plymptons (now Higher Venmore) Cuttysmore (later called Scotsmore but now absorbed in Lower Venmore) and Sparkeshayes, the home of the Lee family who were to make such significant contributions to the story of Woodbury in centuries to come.

The companion to the Malt Book was the Church-wardens' Accounts which start in 1537. From them we learn something about the Church House where the Raters held the two annual Church Ales described above. These entries, picked out of the accounts covering almost a century, tell a tale of their own.

> "1538 for the Standyngs in the Church Howse called the Market Place for a hole year. 8s.
>
> 1538 for gathering of straw for the Church Howse 4d., to the Thaycherher for meyte and Drynke whan he dyd thayche ye Howse 5s.5d.
>
> 1540 for Thaychyn of the Church Howse and Wallys 2s.5d.
>
> 1542 of the Market men for ther Standyngs 6s.4d.
>
> 1546 to Phelypp James for mending of the stondyngs yn the Church Howse.
>
> 1550 for the fyne of the Churche Howse to the Ryght Honorable Lord Marquis Dorset £5.
>
> 1552 to Thomas Barber the Reyff (Reeve) for rent of the Church Howse and the peys of grownd 20d.
>
> 1594 of the bochers and others for the standyngs in the shamells (shambles) 10s.2d.
>
> 1619 to Mr. Jarvis for the Clarke of the Market 6d."

Here we have very much more than the room in which the Vestry Meetings and Church Ales took place. Here, at last, is vital information about the Tuesday Market granted in 1285 and where it was held. One gets the impression of a large building, possibly on two floors, that served both as a market hall and a room in which more than a hundred people could sit down for a meal. The "standyngs" were stalls — many of them, but not all, held by butchers. The building and its "peys of grownd" belonged to the Lord of the Manor who renewed a long lease in 1550 to the Church Vestry who, in turn, maintained the property and paid the market clerk, Mr. Jarvis. Where was it?

The likelihood is that it stood at the bottom of the churchyard on the east side of the lych-gate and the first clue to the whereabouts is contained in the 1540 reference above to thatching. The word "Wallys" probably refers to a tenement which had been the home of the Wille family in 1332. By 1440 the spelling of the name had changed to Wele and the Vicars Choral accounts for that year contains an item concerning "*novi edificii super tenementum Johannis Wele ex parte cimiterii*" — "the new building by the tenement of John Wele from part of the churchyard."[5] These loose ends are nicely tied together by a sale notice which appeared in the Exeter Flying Post on 12th October 1797 — "Lot 3. A tenement, Garden and Orchard called Whales Tenement. Now the White Hart Inn situate in Woodbury..."

So there we have it . "The Church House called the Market Place" is the 'new building' mentioned as being built in the churchyard in 1440 and was by the tenement variously called Wille's, Wele's, Wallys or Whale's, *alias* the White Hart. The old building, finally converted into cottages, stood in the churchyard until the 1870s.

The Church House was used for a multitude of purposes and can really be described as Woodbury's Village Hall. In it was stored the parish property, including "tow beddys" (two beds) among an extraordinary assortment of things. It is thought that parishes acquired these oddments from "mortuaries" — payments to the church of goods when people died — or as gifts or debts — and that the parish kept them to lend or hire out and eventually to sell. And there were "pots, kuppes and treen vessells bought and occupied att the churche ale", that cost 2s. in 1556, as well as props and costumes required for the mummers' plays at Twelfth Night and the May Day Revels. In 1554 the parish spent 12d. on "A viser for a foole" and 7d. for "Bellys for the foole". These were the days of Merrie England and it is quite evident that Woodbury knew how to enjoy itself. If further proof were needed there are two entries in 1575 showing that the churchwardens spent 16s. for timber to make "Robert (Robin) Hoods house" and subsequently netted a profit of 40s. for the ale sold "whan...Walter Holwell was Robert Hood." This interesting entry probably refers to the erection of a stage and the performance of a Mummers' play.[6]

The Malt Rate arrangements were soon in trouble. What had seemed at the outset to be a voluntary rate and a jolly idea for a parish get-together ran into difficulties before the end of the 16th century. One can imagine the ale-wardens had problems in collecting the rate from people who chose to absent themselves from the dinners.

On 22nd October 1599, a great parish gathering in the church thrashed the matter out in the presence of Mr. John Leache, Bachelor of Divinity and Thomas Chaffe, priest of the parish, describing himself as "notarie publique". There was no mention this time of the rate being voluntary, nor about the dinners, but raters were to pay twice yearly:- "viz. the one moyetie or halfendael... this side of the Feast of St. John the Baptist (24th June) then following and the other halfendael between the said Feast and the Sunday next before Michaelmas Day (29th September)". The "refusers" were to be "compelled to paye" or the sidesmen would forfeit 6s.8d. for every defaulter and the ale-wardens £1 apiece.

The church-wardens' accounts make it very clear that life in Tudor Woodbury did not consist mainly of Church Ales. Grief and disaster were never very far away. A series of bad harvests could bring near-starvation and seriously reduce people's resistance to disease. Bubonic Plague, Typhus, Dysentery and Diphtheria were only some of the hazards they had to contend with but undoubtedly Plague was the most feared.[7]

The Plague was strangely selective. Some years were free of it and in others it would sweep the district, or strike one village and not another. In Woodbury, 1563 (before our burial register begins) was evidently a bad year in which the church-wardens paid 2s. "to James Oke and Joane Roo for keping of syck folks in the syckness tyme". In 1578 the head Constable bought a book for 3s. "concerninge medecinne for the plague". Perhaps it worked, for the same year Woodbury subscribed 26s.8d. "to the poore people of Newton Popleford when they were shoute upp for the plague" (plague-houses were boarded up with the people inside them to stop the infection spreading) though Woodbury itself seems to have escaped. Nineteen people died that year — only slightly above average for the decade. But on the whole Woodbury was thriving and the arrival of the register for baptisms, marriages and burials makes it possible to estimate that the population was between 700 and 800, or three times what it had been at Domesday.

Great changes were taking place in agriculture. A few years before her death in 1530, Cecily Bonville, Marchioness of Dorset, had a detailed survey made of all her lands in Woodbury[8] and this, together with the 1536 Malt Rate presents a clear picture of the state of farming. Gone were the Great Fields with their many hundreds of strips side by side; only a few acres of open-field farming remained at Salterton. In their place had come an intricate pattern of small enclosed fields averaging 3 or 4 acres.

In the break-up some farmers had managed to get quite large farms together, e.g. the Westcotts who had farmed at Heathfield since 1441 and Richard Hopping, living on the site of the old manor and farming some of the barton land. The Hoppings were an old Woodbury family and at that time there were two Hoppings named Richard. At first confusion was avoided by referring to them as "Richard Hopping of Woodbury" and "Richard Hopping of Salterton". But the former took the name Holwell, possibly his wife's maiden name. She may have been the daughter of a wealthy and educated man for from that time the Holwells never looked back while the Hoppings of Salterton remained small-time farmers. But for more than half a century whenever Holwells' name was written it was accompanied by "*alias Hopping*" – *or vice versa*.

Woodbury village itself had comparatively few inhabitants and the farmhouses in the main street were separated from one another by paddocks and orchards, each house with its own area of 'waste' for the dung-heap, the woodpile, geese and nettles. It was a comfortably disorganised scene free from hard-edged roads, neat little gates and front gardens. Most of the village farms still had their fields here and there about the place as they had managed to get them together when the Great Field broke up. The big farms to emerge were away from the village – Woodmanton, for instance, with 87½ acres (mostly pasture), and a cluster of five smaller properties round it, presumably small-holders' or labourers' cottages.

The usual form of lease to tenant farmers was for three lives, that is the man, his wife and their eldest child. A typical entry begins: "John Perse and Johanna his wife and Sybil their daughter hold of the Lord (of the Manor) for their lives according to the custom of the manor...one tenement to which pertains 11 closes containing 28 acres of which 26½ are arable and each acre is worth 12d., and 1½ acres are meadow...worth 4s. Rent per annum 10s.4½d. And for customary services 12d. And common rights for 8 animals on Woodbury Downe and for 40 sheep there". Rents were fairly standard throughout the parish — arable 12d. per acre, pasture 24d.

and meadow 32d. — and the old custom of rendering service to the landlord had been commuted to a money payment. The 8 animals were probably John Perse's ox-team and the survey mentions a total of 190 oxen belonging to the landlord's tenants. The ox was still (and for many centuries to come) the working animal and the usual number was 8 — an ox-team — though Andrew Hopping (son of Richard *alias* Holwell) had 12 on his 57 acre farm at Rydon and Wm. Lucas had 20 on his 76 acres at Venmore — both farms on wet clay soil. At much the same time (1538) the church-wardens' accounts give us details of farm prices:- Oats, 2d. to 3d. a quarter, Barley 5d., Wheat 8d.; Fat ox 26s.8d., fat wether 3s.4d., fat calf 3s.4d., fat lamb 12d.

Sheep were the big business of the day, for the West Country woollen industry was at the height of its prosperity. Cecily Bonville's tenants had a total of 1230 sheep on the Common but as she owned rather less than half the parish the grand total was probably nearer 3000. Ebford residents evidently had grazing rights on "le Hethfyld" and it was no doubt for that purpose that the narrow lane from Ebford to Postlake Corner came into being.

The instance of so many sheep makes one wonder if weaving were going on in Woodbury at that time. Almost certainly it was, though there is no written evidence of it. Visual evidence might suggest that the Beal family were weavers. The striking feature of their house opposite the Green, still called "The Beals", is the wide window under an oak lintel of immense length, similar in proportions to those found in weavers' houses of the Elizabethan period in the Cotswolds and the Yorkshire Dales. They were designed to give daylight to the loom. For what other reason would so difficult a form of construction be attempted? And behind The Beals a long cob barn runs at right-angles to the house — highly suitable for the functions of dyeing and finishing the cloth which was made in standard lengths of 24 x 2 yds., or 12 x 1 yd.

With a shift in the balance of farming towards fewer, larger farms it goes without saying that the labouring class increased greatly in numbers. These landless people were highly vulnerable to the changing wind of fortune. With nothing to fall back on, a labourer's death or disability could throw his whole family on the parish. Legislation tried to deal with the poor yet after the Reformation, with no further help coming from the religious houses, the problem became more acute. New legislation sought to distinguish between the "can't works" and the "won't works". The "won't works" were punished by the Constable, sometimes by whipping but even by such drastic measures as turning the culprits over to the "Press gang". The navy complained of the quality of its intake by this method but in 1653 Woodbury paid 4s.6d. "to ye Constables for carrying an imprestman to Torbay..." and he was almost certainly a 'rogue'.

The "can't works" became the responsibility of the parish. An alms-box was placed in the church and priest and church-wardens exhorted the people to give generously for the maintenance of the "impotent poor", resident in the parish.[9] 'Resident' was the key word and to avoid the risk of being overwhelmed by the poor of the entire neighbourhood, the church-wardens had to insist on proof of residence from those who applied. References abound in the accounts but one quotation will serve to show the plight of those who could not establish residence in any one parish:-

> "1576 — to a poore woman that was borne in a barrow from thithen to thithen."

Nobody wanted to accept responsibility for the poor old soul! By the end of the century the poor could no longer be funded from the alms-box alone and it became necessary to introduce special taxation — or Poor Rate. It was collected by four Overseers of the Poor and administered by the Vestry.

As wealth and poverty grew side by side, the nation's conscience showed a growing concern for the less fortunate. Besides well-meaning legislation there was an enormous increase in private funds to set up schools, hospitals, almshouses and all sorts of charities for the poor. Woodbury's first charity dates from 1597 when, in his will, John Haydon left two sums of money and careful instructions as to how it was to be administered. The interest from one sum was laid out yearly in "shirt-cloth for the poor", while the other went "to three poor people inhabiting in the parish of Woodbury, on every Sunday of the year to each of them 5d. viz. 4d. in money and 1d. in bread and so to go round to the poor of the said parish, and 20d. being the rest of the said £3.6s.4d. to be distributed at the discretion of the church-wardens".[10] There are numerous people still in Woodbury who remember going to church on Palm Sunday to receive a loaf of bread with a 6d. stuck in the top of it. The bread was newly baked and the delicious smell filled the church. It was John Haydon's voice speaking across 400 years.

9.
The Reformation and the Armada

The powerful ideas for reform within the Church of Rome which spilled out into a full-scale breakaway movement in northern Europe affected England very slowly. Though Henry VIII surrounded himself by men of the "new learning" his intention was clearly reform rather than breakaway and much was done to prevent the spirit of the Reformation from slipping out of hand.[1]

In Woodbury things went on as before and people were blissfully unaware of the storms to come. Some of the parish's growing wealth was lavished on the church. In 1532-3 Richard Haydon of Ebford had the north aisle of St. Swithin's built at his own expense. In 1539 – the year of the suppression of Torre Abbey and the confiscation of Greendale Barton – the church-wardens spent £4 on "a suyt of vestyments of blacke velvet and a auter cloth of paned wt. damaske crymsyn velvet."

The suppression of the monasteries scarcely caused a ripple among the ordinary people of Devon who thought the monks' grasp upon land and wealth excessive. But if they had hoped the seizure of monastic lands would lead to a fairer distribution they were to be sorely disappointed. In the land-grab that followed the Dissolution, Greendale Barton became the property of Lord John Russell, a leading Protestant and the biggest receiver of monastic lands in the West of England.[2]

Did Henry VIII have qualms about the troubled future as he made his will naming his three very different children as his successors? As he lay dying in 1547 he whispered over and over again "First Edward – then Mary – then Elizabeth" as though he doubted it would happen that way. Woodbury church bells tolled his knell and dirges were sung for his soul – at a cost of 16s., as appears in the church-wardens' accounts. Edward VI, the youngest of Henry's children, was a bright but sickly child of nine when he ascended the throne and Henry had placed him under the protection of his maternal uncle, the Duke of Somerset.

Within two years the drastic effect of Somerset's Protestantism began to make itself felt in Woodbury. The two stone altars were destroyed and the rubble carted away by James Croft who was paid 5d. Andrew Gybb made a new Communion table for 6d. and the "latyn bokys" were removed to Exeter "according to the commandment". The new "salter bokys and the Omely Boke" in English were purchased for 6s. The rood cross was dismantled and its accompanying figures of the Virgin Mary and St. John destroyed. The list of vestments "delyvryd to the Kyngs Comyssyoners" makes one realise the colour and pageantry of feast days in even an ordinary village church like Woodbury:- "Three copes; of blue velvet, of sangwyn cloth of silk, of green silk; vestments of crymson velvet, of black velvet, of green with a cross of gold . . . of tawny sylke with a orynge cross . . ." and so on.

These changes were more than conservative Westcountrymen could endure. The destruction of the sacred figures and the communion service in English which replaced the Latin mass sparked a smouldering discontent and the men of Devon and Cornwall rose in a body to demand a return to the status quo of Henry VIII's time — likening the new communion service to "Christmas games". Their demands were rejected and ten thousand indignant men armed themselves for a hopeless fight.[3]

Lord John Russell was sent with a force largely composed of foreign mercenaries to meet them and during the hot days of July and August 1549 the Western (or Prayer Book) Rebellion took its brave, bloody and fateful course. After defeating 'the rebels' at Fenny Bridges, Russell was reinforced by Lord Grey (Woodbury's landlord and a notable Protestant) at the head of 300 horsemen. They turned off the main Exeter road at Straitway and came over Aylesbeare Common to Greendale Barton where they set up their headquarters, using Windmill Hill as a look-out.

The men of Devon were encamped at Clyst St. Mary where they were busy barricading the bridge and felling trees across the road to block Russell's advance to Exeter. On hearing of Russell's arrival at Greendale they eagerly hurried over to attack the camp without delay. The attack was beaten off and Russell's chaplain preached a thanksgiving sermon among the corpses. This chaplain was none other than Miles Coverdale, one of the translators of the Bible and afterwards briefly Bishop of Exeter. But his sermon was not yet finished when the look-outs at the windmill reported another imminent attack. The stubborn courage of the 'rebels' was praised by Lord Grey as being the bravest he had ever seen.

The main action was fought at Clyst St. Mary on Monday 4th August. It is not known how many Woodbury men were involved but the blacksmith (John Hamon) distinguished himself defending Clyst Bridge with extraordinary tenacity and was killed. Due to a mistaken report that the 'rebels' were bringing up reinforcements from Woodbury, Grey ordered the prisoners taken at Greendale to be killed. Some reports give the total loss of life on those two days as nine hundred. Russell's army swept on to Exeter and the brief rising was all but over. The church-wardens marked the occasion without comment: "Md (minded) that the comocyon was at Clyst thys same yere and then after the pisshies were comandyed to ring but one bell".

During the four years that remained of Edward VI's brief reign the dismantling of the old faith progressed without further protest. With Miles Coverdale now in the Bishop's Palace at Exeter how could the Vicars Choral do otherwise? In 1550 the processional cross was stolen (hidden till it could be safely returned?) together with the censor, two chalices of silver parcel gilt "wt other thyngs". And in 1552 the church-wardens incurred expenses of 6s.8d. "at Exeter when the Church goodds were caryed thether to be delyvered to the Kynggs use."

But in 1553 the 15-year-old king died and Henry VIII's first-born child, Mary, succeeded him. Mary, the daughter of Catherine of Aragon, had been brought up as a strict Roman Catholic and the whole process of the Reformation in England was suddenly and violently put into reverse.

In Woodbury Queen Mary's accession was the occasion for great rejoicing and from the tall tower of St. Swithin's the bells rang out for the first time in four years. £1 was paid "for the bellys to ryng agayne when my Lady Mary was proclamyd Quene which was the XXIII deye of Julie" — obviously a day to remember. And thereafter a great spate of entries tells clearly enough of the enthusiasm with which stone altars were rebuilt, the rood loft set up with new figures, rich new vestments bought, candles, new books and "grese for the bells". In 1555 the stolen cross was triumphantly returned and John Combe was paid 18d. for bringing it home, plus an additional 6d. "paid for his brekefast wt his companye." In 1556 "Thomas Gove the elder gent" paid 5s.4d. "for XI bollys of pewter that did stand upon the Rudlaft to set tapers on."

Yet England was deeply divided between the old faith and the new and the Protestant faction hatched a desperate plot in which Woodbury's landlord was fatally implicated. Lord Grey, Duke of Suffolk, was the grandson of Cecily Bonville and the father of the tragic Lady Jane Grey. Through her mother, Jane was descended from Henry VIII's sister Margaret. Protestant supporters rallied round Lady Jane Grey and tried to overthrow Mary in her favour. The rising failed and the Grey family paid with their heads. Grey's manor of Woodbury was appropriated by the Crown.

The savagery with which Mary tried to stamp out Protestantism — the hundreds of people burnt at the stake, from Archbishop Cranmer to the simplest citizen (Miles Coverdale fled to the Continent just in time) — and the unpopularity of Mary's marriage to Philip of Spain finally sickened England of Mary and when she died in 1558 there were few to lament her passing.

Elizabeth, the last of Henry VIII's three children, ascended the throne at the age of twenty-five and found the fortunes of England at a low ebb. Though brought up as a Protestant, Elizabeth was not a deeply religious woman. She had neither the reforming zeal of Edward nor the blinkered passion of Mary and her immediate concern was for law and order and for healing the old wounds by conciliation and tolerance. So the newly-made bonds with Rome were not severed but allowed to drift quietly away, while the Church of England was restored in a more liberal form acceptable to many shades of opinion.

Woodbury church acquired Cranmer's Great Bible in English. It may still be seen in its glass case at the back of the church. The stone altars, so recently rebuilt, were again ripped out and the rubble carted away. The rood loft was again dismantled but the church-wardens, suspecting no doubt that the measures might be reversed as before, did not destroy the newly-carved figures but discreetly buried them — although the entry is hard to read and it may say "burned". In 1562 the church-wardens paid 4s. "for a newe booke of homelies and another little new book called the booke of prayer". And as far as we know, no serious protest was raised in Woodbury or Devon generally.

Indeed, England was on the threshold of a Golden Age. Elizabeth, perhaps the most charismatic monarch since Alfred the Great, had the capacity to inspire, and the ability to choose, brilliant men to serve her. Under her long and wise leadership England found a new sense of nationhood.

While comparative peace reigned at home Elizabeth faced a growing threat from her brother-in-law, Philip of Spain, who saw himself as the champion of Catholicism. Spain was developing enormous naval power based on Cadiz and Corunna and the final clash in 1588 had long been foreseen.

Through the pages of Woodbury's church-wardens' accounts it is possible to see in some detail the ways in which England prepared to meet such a threat. From the time the accounts start in Henry VIII's time it is apparent that much of the organization for raising, equipping and training a fighting force had fallen on the Vestry. England retained no professional regular army and relied on a militia should the need arise. In each parish the Constable was responsible for drawing up a list of able-bodied men between the ages of sixteen and sixty. The armour and weapons had to be provided by the Vestry (parish armour) and by the more prosperous residents of the parish, referred to as "men of substance". The armour was valuable and was stored in the church where it required a good deal of expert maintenance to keep the rust at bay. In 1580 the parish of Woodbury paid 4s.8d. to the "harnes kower for kepeinge cleane of the pishe armoure" and in 1595 "to one of Exeter for making cleane of the Armor againste the Trayninge, 5s."

Periodic 'musters' for the purpose of inspection were ordered by the Lord Lieutenant of the County and it was the Constable's duty to collect the appointed men, take them to the musters with the parish arms and armour and provide money for their maintenance. In 1546 one such muster took place at Newton Poppleford for an inspection by Sir Thomas Denys of Bicton and the parish paid 2s.4d. "for 12 mennys dyners" and 4d. for "a potell of wyne geven to Sr. Rychard Grenfeld Knyght whan he chose the men." One man from Woodbury was chosen and went to fight the French. Though we are not told his name the church-wardens have left us a colourful description of what he wore: "White kersy cloth for his coat with green, yellow and red ribbons, white fustian doublet, a sword and a dagger, a pair of harness and a bill."

Despite the development of musketry, the English long-bow remained the principal weapon and archery practice was compulsory on most Sundays and Holy Days. Somewhere or other Woodbury had its parish 'butts' though it is not known where. The inspection of these weapons is described in 1584 when "John Periam being Tytheman for going about the pishe to see every mans bowes and arowes" was paid 20d. The present yew trees in the churchyard are no doubt the direct descendants of those that provided the wood for Woodbury's long-bows and have themselves been there for over two hundred years.

A detailed Muster Roll for 1569[4] still exists and it shows that of the 58 men of Woodbury 23 were Archers, while 15 were "Harquebusiers" (or musketeers), 14 were Pikemen and 6 Billmen. Among the archers was Richard Pearce, Reeve of Woodbury.

There was another way in which Woodbury men were called upon to serve their country. As war with Spain became inevitable an elaborate warning system was devised whereby England could be alerted by means of bonfires. For the first time since Saxon days Woodbury Beacon was manned. Detailed instructions were issued. A bonfire must be built in readiness and dry kindling kept always at hand. A rota of men must man the Beacon at all times, three men by day and two by night. To avoid the possiblity of false alarms Woodbury Beacon was to be fired only on a signal from Mamhead across the river.

The real centre of activity at this time was Plymouth,[5] home port of Sir Francis Drake and Sir John Hawkins. Here, in the early summer of 1588, assembled some ninety ships under the overall command of Admiral Lord Howard of Effingham, with Drake as his second-in-command.

The Spanish Armada comprised a total of 130 ships of all sizes, carrying 38,000 soldiers and sailors, under the command of the Duke of Medina Sidonia. It must have presented a formidable sight to Capt. Tom Fleming, in Drake's old ship "Golden Hind", who spotted it at anchor off the Scillies on the morning of 29th July. He raced up the Channel and reached Plymouth late that afternoon as Drake was playing his famous game of bowls. The English fleet began to slip out of port as the tide turned at 10 o'clock that night.

At first light on the 30th July the Armada was seen by watchers on the Lizard and the first beacon fired. Soon the message was being carried past Plymouth, Mamhead, Woodbury and along the coast to Dover, North Foreland and Essex. By next morning even York and Durham knew.

This was the moment Woodbury had prepared for and the excitement and terror must have been overwhelming, for it was confidently expected that the Spaniards would try to put an army ashore in Torbay. Everywhere the cliffs were lined with thousands of spectators as the two giant fleets — the Spaniards maintaining a tight crescent formation — sailed eastward in full view of land; Howard in "Ark Royal", Drake in "Revenge", Hawkins in "Victory" and Frobisher in "Triumph". Spine-tingling names all!

But though there were skirmishes at many points as the Armada made its way up Channel, the expected grand naval battle never took place. During the night of July 31st. Lord Howard in "Ark Royal" with a small handful of ships outstripped the main English Fleet and when daylight dawned on August 1st, found himself unsupported and dangerously close to the Spanish fleet. He had no option but to disengage himself as best he could and withdraw off Exmouth to wait for Drake and the rest to catch him up. Meanwhile the Armada continued on its way towards Portland and for the moment the danger of a Spanish landing in Devon was over.

As the action shifts eastward it passes out of the scope of this book. The fire-ships of Calais, the debacle off Gravelines and the calamitous dash round Scotland all belong to the history of England. In a sense it was an anticlimax and, as many of the Spanish ships did finally get back to Spain, the threat remained. Six years after the events of 1588 the church-wardens paid 12s. "To Thomas Hale for Furses to make the Beacon wt. all." But it was all over bar the reminiscing and one can well imagine how the story was told and retold to children and grandchildren until the lighting of the bonfire on Woodbury Beacon on 30th July 1588 passed into folk-memory.

10.
Woodbury Worthies of the Tudor Period

The Haydons of Ebford

According to Polwhele the Haydons arrived in Woodbury in the 14th century. Peter de Haydon's name appears on one of the Albemarle inventories in 1320 and Henry Haydon's on another in 1361. While we cannot be sure they were living in Woodbury at the time, Henry Haydon is surely the same man whose death in Woodbury is recorded in the Vicars Choral accounts for 1407. There followed two sons, John and Thomas, and a grandson Richard and it is likely to have been one of these who gave Woodbury its Parish Orchard and the land on which the Clerk's House was built. The instructions were that the income from the property was to be used for the maintenance of the church but no documents survive earlier than 1699 in which the "ancient uses" are referred to.[1] It has been said that the money was to be used to maintain the clock in the tower and that, too, may have been a Haydon gift.

Richard Haydon II, who now followed his father in the old Barton house at Ebford, was the benefactor (so tradition says) who built the North Aisle of the parish church and was buried there in 1533. From the time the parish records start we find the Haydons wherever there was anything to be done. Richard had two sons, John and Thomas. John married the Cadhay heiress in 1527 and moved to Ottery St. Mary. He was a highly successful and wealthy lawyer, Steward to Bishop Veysey and Legal Adviser to Exeter City Council[2]. But he remembered the poor of Woodbury in his will. Thomas, also a lawyer, stayed on at Ebford, playing the role of go-between in the tricky years of the Reformation when the "church goods" were confiscated, and appearing as one of Woodbury's "men of substance" in the Muster Roll of 1569. He died in 1576 at the age of 65 and is buried in the Haydon vault. When Thomas's grandson inherited Cadhay in 1587 Ebford Barton became the home of a junior branch of the family who continued there for another hundred years.

The Goffe or Gove family

Of Irish origin, the Goves were in Ottery St. Mary by 1332 and probably moved to Woodbury about the year 1500. Their name does not occur in the 15th century Vicars Choral accounts but by 1515 'John Gove of Woodbury, gent'[3] was established at Bridge Farm, Salterton, which became the nucleus of their estate for the next 100 years. John's son Thomas, and his wife Alice, also held land in Woodbury from Cecily (Bonville), Marchioness of Dorset, in 1526.[4] From the first they were good and generous parishioners and one of the earliest entries in the church-wardens' accounts records that "Thos. Gove the Elder, gent" gave to the church "XI bollys of Pewter that did stand upon the Rudlaft to set tapers on" — in other words, eleven pewter candlesticks representing the eleven Apostles. It was the beginnning of those turbulent years of the Reformation and in 1546 Thomas the Younger was one of the men chosen to deliver the church valuables up to the King's Commissioners. The entry reads: "Dinner for Thos. Haydon, Thos. Gooff gentlemen, Andrew Hollwyl, Thos. Young, John Trosse and John Wenman, whan they weyed the Church Jules (jewels) at Exeter 3s.4d." They needed some cheer on so sad a day!

Thomas's son John and his wife Agnes Cary had ten children in the fourteen years between 1561 and 1575, all of them baptised in the parish church. Gregory, the eldest, took on Bridge Farm, married twice and raised two families; John the 3rd son married Jane Haydon of Ebford and was buried in the Haydon aisle where his stone is still to be seen — the only member of his family whose grave is now known. It was probably Richard, the 4th son, who built Govetts in the 1580s (the house was known as Goveshayes).[5] He was church-warden in 1609, the year in which his son, John, married Joan Hoole. But the Goves' time in Woodbury was running out. Neither Gregory nor Richard appear to have been buried here. Gregory sold Bridge to the Carys, his mother's family, and his son John went back to Ireland. John Gove was still in the parish in 1624 but by 1631 Joan Hoole was described as 'widow' and their son John married an Ottery girl and disappeared from Woodbury. Finally only Joan was left at Govetts and her death in 1635 is the last family entry in the register. It has been suggested that they were staunch Puritans and emigrated to America to find religious freedom, as so many did at that time, and it is a strange coincidence that the Goffes of Bedford U.S.A. married into a family called

Woodbury. But there is no real evidence to connect them with the Goffes of Govetts.[6]

Govetts is remembered now as a group of shabby cottages clustered round a large cobbled courtyard in the centre of which was a well with a pump and a handsome stone trough, worn away on one side by the passage of thousands of buckets of water in its 400 year lifetime. Yet beneath the sad decay of its last years (demolished in 1965) it wore proudly the indisputable evidence of its hey-day. The beautiful oak panelling of its parlour is now to be found in No. 1 Gilbrook Cottages and the old stone trough from the courtyard is a feature in the garden of No. 3.

John Prideaux

John Prideaux made an all-too-brief appearance in Woodbury in the middle of the 16th century. The son of Thomas Prideaux of Ashburton, he was the first of four generations whose occupation of Nutwell spanned almost a hundred years. In 1554 the manors of Woodbury and Lympstone came into the hands of the Crown and were bought by John Prideaux who had already purchased Nutwell from the descendants of Lord Dinham.

John Prideaux, in his mid-thirties, was already on the road to success. He was a Member of Parliament for Devon and a Serjeant-at-law (a higher echelon of lawyers from whom judges were chosen). There is no knowing how high he would have climbed on the ladder to fame and fortune had he been spared. But he died in 1558 at the age of thirty-nine and was succeeded by his son Thomas, then nine years old. It is probably John's effigy, and that of his wife, Mary Stukely, to be seen in the parish church, on the North side of the high altar.

Nicholas Stone, sculptor[7]

Perhaps the most imperishable Woodbury Worthy of the 16th century was Nicholas Stone, though he was not truly a Woodbury man and did not become famous until the following century. Nicholas was born in Woodbury and baptized here on 25th July 1587, the year before the Armada. His mother, Alice Strong, was a Woodbury girl and she and Robert Stone had been married in St. Swithin's just nine months previously. As was usual, Alice probably came home to her mother for her first confinement. Nicholas was registered as 'Robert', his father's name, but that is likely to be a slip of the pen.

Some mystery surrounds Nicholas's childhood but it is possible that the family came from Sidbury, where there are several monuments to members of the Stone family, though the parish registers were unfortunately destroyed by fire. It would mean that Robert was well-placed to carry on his work as a quarryman, for the famous quarries at Salcombe Regis and Beer are within reach, and there the young Nicholas could have become acquainted with the tools of the trade that were to make him famous.

Nicholas showed early promise and was apprenticed to a monumental sculptor in London before moving to Amsterdam where he married 'the boss's daughter'. Returning to London, he worked closely with Inigo Jones on the Banqueting House in Whitehall, for which he was paid 4s.10d. a day, and finally succeeded Jones as Master Mason to King James I.

Though Stone's delicate and sensitive work graces some of England's finest buildings, from Westminister Abbey downwards, it is sad that not a single known piece of his exists in his native Devon. However, his wall monument to Sir Thomas Bodley, fellow Devonian and founder of the Bodleian Library at Oxford, can be seen in Merton College Chapel and is regarded as among his finest works.

11.
Towards a Civil War

When Queen Elizabeth died in 1603 the throne of England could hardly have been more secure nor its occupant more popular. In a few short years her inept successors were to bring the country to civil war. Son of Elizabeth's Catholic cousin, Mary Queen of Scots, King James I of England had no feeling for the English mood. His despotic rule, gross extravagance and Papist leanings soon brought him into conflict with Parliament, while his determination to seek an alliance with Spain affronted most Englishmen.

Sir Walter Raleigh had been an idol in Elizabethan England. A true son of the Reformation, Raleigh regarded Catholic Spain as England's natural enemy. But now his daring exploits against Spanish shipping which had so delighted Elizabeth were a grave embarrassment to James's plans and Raleigh soon found himself in the Tower of London on a charge of treason. There he mouldered away for twelve years, until in 1617 James contrived an excuse for sending him to the scaffold and, amid scenes of national grief and anger, Raleigh lost his head and England lost the last great Elizabethan.[1]

The removal of Raleigh opened the way for James's next objective — the hand of the Spanish princess for his son Charles. English opinion was so inflamed by this move that when the lady turned him down and Charles returned from Madrid empty-handed spontaneous rejoicing broke out everywhere — bonfires were lit and Woodbury's bell-ringers pealed out the glad tidings to everyone within earshot and the church-wardens stood them all a round of beer. Within a few months James was dead and Charles I was king.

While the struggle for power between the despotic king and his House of Commons went on and the rift between them widened, Woodbury was concerning itself with making a new survey for the Malt Rate. Made in 1631,[2] it contains 192 surnames — more than twice as many as the 1536 list — though it does not mean that the population had doubled. It is more likely that the survey was more thorough and that greater prosperity brought more families into the tax net, which no longer seems to have been voluntary. However, it clearly shows that there had been an enormous turnover in surnames in the century that divides the lists. Two-thirds of the names are different. In "Wester Parte of Woodbury Towne" not one name from the earlier list survived in 1631 and the only link between the later list and today is the appearance of the name Smeath.

A collection of wills of the Holwell family[3] illustrates this movement. Of the two brothers, Edward and John Holwell, who died in Woodbury in the mid-1600s, Edward's elder son moved to Littleham while his younger son stayed in Woodbury. John's son John went into business as a clothier (weaver of cloth) at Bradninch and Robert moved to Kentisbeare. Only Andrew remained at his father's property in Woodbury.

Here in the new list we find the first mention of Mallocks Farm (Rich. Mallucke) rated equally with Woodmanton and Coombe Farm at 3s.4d. Jane Holwell, widow, was at Rydon Farm. Sir Thomas Prideaux paid the highest rate, 16s.8d., "for his aunchaunt Barten of Nutwill". The list also provides a first mention of John Leate's "tenement called Gilbrooke", rated at 1s. — obviously a small cottage and probably the single-storey cob building which revealed itself in the core of Gilbrook House during the recent refacing.

Rydon Mill made its first appearance in the list. Not since about the year 1300 had there been a cornmill on the Gillbrook, other than at Exton. This new venture was yet another attempt to improve milling facilities in Woodbury and the earlier water shortage could now be overcome by a mill-leat, mill-pond and over-shot wheel. The leat came off the Gillbrook in Ham Lane, carried the water past Rydon Farm and, following the contour of the land, fed into a long, narrow mill-pond above the mill. Here, by means of a sluice gate, the meagre water supply could be dammed up during the night so that there was sufficient to keep the mill working by day. After passing through the mill the water rejoined the Gillbrook to be used again at Exton Mill. Almost certainly Rydon Mill was brand new in 1631. The miller, William Cooke, was rated separately for his house and does not yet appear to have been living on the job as later millers did. And the Rate List is the one and only time the "myll-leates" are specifically mentioned — so new and noteworthy were they! Edward Holwell held the lease of the leat and, as it could not have been constructed without considerable disturbance at Rydon Farm, it looks as if Holwell had a hand in the new venture, as in so many other things in Woodbury.

Few farms formed compact blocks of land as, say, Greendale which had been an entirity since early days, or Woodmanton which had been carved out of the wood at a later date. Most of the farmers had odd fields dotted about all over the parish as they had managed to acquire them from time to time — from enclosures as the Great Field broke up, from swopping, buying, clearing or inheriting.

This curiously complicated form of land-tenure (which still goes on today) necessitated a considerable amount of to-ing and fro-ing on Woodbury's narrow, muddy roads and lanes. The constant driving of animals for pasturing, the plough-teams and the solid-wheeled ox-waggons put continuous pressure on the lanes that had somehow to be dealt with. Needless to say, it came to rest on the shoulders of that hard-working body, the Vestry. In earlier times the repair of the roads had been a matter for the Manor Courts. But in 1555 the first great Highway Act set out a frame-work of regulations which remained the foundation of highway law for three centuries.[4]

Every parishioner above a certain level of land-holding had to provide for four days a year "one wain or cart furnished after the custom of the country....and also two able men with the same". Lesser householders had to provide four days' labour a year and there is a reference to this as early as 1606 in Woodbury's church-wardens' accounts when 4d. was paid "to Mr. Hole for writting of a Coppie of the Statute for Laborrers".

Their jobs entailed hedging and ditching, filling in holes, resurfacing and draining surface water and the supervision was entrusted to unpaid surveyors appointed by the parish (later by magistrates). It was the surveyors' — or way-wardens' — job to report people to the magistrates for not "mending their ways", the origin of that expression, and it is not surprising that of all the parish jobs this was the most unpopular. On the whole the system did not work well and the state of the roads and lanes was terrible.

Woodbury's roads fell broadly into three catagories:- those designed to carry wheeled traffic — then something of a rarity — and required by law to be not less than 8 ft. wide (e.g. the Woodbury — W. Salterton road); the many country lanes used for driving animals to pasturage or for the pack-animals most farmers still used

— 3 ft. wide (e.g. Watery Lane) and the roads that ran unfenced through open heathland (e.g. the B3180 over the Common and probably much of the Exeter road at that time, B3179). Our roads were surfaced with stones and gravel dug from numerous small pits along the west side of the Common and were made to slope towards a central drainage gully. Every heavy storm gouged out deep gullies in such roads as Castle Lane.

The onus on landholders to be responsible for the roads bordering their own land fell heavily and unfairly on some. For instance, the tenant of Greendale Barton had continuous roads and lanes on three sides of his property, totalling almost exactly two miles. Of this total three quarters of a mile was the main Dorchester—Exeter road carrying a great deal of wheeled traffic which had nothing to do with Woodbury. Though he would have had the loan of carts and labour from less burdened farmers, yet the responsiblility remained his. Small wonder that travellers to Devon in those days complained so vociferously about the state of the roads!

The Gathering Storm

Puritanism had been quietly gathering strength in England since the break with Rome in the previous century. There were many who thought the Reformation had not gone far enough. For followers of Luther and Calvin the Church of England was still too close to Rome and they wanted the freedom to worship as they chose. They sought a plainer way, without bishops, without ostentatious ritual. But both James I and Charles I set their faces resolutely against toleration and families of Puritan conviction had to choose between accepting the Church of England as it was, or punishment, or emigrating to America — which many thousands did.

Here in Devon a great change had taken place since the days of the "commocion". The great-grandsons of the men who had so vehemently clung to and fought for the old Latin mass in 1549 were now in the forefront of those demanding greater tolerance in matters of conscience. The leaders of the movement were to be found among the country squires. The Prideaux of Nutwell were Puritans and in 1583 Woodbury Church witnessed the marriage of Catherine Prideaux and Richard Duke of Otterton — another Puritan.

The Church of England was in some disarray and the general dissatisfaction and uncertainty was reflected in the poor quality of men coming forward for ordination. In 1633 King Charles appointed William Laud to be Archbishop of Canterbury. It was a very unpopular appointment. Laud was a High Churchman and his aims were to raise the status of the clergy and, ultimately, the re-unification with Rome. It was not long before villages as remote from Canterbury as Woodbury began to feel the pressure. Since Elizabethan times, the Communion Table in most churches had been brought forward into the nave. Laud now ordered that Communion Tables must be moved back to the position they had occupied in the Sanctuary before the Reformation, and that they must be enclosed by railings to protect them from profanation. Woodbury complied in 1640 when a second-hand Communion Table and a set of altar rails were purchased for £2.10s. (not the present rails).

During these restless years the Vicars Choral were having their own problems. The Parliament of 1545 had stripped them of all their endowments except Woodbury. By 1547 the old quota of 24 Vicars had shrunk to 8 priests and 12 lay-vicars and, since the clergy could now marry, many of them no longer lived their bachelor lives in the little "chambers" of the College in Kalendarhay.

Furthermore, a trouble maker in their midst (one Robert Withers, a lay-vicar) had pursuaded his fellow-vicars to let their manor at Woodbury to a certin Philip Sture at too low a rent. The Dean and Chapter of Exeter Cathedral were obliged to intervene and in 1613 an agreement was made that the College would not grant "any lease of Woodbury mansion house, called the Parsonage, orchards, gardens, water rights, offerings, oblations, meadows, marshes etc., now or late in the occupation of Philip Sture". In return the Dean and Chapter pledged themselves for eleven years to contribute £20 quarterly at the four principal feasts "for their old rent of £54.4.2 less £20 wages of the curate and a compassionate allowance for his house".[5] In the general shake-up the vicars lost the right to use Parsonage as their vicarage and from that time until 1849 each vicar of Woodbury had to find his own accommodation.

All these changes left affairs in the College in some state of neglect and Archbishop Laud personally dispatched two trusted priests to Exeter in an endeavour to pull things together. One was William Hopwood, an excellent man from St. Paul's Cathedral, who survived the upheavals of the Civil War and the Commonwealth to remain Custos for many years.

But it was too late. The king's policies ran totally across the feelings of the times and were accompained by an ever increasing determination on the part of the king to have his own way — with or without the consent of Parliament. Gradually the lines were being drawn between a majority of the country squires and the common people on the one hand, seeking to limit the powers of the king and the bishops, and the king with most of his peers and bishops on the other hand, supporting the authority of the crown and the shift towards Rome. Members of the House of Commons, drawn from the former class, began to see themselves as the only legal means by which the ancient laws and liberties of England could be preserved against the tyranny of the king. Politics and religion became inseparable and the mood of the country moved towards civil war.

12.
The Troubles and After

The Civil War broke out in October 1642 and, as with other wars, there was a popular belief that it would all be over by Christmas. After all, Parliament held the royal arsenals and all that King Charles needed was a short sharp shock to bring him to his senses. Or so they thought. But Christmas came and went without more than a few confused local skirmishes and Royalists rallied to their King to form an army of surprising strength.

At first all was quiet in the South West. Cornwall was predominently Royalist while Devon was fairly evenly divided. Plymouth supported Parliament throughout the campaign, while Exeter was for the King and Exmouth built Royalist forts and gun-emplacements at the mouth of the Exe to prevent Parliamentary forces from going up-river to Exeter.[1] By 1644 King Charles considered Exeter safe enough to place his family in the care of the Earl of Bedford, in whose house the Princess Henrietta was born. The presence of the royal family no doubt strengthened Exeter's resolve and when the tide of battle turned against Charles in the following year it was Exeter's resistence that delayed Generals Fairfax and Cromwell in their drive to relieve Plymouth.[2]

Headquarters were set up first at Ottery St. Mary in December 1645. A council of war on December 7th decided that Exeter must be "straitened" before the Parliamentary army could proceed westward and as a result Exeter was ringed about with garrisoned country houses, of which Nutwell was one.

The Prideaux of Nutwell, for Parliament, and the Courtenays of Powderham, for the King, had been glaring at each other across the Exe since the war began three years previously. Now was the time for action. On December 14th the Nutwell garrison, under Capt. Farmer, sallied forth across the river by boat to attack Powderham. But, unknown to them, Powderham had been reinforced some hours previously by 150 troops from Exeter. Being determined not to withdraw without some show of strength, the Nutwell men occupied

Powderham Church and held it till the next day, despite hunger and extreme cold — as they had broken the windows to fire their muskets through! The following morning Nutwell got another boat across bringing provisions to their men in the church. But, although they managed to beat off an attack from Exeter, it was decided to withdraw to Nutwell — which operation was achieved without loss.[3]

Still Exeter held out and it was not until Devon was firmly in Fairfax's hands that a surrender was negotiated. So far as Woodbury was concerned the Civil War was over though the church-wardens' accounts remind us that a military dictatorship kept the fragile peace. In 1647 Henry Perry was paid 1d. "for going over to Major Parking's to prevent his troop from coming" (plague was rife in the army), and in 1648, 10s. was paid "to Henry Martyn for Curinge the Horses wch were hurt in John Spares ground that did belong to Lieutenant Colonell Arrendalls Troope".

Woodbury had been deeply divided by the Civil War. The Prideaux' near neighbours, the Haydons, were for the King. A member of the Ottery St. Mary branch of the Haydon family in 1649 paid a fine of £69.4s.6d. "for delinquency in adhering to the forces raised against Parliament".[4] But whether Woodbury men were mustered and the 'Parish armour' brought out is not revealed in the church-wardens' accounts.

Even the College of Vicars Choral was divided. Under the strong Royalist influence of William Hopwood the College plate was sold in 1644 for £33-7s.4d. and the money given to help the Royalist army. But Hopwood could not stem the tide of Puritanism and as Exeter surrendered to the Parliamentary forces Woodbury's high church minister, Barnaby Gouche, was suspended from office and a Puritan, Samuel Fones, arrived with his family to take up residence in Woodbury. Barnaby Gouche was a scholar who, so Matthew Lee tells us, translated "The Art of Husbandry" and "Lives of the Poets" from the Latin.[5] He stayed on in Woodbury for a short while, a sad ill man, and died here in April 1646.

Hopwood, in 1647, arranged the sale of the College buildings to Exeter City Council, possibly as a means of preserving them, and the splendid barrel-vaulted Vicars' Hall became a wool market, while most of the 'chambers' housed poor people whose homes had been destroyed during the siege of Exeter. By 1660 only two vicars remained in Kalendarhay, of which Hopwood was one, though old and sick.[6]

Sam Fones and his wife had at least ten children, eight of them born in Woodbury, as the register shows. Their eldest son, Samuel, was born soon after their arrival here in 1646 with two daughters, Elizabeth and Mary. But the Foneses had a sad family life. Elizabeth died in 1647 and Mary in 1656. In 1651 their third son John died, aged just one week, and in 1659 their second son Henry died at the age of eleven. Their last daughter, Sarah, born in 1663 died shortly after her second birthday. Of the ten children only Samuel, Anne (born 1657), the twins (born 1652) and a second Mary, born after the death of the first, survived to accompany their parents into the wilderness after the Restoration.

With the return of King Charles II in 1660 life once more became difficult for Puritans. The Act of Uniformity in 1662 tried to compel the clergy to conform to beliefs and practices that many honest men could no longer in all conscience obey. Sam Fones was one of the 121 clergy in Devon who did not sign the declaration by St. Bartholomew's Day, 24th August 1662, and was ejected from his living and deprived of his right to preach. We are told that he was a good man, universally beloved by his parishioners. The self-same pulpit still in regular use today is the one whose steps Fones sadly climbed to preach his farewell sermon, after 16 years as vicar of Woodbury. And his congregation wept.[7]

Fones did not immediately leave Woodbury. In 1663 his daughter Sarah's baptism was registered and the family were still here two years later when her body was laid to rest with their other children — though the register no longer refers to him as "minister" but as "gent". It has been said that Fones gathered round him a small congregation of Presbyterians who met at his house and that these "dissenters" eventually formed the nucleus of the community at Gulliford Meeting. It is very likely the case, though not proven.[8]

Despite Sam Fones's popularity the Puritans were inclined to be a solemn, joyless lot, much preoccupied with the sins of the flesh and the wrath of God, and life in Woodbury was cruelly deprived of its old traditional merry-making. The celebration of Christmas was forbidden. There were no more Twelfth Night frolics nor May Day Revels nor games of Robin Hood and the church-wardens' accounts are silent about such things as "a mask and bells for a fool" and the "cups, pots and treens for the Church Ale". By 1660 only Woodbury's older inhabitants could remember all the jollifications that used to go on "....to the dishonour of Almighty God, increase in bastardy and of the dissolute life, and very many other mischiefs...." as the Puritans described such events.[9]

In fact, Woodbury's register of baptisms, in so far as it can be relied upon, provides no evidence to support the "increase in bastardy" claim. Rather the reverse. During the 1620s the illegitimacy rate was 1 per 66 of the baptisms. During the 1640s and 50s it rose to 1 per 62, while after the restoration of the monarchy in the 1660s it dropped to 1 per 75. One is left to draw the conclusion that during the joyless years there was little other fun to be had!

During the curacy of Sam Fones there was a continuity in the keeping of the registers which few parishes enjoy, though it is interesting that the marriage register shows a drop from an annual average of 12 to one or two. There are four years in which no marriages are recorded. The Puritan Government favoured civil marriages and, thanks to a note in the register, we know that some Woodbury marriages at that time were being performed by magistrates Wm. Bamfield, Rbt. Duke, Wm. Putt and John Tyrling, while others were taking place in Clyst St. George church.

The people of Devon had been highly suspicious of the registers when they first became law back in 1538, fearing (quite rightly as it happened) that they would be used for taxation purposes.[10] Firstly, charges for compulsory registration were imposed. Now another ingenious way was thought of to raise revenue from the registers. It was known as "Burial in Woollen". The woollen industry was booming and all cloth had a government tax on it. The more cloth sold, the more revenue rolled into the treasury. An act of 1666 had been largely ignored but in 1678 a successor provided that: "no corpse of any person (except those who shall die of the plague) shall be buried in any shirt, shift, sheet, shroud or anything whatsoever made or mingled with flax, hemp, silk, hair, gold or silver, or any stuff or thing, other than what is made of sheep's wool only.....or be put into any coffin faced with.....any other material but sheep's wool only."[11] The act came into force on 1st August 1678 and percolated through to Woodbury in time for the funeral of Richard Scott of Greendale, buried on 20th September. In the margin of the register is written in the clerk's hand "first in woollen".

The Vestry officials of the 17th century continued to concern themselves with the poor and now for the first time we begin to find reference to an Almshouse in Woodbury. It seems to have been the responsibility of the Vestry and a careful look at the entries in the church-wardens' accounts may provide a clue to its whereabouts. The first reference to the Almshouse appears in 1619 — the year which also contains the last reference to the "Clarke of the Markett" and the Church House. In that year the Vestry paid 3s. for "altering the Doore and Stayers of the Almshouses" and 7s.6d. for alterations to the roof and rethatching; obviously not a new building but alterations to an old building and as they occur in the year that saw the end of the market they point to the conversion of the now redundant Church House "*ex parte cimiterii*" (see p. 66). Behind the Almshouses the churchyard rose halfway up the walls while the front doors opened on to Church Street and the stream over which a little wooden footbridge gave access to the Village Green. One can imagine the old folk climbing the steep church path from their cottages to the seats in the porch, there to receive Haydon's Charity.

The Overseers for the Poor were four in number and responsible farmers and tradesmen of the parish held the posts in rotation with the other voluntary offices of the Vestry. One of their functions was to place poor children in apprenticeships, to learn a trade, and details were entered in the Malt Book. Unfortunately the entries do not tell us the trades to which the children were bound. For certain Woodbury had a great variety of trades but there were never enough to go round and no doubt in Woodbury, as elsewhere, poor boys were usually bound as farm labourers and girls as domestic servants.

The children usually started their apprenticeships at 10 or 11 years of age and in the early years of the 17th century were apprenticed until they reached the age of 24. But this placed too much of a strain on both parties to the bargain and the age was lowered to 21. The parish fitted out the poor children with "two suites of apparell" — one for working, one for best — and paid the family who took them in a lump sum varying from £2 to £4. The family had no choice in the matter, all families of a certain standing having to accept the children when their turn came. In 1666 Daniel and John Scott were prosecuted for refusing to take apprentices.

The wording in the Malt Book follows a strange quasi-legal formula and one can see that there were ways of getting rid of unwanted apprentices. One such reads:-

"November the 17th 1694.

Whereas there was An Apprentice Improfer upon Mr. John Holwell for Churchstill (Churchstile) Tenement the name of the Apprentice was Mary Sanders which the sd Mr. John Holwell did give unto Thomas Lovering to free him of the sd Apprentice the sume of two pounds of good & lawful money of England to be freed from the sd Mary Sanders for the sd Mr. John Holwell is to be freed from having any other apprentice from the parish until the sd Mary Sanders doth attain the age of one and twenty years".

Poor Mary Sanders! The previous year she had been discharged from Dorothy Trapnell of Exton on payment of £2. Mary was eleven years old.

One of the strangest entries concerns William Haydon, illegitimate son of Anne Haydon. William had been baptized in Woodbury in 1681 but there is no sign of his mother having been born in the parish. The main branch of the Ebford Haydons were now in Ottery St. Mary and a daughter of the family was christened Anne on 20th December 1652 in St. Mary's church. Anne never married and it is not known what happened to her. Did she fall from grace in her thirtieth year and was she disowned by her family and left to the care of Woodbury parish? Or was Anne Haydon a foundling child, reared in the Haydon household at Ebford and given the family name, as often happened with foundling children?

The Malt Book entry runs as follows:-

"September the 9th 1692
William Webber of Pilehayes then took William the sonne of Anne Haydon a poor child of the parish of Woodbury with the consent of the Church Wardens and Overseers and do hereby discharge him from another apprentice during the term of his apprenticeship
Witness our hand this day and year above said — John Lee and Matthew Lee — Churchwardens.

Edward Hollwell, George Venn)
Nicholas Nut, Samuel Stogdon) Overseers"

Though the apprenticeship scheme cannot properly be called 'education', there was a growing movement to make education more widely available. There had always been schools for the few, run in early times almost exclusively by the Church as a means of supplying the priesthood with educated boys. In Exeter the Cathedral Song School and the Grammar School were both in being before 1200. Bishops Stapleton and Grandisson did much to further education and, between 1314 and 1338, Exeter College Oxford was founded with places for eight scholars from Devon, St. John's Hospital School in Exeter (the Bluecoat School) was not only founded by Stapleton but was linked with Exeter College Oxford, and Bishop Grandisson founded the famous school at Ottery St. Mary.[12] At the Reformation, Ottery School was threatened with extinction but through the good offices of John Haydon, King Henry VIII was persuaded to refound it as "the King's New Grammar School of St. Mary of Ottery". Haydon became one of the first Governors. [13] All these establishments survived the upheavals of the Reformation in some shape or form and were joined by others — Blundells at Tiverton in 1599, for instance.

Those Woodbury men who achieved eminence as lawyers and merchants received a good basic education in classics and "the 3 Rs" and attended one or other of these schools. Yet we know from the church-wardens' accounts that ordinary farmers and tradesmen could also write (sometimes very beautifully) and could keep simple accounts.

The early pages of the accounts are kept in Roman numerals — difficult to read and almost impossible to reckon in (i.e. Lxviij = £18). Suddenly in 1632 the accounts appear in Arabic numerals such as we use today. The change was so totally dramatic and fundamental that it is unlikely anyone could have picked it up for himself. Where did Woodbury farmers' sons receive their education? We know of no school nearer than Exeter. Yet educational facilities must have been more widely available than the sparse evidence suggests.

In 1691 Woodbury's first educational charity was set up. Known as "Weare's Gift" it provided 15s. yearly for each of six poor Woodbury children, to pay for their education to the age of nine. Its main aim was to teach them to read the Bible and those children who went on to take up apprenticeships were presented with a Bible on leaving. But we are not told in what form this education came. The charity did not itself set up a school as the Broadmead Charity did in the next century. Did the six poor children attend some small fee-paying school here in Woodbury? Or did some individual tutor them in his (or her) own home? The setting up of the charity presupposes that the object was to extend to poor children an education which fee-paying children already enjoyed and that it could be had in the village if the necessary fees were available. Several people are known to have obtained the Bishop's "licence to teach" during the 17th and 18th centuries, including two vicars and a member of the Beal family, and the likelihood is that Woodbury children, both fee-paying and 'charity', were being taught in private houses in the village.

Education was only one of the ways in which Woodbury was changing with the times. The last years of the 17th century brought a great step forward in religious tolerance. After the swing to Puritanism during Cromwell's time, the restoration of the Stuart kings brought renewed persecution of Non-comformists and Catholics alike. It was not until James II fled to France before the forces of his son-in-law, William of Orange, that matters could improve.

"Dutch William" sailed into Torbay with 600 transports and 50 men-of-war on 5th November 1688, at the request of an influential faction here in England. Not since the Armada just 100 years earlier had there been such excitement or so much to see from the Beacon. Everywhere people rallied to William as he marched via Exeter, Oxford and Salisbury to London where the capital greeted him with wild rejoicing.

One of William's first acts was to grant freedom of conscience to religious "dissenters" of all shades. The Toleration Act of 1689 came as a great relief to those families in Woodbury who, since Sam Fones's days, had secretly kept Puritanism alive at great personal risk to themselves. It is very possible that they had been meeting in the home of Thomas Lee at Sparkshayes. When the Toleration Act became law Lee and his friends were ready and waiting to begin building their chapel in the corner of a field Lee owned at Gulliford. A lease of 300 years was granted at an annual payment of £6, to be paid only if demanded, and although the foundation deed has not survived it is quoted as bearing the date 10th April 1689.[14] "Thomas Lee of Sparkshaies — yeoman" was one of the original trustees, and the first minister was Samuel Tapper, a scholar and former parish priest who, like Sam Fones, had been deprived of his living after 1660. Murch tells us that Tapper's "warm practical preaching and holy exemplary conversation gained him universal love among his people. His congregation increased, and he was blessed with success in the conversion of many souls.....But his good qualities did not secure him from the fury of High Church bigots, who, during the times of persecution, violently entered the meeting-house and broke the windows. On the next Lord's Day, he prayed earnestly for his enemies, that God would forgive their sin and turn their hearts".

All expenses for the running of the Meeting and paying the minister were met by subscription and, though early lists have been lost, later lists tell of the rise and eventual fall of Gulliford Meeting over a period of a century and a half, and of the part played by Woodbury families who shared the chapel with their brethren in Lympstone and Exmouth. Many of Woodbury's wealthy yeomen supported Gulliford and one senses a spirit of total commitment reminiscent of the early Christians. Beside the Lees, who were probably the prime movers from the beginning, there were the Dagworthys, Saunders and Braddicks, the Webbers from Heathfield, and the Stogdons, Daleys, Darbys, Beals and Chowns. Other families can be discovered from Gulliford's registers of christenings and burials which survive from 1773.[15]

The chapel itself has long since disappeared but the overgrown site, with its half-buried tomb-stones and dark yew trees, is a nostalgic place. Spying through the chinks in the gate in Meeting Lane and studying the scene once so familiar to Woodbury's first Non-conformists one can see again those fervent congregations arriving in their sober Sunday best, undeterred by the length of the journey or the hour-long sermon that might await them.

13.
Matthew Lee of Ebford

By the year 1700 the Haydons had left Ebford Barton, though the family continued to thrive at Ottery St. Mary. The long, low, cob farmhouse which had been their home since the 14th century passed to the Venn family. There was some relationship between the Haydons, the Venns and the Lees of Sparkshayes, into whose hands Ebford Barton was soon to come.

The Venns were originally a Topsham family, though by 1682 George Venn was churchwarden here in Woodbury. In 1701 he was described as "of Woodbury — clothier" while his sons, Michael and George junior, were "woolcomber" and "sergemaker" respectively.[1] This is the first positive evidence we have that Devon's woollen industry was affecting Woodbury, though where they carrried on their business we do not know.

The wool trade was having a profound effect on the country districts around Exeter at that time. Westcote, writing in 1630, had complained of the drift of country people to the towns and the difficulty in obtaining good labour on the farms. It was more profitable to spin and weave, comb and full, or engage in one of the many processes of the cloth industry, than to carry on husbandry. Many labourers worked for employers and helped to make them rich. Others started in small ways, little family entities working in their own homes, and eventually made fortunes.

The Woolstaple, or Market, in Exeter regulated and co-ordinated all these activites. Every market day farmers brought their wool to market where it passed to the spinners. Spinning with a distaff was generally considered women's work and it required eight "spinsters" to keep one weaver's loom going. There must have been countless homes in Woodbury where the womenfolk span yarn to supplement the family income.

On the following market day the yarn was passed on to the weaver. One week later it had been woven into cloth and, if the weaver were not to dye and finish it himself, it came to the market yet again, and finally the finished product was bought by the merchants who marketed it — much of it going to London or abroad. Serge was the cloth for which Devon was famous and large quantites of it were shipped to Holland from Topsham. Merchants were making huge profits, some of which they invested in setting up weavers in business and lending them money with which to buy the looms and tools of their trade. Thus the money was kept in circulation and trade grew.

By the time George Venn's brother Robert acquired Ebford Barton he was already prosperous. The old cob house of the Haydons was too humble a dwelling for a successful 18th century businessman and in 1710 he built the fine mansion house we see today. It was designed in the new classical style, first seen here in Exeter's Customs House, built a few years earlier and well known to Robert Venn. Its locally produced bricks and stucco quoins, the elegant pillared porch and pedimented gables and the striking array of large sash windows must have been the talking point of the

Ebford Manor

decade. While most of Woodbury had only recently accustomed itself to living on two floors and having a kitchen chimney, here was a house such as was never seen before, on three floors, with a maze of attic bedrooms for servants, and a chimney to every room. The new house adjoined the old, in front of and at right-angles to it, and the old house became the home of Venn's tenant farmer.

It will be remembered that the Lee family had been farming at Sparkshayes since at least 1526 and by 1700 branches of the family were also farming at Gulliford and Salterton. Thomas Lee's grandson, Matthew Lee senior, was born at Sparkshayes but forsook the land for the wool trade. He married George Venn's sister, Jane, and set up home in St. Leonards, Exeter, where he carried on the business of fulling cloth; and there his eldest son, Matthew the younger, was born in 1715.

Robert Venn died in 1728 and left his estate at Ebford and other lands in Woodbury to young Matthew, his nephew, then a schoolboy of thirteen.[2] It was administered for him by trustees until he came of age.

In the meantime, Matthew (known as 'Mat') had to learn his father's trade and so, at the age of eighteen, he was dispatched to Holland to learn the language and generally to become acquainted with his father's customers there. During the 8 month visit he kept a daily diary which has survived[3] and is a mine of information on topics ranging from food and fashion to religion and international trade. It shows Matthew to have been a serious young man, curious about everything he saw and painstaking in all he did.

He sailed from Exmouth with Capt. Bishop in "the Friendship" on 15th May 1733, accompanied by a Mr. Elliot of Woodbury Salterton, probably one of his father's employees. Matthew carefully lists the clothes he took with him:- "3 coats, 3 waistcoats, 4 pr. breeches, 7pr. stockings, 7 pr. shoes, 10 ruffled shirts, 5 plain ditto, 3 hankerchiefs, 2 periwigs — etc." During his stay in Holland he acquired, amongst other things, another wig and a special box to keep it in, a fishing rod and a cane, Obviously Mat was a sophisticated and fashionable young man, even at eighteen, and the wearing of a periwig would immediately distinguish him as a gentleman.

One of Mat's first duty-calls was on his aunt, married to a very substantial Dutchman living in style in Rotterdam. One feels, reading the beautiful copperplate handwritng, that he was suitably impressed as he recorded:- "My aunt sent her footman to desire me to drink a dish of tea with her in the afternoon". Tea-drinking was a new fad which had taken a firm hold on Dutch social life and Mat was fascinated by the many varieties of tea, which he bought to send home, and by the pretty china teapots and novel "tea-kitchens" (kettles).

The prosperity of Holland astonished him and he was agog at "the finest Country Houses that ever eyes beheld", where his father's business friends lived. He also had a special word for the splendours of the gardens and his mind may have recalled these early impressions when at a later date he enthusiastically set about redesigning the garden at Ebford.

Mat attended a school to learn Dutch and lodged with the master, though his time was divided between studies, sight-seeing and visiting the 'Change (Wool Market). By August 14th he was ready to attempt to write his first letter in Dutch, to a young friend, Mr. Jan Verbeck. On September 15. "Mr. Jan wrote me the faults that were in my Dutch letter.....and desired I would show him the faults in his".

All the while letters were being sent back and forth by ship to Topsham and from his father Mat was hearing the disturbing news that all was not well with the woollen trade in Exeter.

"October 25th Received a letter from my Father.....he advised me.....of the failure of Mr. Edm'd Cock Jun. for a great sum. The most surprising thing I ever heard". A previous letter had told him of the bankruptcy of Messrs. Lavington and Paull, also of Exeter, while in December came news that Digory Cock had also failed, "with assets of £600 and debts of £2000". Matthew Lee senior wrote "these failures of late have made such a rupture in the town that almost every person that owes money on interest is now called for it". No wonder that Mat later saw fit to insert clauses in his daughter's marriage settlement in case his future son-in-law should land up in a debtors' prison!

But the Lees' business seemed secure enough and the father wrote to the son that he should "do nothing with van der Bosch.....because there is now no other person in Exeter (but Lee) that sends goods (to Holland) or understands the Holland trade", so that he could "pick and choose".

On January 17th 1734, Matthew set sail once more for England, in the same ship, after a long delay due to bad weather. His diary records "about 200 ships more, out of the Texel, bound for Topsham". Then "by the rolling of the ship some of the china was broken" — not, one hopes, the teapot he was taking home for his mother.

His account ends: "Passed by Portland and about noon came before the bar at Topsham. We waited for the tide till evening and then sailed in and about Starcross.....Mr. Elliot and I went up to Topsham by boat.....and the next day went home and found all my relations in good health. Thus being wanting from England.....I came at length safe again to England. Bless ye the Lord, O my Soul, and forget not all his loving kindness".

In 1742 Mat married Jenny Huckell, the daughter of a rich London linen draper, and from then on spent much of his time in London where they had a house and business in St. Martin's-le-Grand. Ebford Barton was let on a fourteen year lease.

His diary tells us "My Father made me worth at marriage (including the Estates and Money left to me by my Uncle Venn) £5000, and Mr. Huckell gave me with his daughter £3000".

The wedding in London occasioned much detailed expenditure in the diary. Throughout February and March there were clothes to be made.

Embroidered Waistcoat, buttons etc.	£11.6s.0d.
Making 8 ruffled shirts	£1.8s.0d;
Irish Silk Nightgown	£2.2s.0d.
2½ yds Gold Lace	15s.0d.

Jewellery for the bride included:-

Diamond ring with 24 stones	£16.0s.0d.
Plain gold hoop	9s.0d.
Pair 3-drop brilliant earrings	£105.0s.0d.

Then the wedding itself on April 6th, 1742:-

A marriage licence	£1.4s.6d.
Pd. the Parson for Marrying us	£1.16s.
Clerk, Sexton etc.	9s.6d.
Charges on the Road & Turnpike	11s.6d.
Coach Hire (to Uxbridge & Andover)	£3.5s.0d.
Pd. to the Ringers at Andover	£1.1s.0d.
Drums and Fiddles	5s.0d.

The newly wedded Lees employed two resident maids, both Woodbury Salterton girls, Peggy Channon and Betty Cooke. They were paid 25s. a quarter and stayed until 1747, travelling frequently with the family between London and Devon.

The birth of their first child, Matthew (Matty), in 1744 was followed in 1745 by the arrival of a "strong healthy girl ...baptized...by the name of Jane" (Jenny). Throughout the diary Matthew refers to his wife invariably as "Mrs. Lee" and it is probable that is what he always called her.

There are many references to the children's health and these shed light on the medical matters of the time. In the latter half of the 17th century Bubonic Plague lessened and petered out. Its final fling was the Plague of London in 1665 and that never reached Devon. But Plague as a killer was being replaced by the rising incidence of Smallpox, which claimed the lives mostly of children (though Queen Mary died of it in 1694) and Typhus, which tended to kill the elderly.[4]

The 18th century was remarkable for its improvements in housing standards and personal hygiene (Mat's accounts contain copious items for laundry) and for better diagnosis and treatment of infectious diseases. In May 1746, says the diary, "my two children Matty and Jenny had an eruption come out on them.....First appearance Small Pox but afterwards concluded it must be measles. Matty has had Chicken Pox and both have had Hooping Cough". But there is an unusually interesting entry in October 1748 when Matty developed the Smallpox. Fortunately it was a mild attack from which he recovered. But the parents were anxious to keep Jenny, aged three, from so disfiguring a disease and she was immediately sent to the house of her grandmother Huckell to avoid infection. There, on October 28th, she was inoculated against Smallpox by a Mr. Baker, Surgeon,(later Sir George, President of R.C.P.) who attended her over the next six weeks through a mild attack presumably brought on by the inoculation. This was almost thirty years earlier than the first experiments in Smallpox inoculation in Devon.

Alas for the Lee family: "February 3rd 1749/50. About 12 at night it pleased the Almighty to take from me, after 48 hours illness of a sore throat, my dearest child Jenny, in her 5th year. A child of a most remarkably sweet and amiable disposition. She was buried in St. Anne's Church, Aldersgate, in a grave with Mr. Huckell's children". Jenny's death came hard upon the heels of the disappointment of a still-born son: such was the frailty of life even among the wealthy.

The Lees were blessed with two other children; Thomas Huckell Lee, born in 1753, was to inherit Ebford and play a major role in Woodbury. Jenny was born at Ebford in 1757 and it is clear that after the 14 year lease expired the Lees made Ebford their home.

THE LEE FAMILY

Thomas Lee of Sparkshayes — Yeoman
b.1623. Founder-Trustee of Gulliford Meeting.

Matthew Lee of Sparkshayes — Yeoman
b.1642 m. Agnes Haydon of Ebford.

Six other Children

Thomas Lee of Sparkshayes b.1680

Matthew Lee of St. Leonards, Exeter — Fuller. b.1681 d.1742 m. Elizabeth Venn of Woodbury

Matthew Lee of Ebford b.1715 d.1774 m. Jenny Huckell of London

George Lee m. Anna Waldron d.1750

George (died in infancy)

Elizabeth m. Ben Withers b.1713 d.1756

Matthew Lee of Ebford b.1744 d.1788 m. Hannah Wakeford

A son b.&d. 1768

Jenny b.1745 d.1749

Thomas Huckell Lee b.1752 d.1822 m. Mary Greir Wakeford

Jenny b. 1757 m. 1 Rbt. Yeates 2 Nat. Wakeford

Matthew Lee Yeates b.1777

Rebecca Huckell Lee b.1775 d.1841 m. Rich. Pennell (Capt. Mer. Navy)

Richard b.1793

Henry m. Anne

Emma Pennell b.1829

Frances Pennell b.1831

Mary Jane Pennell

Mary Grier Lee b.1776 d.1798 m. Col Jackson

Thomas Huckell Lee b.1782 d.1798

George b.&d. 1787

Brice Wakeford Lee (Maj. General: Madras Army) b.1786 d.1871

Jonathon b.1788 d.1798

George Lee (Maj. Indian Army) b.1793 d.1853

Ann Greir Lee b.1796 (still living 1883)

Money was lavished on the house and garden. Full-time gardeners were employed, nectarines and other exotic fruit-trees planted and a "Pleasure House" built on the high ground, south of the house, where Mat could sit and watch shipping in the estuary through the telescope he had earlier bought in London.

Now a wealthy man, Matthew was able to indulge some of his wide interests to advantage. He became Treasurer to the new Devon & Exeter Hospital in Southernhay. In 1765 he and his business friend John Baring of Exeter gave fincancial backing to Benjamin Donn to enable him to bring out the first detailed and properly surveyed map of Devon. It appeared in a handsome book, engraved and illustrated by Thos. Jefferys, "Geographer to His Majesty" and included Donn's thankful dedication:-

> "To John Baring of Mount Radford, and to
> Matthew Lee of Ebford, near Exeter, Esqrs.
> This Map, as a grateful Acknowledgement of
> the great & generous Assistance which they
> have given thereto, -
> Is humbly inscribed
> By their most obedient Serv.t.
> Benjamin Donn"

One imagines that it was partly for reasons of gratitude that Donn carefully included not only "Ebford — Lee Esq." but also Matthew's "Pleasure House" and, of course, Gulliford Meeting on his map.

Like his forebears, Matthew had always taken a lively interest in the Gulliford Meeting, of which he was now a trustee as well as subscriber, although he was also closely associated with George's Meeting in South Street, Exeter, in company with John Baring and a large number of his business friends. Of late the congregations at Gulliford had been increasing, thanks to the popularity of their talented minister Thomas Jervis. It became necessary to build a larger chapel and this was done in 1774.

It is likely that Matthew had a considerable hand in it, for the style and materials echoed both Ebford and George's Meeting, the chapel being built of red brick with stucco quoins and classical details — as can be judged from the surviving illustration. (See opposite).

Yet Matthew barely lived to see the new Meeting completed. On

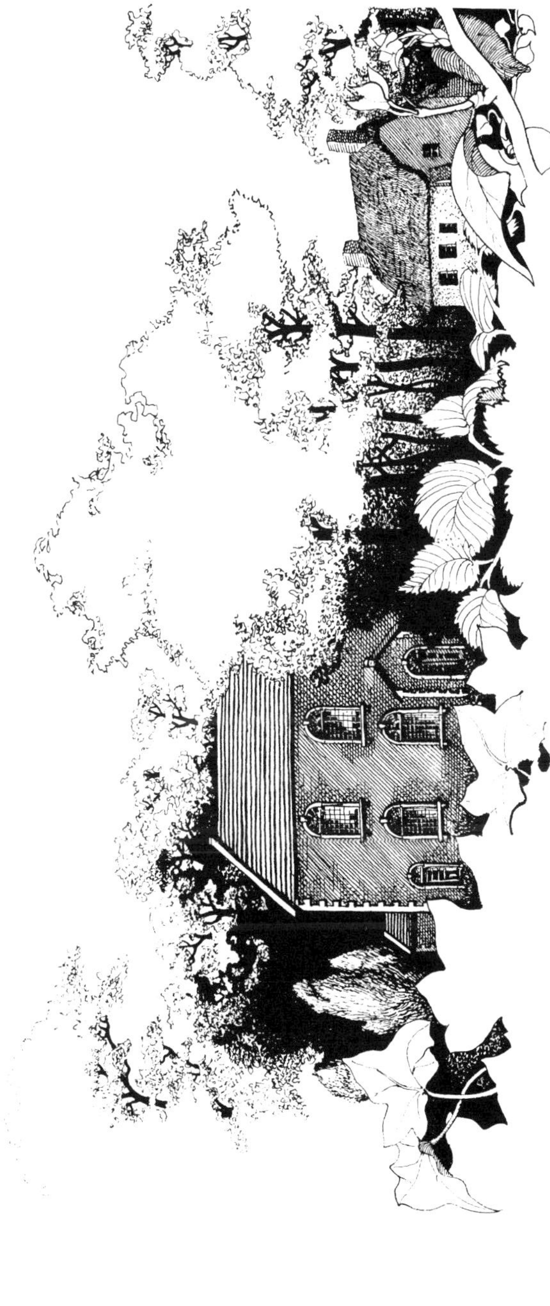

Gulliford Meeting and Boundary Cottage seen from Harefield Cross, mid 19th century.

30th July of that year, 1774, he died at the relatively early age of 59. He was buried with other members of his family in the little graveyard at Gulliford and there his grave is still to be found, guarded secretly by the brambles which have overrun the place and laid upon it a tranquility disturbed only by the songs of the birds that live there.

The Exeter Flying Post for 5th August, 1774 paid this tribute. "Saturday last died at his seat in Ebford, Matthew Lee Esq., much lamented. He was a gentleman of solid judgement and considerable reading. Part of his ample fortune he generously employed in encouraging learning and supporting what he esteemed, the Cause of Religion, Liberty and Truth. In his conduct he discovered Complaisance without Flattery, Hospitality without Profuseness, Justice without Oppression.....an affectionate husbsand and tender parent, the kind master, liberal benefactor and valuable friend."

His had been an exemplary life: small wonder that he was widely mourned. One recalls words from Matthew's diary: "Lord! may I be prepared for the awful summons." Assuredly the trumpets sounded for him on the other side.

Glass seal of cider bottle.

14.
People & Events in the 18th Century

Matthew Lee owned the freehold of Ebford Barton as the Haydons had done before him. But his other farms, Lower Bagmores and Rydon, he held on long leases from Woodbury's ground-landlords, the Rolles[1].

The Rolles were a North Devon family who amassed vast estates through a series of profitable marriages and shrewd purchases. In 1630 Henry Rolle married Anne, daughter and heiress of Sir Thomas Denys of Bicton, and this gave him a toe-hold in East Devon which he lost no time in consolidating. In 1632[2] he bought the manor of Woodbury from Sir Thomas Prideaux of Nutwell and the Rolles continued their acquisitions until, it was said, one could travel from Woodbury to Seaton without ever leaving Rolle Estate land.[3] Prideaux kept Nutwell and Coombe Farm for himself and by 1700 the Nutwell Estate had passed, via his great-nephew Sir Henry Ford, to the Pollexfen family.

Woodbury was short of resident landlords to take a personal interest in the village. The Putts, who owned most of Woodbury Salterton, lived at Combe House, Gittisham. The Rolles continued to live in North Devon. And while the Nutwell people were here for important family occasions, such as weddings and funerals at St. Swithin's, they were busy London lawyers and it is doubtful if Woodbury saw very much of them. When their turns came to be church-wardens more often than not they were represented by proxies.

In the closing years of the 17th century a new family of private means arrived from Somerset to make a brief stay in Woodbury and leave their name in the recorded history of the parish. Samuel Broadmead's name first appears in 1677 when his wife Martha gave birth to a son and they had him christened Samuel in the parish church. On the death of Martha in 1693 Samuel senior married again and he and his second wife Charity proceeded to have a large family between 1695 and 1704. Their first-born was Isaiah, or

Esaias as he preferred to be known. The family lived at Sproutshayes (or Spratshaies) — the old name for Springhayes, so-called on account of its abundant fresh-water springs. The present owners of Springhayes possess a remarkable collection of twelve documents which trace the fortunes of the property from 1696, when it consisted of two cottages, barns, orchards and fields, with common rights, to 1810 when "the House and Edifices newly erected" are referred to (the present house). These documents supplement the very little we know about the Broadmeads. When Sam senior died in 1716 his son Esaias inherited the property and when Esaias died in 1728, at the early age of 33, Sproutshayes went first to his sister Charity, then by sale to their brother John who had returned to Somerset. By 1730 Sproutshayes was in other hands. So the Broadmeads' brief stay of 53 years was over and might have gone unnoticed but for the fact that in his will Esaias left a bequest of £120 for education in Woodbury which resulted in the setting up of the Broadmead Charity School.

The object of the charity was "for instructing the poor children of such day-labourers, or other inhabitants and parishioners of the parish of Woodbury as should be least able to pay for the instruction of their children....to read English until such children should be able to read the Bible, and....to purchase books....proper to that purpose, the children....to be nominated by the said trustees and by....the vicar....and church-wardens and overseers....". So says the will of Esaias Broadmead. He appointed as Trustees "Thomas Lee and seven other persons of Woodbury....and their heirs". Among the original seven trustees were also John Lee, John Stogdon (Broadmead's brother-in-law), another member of the Stogdon family and Edward Holwell, through whose influence, no doubt, money left for a similar purpose by Dr. William Holwell of Exeter in 1707 was added to the Broadmead Charity[4]. In time to come the hereditary nature of the trusteeship was to cause problems but for the moment it worked quite well.

In 1743 the trustees laid out £175 in land, the rent from which would provide the income for the school. A small farm was bought called Edmonds. It consisted of nearly 14 acres in 7 fields, an orchard and cottage, lying between the two lanes at Exton known as Porters Lane and Ridgeway Lane. The land adjoined John Stogdon's farm, called Ash Trees Farm (now gone), and it was Stogdon and his successors who farmed Edmonds and paid the rent.

The first account of the school emerges from a questionaire sent out by the Bishop of Exeter in 1746 to Woodbury's vicar, the Rev'd Charles Williams M.A.[5]

Question: "Is there any Public or Charity School, endowed or otherwise maintained in your Parish? What number of children are taught in it? And what Care is taken to instruct them in the Principles of the Church of England, and to bring them duly to Church as the Canon requires?"

Answer: "Yes — sixteen children are taught in it. They are nominated from time to time (according to Directions contained in the Wills of the Benefactors) by the Minister and Churchwardens for the time being. The children are carefully and legally instructed by their master, and duly brought to church." Strange as it may seem, we have no idea where this school was held during the first 70 years of its existence and its later history belongs to another chapter.

In the year in which Esias Broadmead died Woodbury had another matter on its mind. In concerned a murder. Nathaniel Langley arrived in Woodbury with his young family in the early years of the 18th century, settling at Mallocks Farm which he leased from the Rolle Estate. He prospered and was well-liked and respected. In 1706 he was elected church-warden and served in that capacity 15 times in the next 20 years. In 1719 he joined Jonathon Snow in his milling business at Exton Mill.[6] Snow was a member of an established Woodbury family and had first leased the mill from the Rolle Estate in 1697. Now, when the 21-year lease came up for renewal, Nathaniel Langley's name appears as Snow's partner. Langley was re-elected church-warden in 1726 and all seemed to be going well. But in that year he was indicted for murder, found guilty at Exeter Assizes and imprisoned in Exeter Gaol.

There he languished for two years, his name appears in The Exeter Gaol Kalendar[7] against the words "to remain according to his former commitment". This was unusual, to say the least. Murderers were normally executed within days of conviction and a sinister "sus" (for "suspendit"), or sometimes just plain "s" added after their names. In Langley's case there must have been sufficient doubt to warrant a stay of execution. Early in 1727 Langley's two apprentices, Thos. Challice and Rbt. Leroy, applied for, and were granted a discharge from their apprenticeships and the Rolle Estate called in the leases of his properties and sold off his goods and chattels. The sale seems to have attracted a good deal of sympathetic interest; his fellow-farmers crowded the event and Edward Holwell gave £3 14s for "an old blind mare". One item without a price against it reads "a large silver tankard – sent to Bicton".[8] The landlord's perks!

Eventually Langley, having served his time, was released and returned to Woodbury where he died, a broken man, in 1734 and was buried in Woodbury churchyard.

Edward Holwell, Langley's friend and fellow church-warden, held the lease of Thorn Barton where he probably carried on his trade as Master Butcher. A branch of the family may have been there in the previous century when the ancient house had been much improved by the addition of a new wing at the back with a handsome bay-window looking out on the garden and churchyard. And the fine plaster ceilings which adorned the big upstairs rooms marked it as the home of a well-to-do family with money and taste to lavish on improvements. However, in 1762 the property passed from Holwell to "Philip Lemprière of Lymington in the County of Hampshire.

The Lemprières were Channel Islanders and had played a significant, if stormy, part in the administration of Jersey for centuries. Their strong arm and their power-politics did not always make them popular at home and they very wisely sought out comfortable bolt-holes in Lymington and Woodbury in case things got too hot for them in Jersey – which is precisely what happened in 1769.

Philip Lemprière, born in Jersey in 1718, became Attorney General of the island at the age of 40. In 1769, after eleven years of continual rumpus, he fled to England and settled in Woodbury.[10] But even here he could not endear himself. He married Mary, daughter of Charles Weeks, (whose family ran the tannery at Gilbrook) and Charles promised Philip £1000 dowry with his daughter. Not being able to pay the money in a lump sum, he begged to be allowed to pay it in instalments. But payment fell behind and an unedifying legal wrangle strung out for years until Weeks died and the money was never paid in full.[11] Poor Mary!

Philip Lemprière was not content with Thorn Barton for long. He owned a small-holding opposite Thorn then known as Axes Tenement and in 1781 he built himself a comfortable house there, amalgamating the land of Axes with some of the barton land. For a while the new house was referred to simply as "The Brick House" (Land Tax Assessment) but when Thorn ceased to be a farm the old name was transferred to Lemprière's new house. It is now known as Woodbury House and remains very much as Lemprière built it, with his initials and the date embossed on the lead hopper-head, a fine Georgian fanlight and canopy over the front door and the first triple-light sash-windows to be seen in Woodbury.

Woodbury House in 1981, built by Philip Lemprière in 1781.

As for Thorn Barton, it began to fall on evil days. Lemprière renewed the lease in 1784 and it may have become Woodbury's second tannery shortly after that date. For a while it clung to the old name, being referred to as "Part of Thorn" in the Church Rate Lists which show that the rateable value fell from 3s.8d. with the land (1779) to 7d. without it (1816). The new bay window, which had enjoyed the view of the church, now looked out onto the stinking tan-pits. Soon its old dignity and historic associations were to be quite forgotten and it became known simply as "the Tannery".

The Tannery, formerly Thorn Barton c. 1865.

Games at Exton

It has already been seen that Matthew Lee was a meticulous keeper of diaries, note books, accounts and legal documents. It is fortunate for Woodbury's historians that his younger son, Thomas Huckell Lee, not only kept his father's papers but added to them. Through these we make the startling discovery that Exton had its own Village Green "otherwise called the Bowling Green", owned by Lee. In 1793 a dispute arose about the use of the Green. Nobody disputed Lee's "right to the soil of the Bowling Green". It concerned the grazing rights which John Wheaton of Venmore said he had. On April 10th that year a young lad was minding 19 ewes and lambs on the Bowling Green when John Wheaton came up to him and asked whose sheep they were. Wheaton's dogs, much to the consternation of the lad, then chased the sheep out of the field and finally drove them into Exton Pound. To settle the matter the oldest inhabitants of Exton were called to give Testamonies as to how the field had been used during their memory. Was it common grazing land or was it not?[12]

Thomas Cantlebury, aged 76, "says he remembers the....Bowling Green a sporting place....and the fact of someone's cutting furze there — he thinks twas by Wheaton's Granfer".

Richard Hall was 63 and landlord of the New Inn at Exton. He "remembers the remains of a shed or Bowling House standing ...The Bowling Green was always since his time a Common".

Next came John Braddick, shipwright,[13] who lived at Exton House, then called Braddicks. He was 80 and had known the Green for 70 years. "It had been open...used for the sports of Easter Monday and wrestling and always considered an Open Common.

Surprisingly, the case was awarded to John Wheaton, subject to its ancient rights being observed.

The Tithe Map of 1839 shows a field at Exton called "the Bowling Green" and this is undoubtedly the same field. It is situated near the outfall of the Gillbrook into the Exe, between the stream and the Royal Marine Camp. (It is interesting to note that, as at Topsham, the bowling green was situated on land which would sometimes be inundated at high tides. "Sea-washed turf" is still considered the finest for that purpose). Here on Easter Mondays, probably since "time immemorial" the local inhabitants (and some not so local, no doubt) had gathered for a Sports Day of which the high-light was the Wrestling Match.

Devonshire wrestling was tremendously popular in the 18th century. It amounted to a passion – an addiction. The contestants were usually young farmers and farm-workers and they wrestled for purses of anything up to 10 guineas put up by the local gentry who often promoted the contests. The contestants fought in a ring 15 to 20 yards in diameter and marked out with stakes and a rope. They could take hold of each other in any way they liked, providing it was not below the belt, and could kick as hard as they liked but not above the knees. It was a common sight to see their shins streaming with blood but they made little of it. Sixteen wrestlers were required for a match so the eventual winner had to be successful in four bouts. Sometimes fighting went on far into the night.[14]

Bowling was a very different matter and not a game for the hot-blooded youngsters. Yet the dim recollection of a "Bowling House" seems to suggest that bowling had come to an end before 1793. It had been the popular sport of the Elizabethans and the story of Drake's famous game on Plymouth Hoe was a legend even in his own lifetime. It was played everywhere. There is even a reference in the Tithe Map to a "Bowling Green field" on Woodbury Salterton and it must surely have been played on Woodbury Village Green on many a fine summer's evening. Certainly there was wrestling there, at Fair Time and on other occasions.

Exton Pound, into which John Wheaton so unceremoniously drove someone else's ewes and lambs, was not at Pink House Corner as it is now. In fact, there was no corner, nor was there a road to Woodbury at that point. The road from Woodbury to Nutwell, such as it was, followed the line of the present road past Venmore to the place where it now makes a left-hand bend before Barclayclose (usually called 'Barnacles') Hill. Here, instead of bending left, the old road went straight on to join the lane that runs past the Brake and comes out at Upper Nutwell (Porters Lane). The pound was immediately opposite this road junction, as can be seen on Benjamin Donn's map.

It was not the only pound in the parish. There was one at Woodbury Salterton opposite the gate of Greendale Barton and the

The Vicars' Pound with thatched cottages, (L) Chowns & (R) Leaches. c.1900.

Vicars Choral had one known as the Vicars' Pound or Parsonage Pound. It occupied the green triangle where Parsonage Cross now stands, on the corner of Pound Lane. Straying animals were driven into it and the owners had to pay a fine to get them out.

However, there may have been a fourth pound whose site has been entirely lost and forgotten. A ghost of it is to be found in a Rolle Estate lease for 1751 which granted "to Robert Cooke of Woodbury,

Innkeeper…a cottage near the old pound and the Herb Garden and the piece of land near thereto where the pound did stand"[15] This cannot be a reference to any of the other three, still is use in 1751, but perhaps to a manorial pound already gone but still well remembered as a landmark. And the Herb Garden? In 1839 the field opposite the corner of Fairfield (now the site of "Thurle") was called Pound Park. It may well have been a long echo from the days when Fairfield was the site of the Albemarles' manor house, and their cattle pound and herb garden was a short stone's throw away.

15.
Turnpikes, Travelling and Trade

In the year 1731 a new family arrived to take up residence at Nutwell Court. On the death of Sir Henry Pollexfen the estate passed to his brother-in-law Sir Francis Drake, a descendant of the famous admiral's brother John.[1]

The Drakes were a family very much aware of rank and wealth. They found Nutwell lacking in the grandeur and privacy which people of their quality had come to expect. Times had changed since the days when the Albemarles had lived side by side with their tenants in Woodbury village and sat at meat with their servants at the long table in the hall. As one generation of Drakes succeeded another they created a well-timbered park between themselves and the prying eyes of common people and did not make themselves popular in so doing.

Benjamin Donn's map shows no park in 1765 but already, in preparation for it, the old mediaeval gate-house had been demolished stone by stone. The chapel built by the Dinhams in 1371 no longer provided services for the estate people — nor anyone else for that matter[2] — and the road that led to it was closed in an endeavour to prevent people passing within view of the house.

But in 1785 the Drakes struck tough opposition. In that year the 5th baronet's attempt to close the footpath along the river-bank was blocked by the stubborn action of the Vestry. A full, official session of the Vestry Meeting and parishioners was held at Richard Hall's "New Inn" at Exton to hear the Overseers of the Highways complain that "the old footpath run along the Bank of the River Exe where foot-passengers daily go between Topsham and Lympstone and the fishermen, fishing boats and see-persons (*sic*) resorting to the river have always gone this way which Sir F. Drake wants now to appropriate to himself to the great prejudice of the Public and Trade and this he would do at the expense of the Public". He was obliged to abandon his scheme for the time being and to allow a path 3ft. wide to remain.[3]

Even in 1785 local traffic mainly went on foot. Wheeled traffic was still rare. Most goods were still shifted by pack-horse and a string of six or seven of these creatures, fully laden and in charge of an experienced driver, was a formidable obstacle to meet on any road. They gave way to no-one and moved incredibly fast so that wise travellers would flatten themselves against a gate or jump into a field to let them go by.[4]

Nevertheless, the population was becoming more mobile and wheeled traffic was used increasingly for long journeys. Matthew Lee had his own chaise in which he and his family travelled between London and Ebford. The old method whereby every parish was responsible for its own roads could no longer cope with growing demands and it was essential that main traffic routes found a new form of maintenance. The turnpikes were the answer.

The Turnpike Trusts were semi-official, regulated by Parliament but run by local people on a non-profitmaking basis. Tolls were charged on most classes of wheeled traffic and the money used for improving main roads, payment being made according to the number of wheels and horses per vehicle at gates and toll-houses specially set up at intervals.[5]

East Devon was covered by the Exeter Turnpike Trust set up in 1753 and one of the first roads to be turnpiked was the Exeter-Newton Poppleford-London road. This skirted the northern boundary of the parish at Greendale Barton. There followed the turnpiking of the Topsham-Exmouth road as far as Bronte House, Lympstone, where there was a gate, and the Clyst St. Mary to Woodbury road as far as "Woodbury Hill" (Four Firs?). These roads were described as having "become so ruinous....that....they cannot be effectually amended and kept in good repair....unless money is raised for that purpose".[6]

For Woodbury an important development came in 1771 with the turnpiking of a link-road from Topsham to Newton Poppleford. It came by way of the George and Dragon where there was a gate. (Though this road was finally disturnpiked in 1884 the late Mrs. E. Allsopp of Woodbury could remember the gate-posts still in position and the gate, lifted off its hinges, lying against the hedge-bank.) After following the Clyst St. George-Woodbury road, still called "the Turnpike" by many old residents, and continuing up Broadway to Four Firs, the route turned left along what is now the B3180 as far as the Beacon. Here it turned right near the junction with Castle Lane and ran where no road now exists in a long curve round the basin of the valley. Gorse grows thickly on what were once the drainage ditches at the side of the road, leaving a tell-tale line of bright yellow across the dark heather.[7] The road now emerges as a stony track beyond the clump of trees that marks the parish boundary and this section is still kept roughly usable by Royal Marine vehicles. It snakes down over Colaton Raleigh Common to join Hawkerland Lane at Stoneyford and thence by the back lane to Newton Poppleford. The road is an impressive sight as it leaves the Common, looking, one imagines, very much as it did when coaches plied the route regularly, carrying fare-passengers from Topsham and Woodbury to join the London coach at the Toll-gate house, Newton Poppleford — now an antique shop.

Once the main roads were improved the way was open for the development of public transport. By 1777 a coach with six passengers inside and as many on top could make the journey from Exeter to London in 2½ days. But it was expensive. For poorer people there were the "Fly Wagons" that took 4½-6 days and cost 18s.[8], (3-weeks' wages for a labouring man.)

The growth of traffic on the roads brought about a great increase in the number of inns where passengers, driver and horses could be rested and refreshed. Such a one was Woodbury's famous Globe Inn. Standing on the corner of Globe Hill and Rydon Lane, it was a fine cob building, thatched, with stabling for horses at the back and a prominent bay-window in front to give a good view up and down the road. Outside the door was a stone-stepped mounting block. The name, "the Globe", probably makes it contemporary with the Globe Inns at Exmouth, Lympstone, Topsham and Exeter and may indicate that port wine in the barrel was being imported direct from Portugal — a globe being the national symbol of Portugal.

So far as Woodbury was concerned the main feature of the Globe Inn was the large upper room, scene of many village functions. It became the headquarters of the Woodbury Volunteers — a contingent of the yeoman army raised in 1794 to meet the threat of invasion from France. Here, under their captain, Thomas Huckell Lee, the young men of Woodbury met twice a week for training and their recruiting posters were prominently displayed outside the door.

The Globe also became the home of the Woodbury Bench of Magistrates and the Petty Sessions were held in the upper room every alternate Thursday (alternating with the Globe at Exmouth). "Petty" is certainly the word! An examination of the proceedings reveals a steady trickle of cases — apple-stealing, rabbit-netting, "drunk and disorderly", affiliation orders, non-payment of turnpike tolls ("I didn't know I had to pay!"), using obscene language and squabbles between neighbours. Anyone hoping to uncover Woodbury's lurid past would be disappointed![9]

Perhaps the most colourful and best-loved memories of the Globe concerned "Visitation Day". This was a survival of the old Church Ales of Tudor times. Every year, on a Saturday in May or June, the Church Vestry held the equivalent of its annual general meeting and the jollifications lasted most of the day. They began with a service and meeting in the parish church at eleven o'clock in the morning at which parishioners chose their church-wardens and overseers. The Steward of the College of Vicars Choral was there in his best wig

The Globe Inn, Globe Hill c. 1900, showing recruiting posters for the Woodbury Volunteers and Mr. Skinner's wagonette.

and gown to inspect the church accounts, after which they were open to public inspection and were approved — and occasionally disapproved, argued over and amended — by the parishioners at large[10]. Then, to the sound of the church bells pealing, the entire company repaired to the Globe, there to enjoy the "Visitation Dinner" at the ratepayers' expense. The dinner grew in popularity to reach a peak in 1811 when £10.18.9. was thus spent, after which it dwindled and ended in 1849. During its last years the venue alternated between the Globe and the White Hart.

There is no doubt that the Visitation Dinner was finally killed off by the fearful growing poverty in the village. But way back in the mid-18th century there were no such thoughts troubling the minds of Woodbury people. True, there were always the poor, the old, the sick and the unfortunate. But they could be coped with as they always had been: one paid one's Poor Rate and remembered them in one's prayers. For the most part Woodbury, along with the rest of East Devon, was still enjoying the prosperity of the wool trade and when one industry flourished it drew attendant services along with it.

The growth in population brought with it the need for more housing. In 1741 Josiah Teed, a mariner of Lympstone and a subscriber of Gulliford Meeting, bought a strip of land in Gillbrook described as "a cottage and garden" from his fellow-dissenter John Darby, baker of Woodbury, and built the row of cottages that bear his name. It was a profitable speculation and he could be sure of his rents.

There was a nucleus of activity along the Gillbrook. In addition to the tannery already mentioned there was a field somewhere near Brookside called the Rack Field.[11] Rack fields were associated with the fulling of cloth — a process requiring water. The lengths of serge were spread out to dry on special wooden fences and the name Rack Field tells us that there was a fulling mill on the Gillbrook of which we have no other record. Further up the village street John Beal was carrying on business as a "fell-monger" — dealing in sheep-skins and fleeces.[12] Sheep-skins were much in demand for book-binding and all Woodbury's parish registers of the period are thus bound. Elsewhere in Woodbury lived William Hart whose will, dated 1719, describes him as a "wool-comber". It is likely that these chance references to the woollen industry represent only the tip of the iceberg and that a great many people in Woodbury were profitably engaged in it. But it is through the Dagworthy family of Woodbury Salterton that we get a sudden, intimate glimpse of the woollen industry actually at work.

The Dagworthys had been in Salterton since the 16th century and it is probable that a branch of the family moved into their present home, Browns Farm, soon after 1684, the year in which John Dagworthy married Joan Brown. They were dissenters from the beginning and trustees and subscribers of Gulliford Meeting. There they would have known Matthew Lee and it is perhaps not surprising to find that Samuel Dagworthy was lured away from farming into the woollen trade. By 1753 he had set himself up at Browns as a sergemaker.

Looms were expensive and, as there had recently been disastrous fires in the woollen towns of Honiton and Tiverton, Samuel prudently took out an insurance policy with the Sun Fire Office.[13] The company's records give a clear description of the premises:- "Dwellinghouse and dyehouse, comb shop, tending shops and rooms over all adjacent in the village of Woodbury Salterton...., stone, cob and thatched £150; household goods and stock in trade therein £150". A second policy in 1760 also mentions the "cellar", the name by which the long barn at Browns is still known. But for these policies we should have no idea that serge-making was being carried on in the village. How many more were there whose names we do not know?

From this description it is clear that Sam was carrying out the processes of combing the wool prior to spinning, and dyeing the cloth after weaving at Browns and to do so he must have had workers outside his immediate family. A verbal tradition in the Dagworthy family says that about eight people were employed. In addition to those directly employed, his busy looms provided work for many dozens of women and children, spinning yarn in their own homes, whereby they could earn as much as 3s.6d. a week. To people passing by on the road the sight of Sam's lengths of serge hanging out to dry after dyeing and the steady click-clack of the looms wafting out through the open windows of Browns were familiar everyday sights and sounds. For a while Sam Dagworthy prospered and Woodbury Salterton prospered with him.

Although the serge industry in Devon was beginning to decline by the time Sam got going, he made enough money in his early days to build a new house near Greendale Barton which he called Higher House. It first appeared on Donn's map (1765) thanks, no doubt, to the prompting of his friend Matthew Lee, and was his principal property in the Church Rate List newly made in 1779. Browns Farm was probably given over entirely to weaving. But by the time Browns Farm account book starts in 1786 Sam Dagworthy was almost certainly out of business. Nowhere in those pages is there anything that might relate to wool. The fields had been let out to others and the process of getting the farm on its feet again and going over to dairy-farming was slow and painful. The apple orchards produced some income and the horse and cart transported commodities for others — lime, turf, corn and so on. These slender means, and the rents from the fields, kept Browns ticking over for the time being and one hopes Sam was able to leave enough money — made in the palmy days — to provide for his successor.

Sam Dagworthy senior died childless in 1797 and was buried in the graveyard at Gulliford. Browns Farm passed briefly to his nephew Sam Dagworthy junior. Five years later young Sam too was laid in the ground at Gulliford. His death must have been sudden — perhaps an accident — for he signed the rate book on March 5th and was buried on April 5th 1802. His young widow was five months pregnant with their third child, Richard, baptized at Gulliford on September 25th 1802. In 1805 Mrs. Dagworthy remarried. Her husband was Daniel Sanders and through the account book we see Browns Farm being built up again and handed back to young Richard on his marriage in 1826.[14]

16.
The Bad Years 1800-1832

The decline and eventual collapse of the serge industry in Devon was a terrible catastrophe. Samuel Dagworthy had the good sense to get out of serge-making before bankruptcy could overtake him. The Lees wisely invested their money in the East India Company and in ships plying the trade routes of the Far East and in Greenland Whalers — both sailing from Exe ports.

Others were not so lucky. As the Devon woollen trade shrank and large-scale sheep-farming became less attractive other small subsidiary industries found themselves on the rocks. 1770 saw the bankruptcy of Joel Hayman, tallow candle-maker, of Cooke's Farm, Woodbury Salterton, and his failure was followed in 1779 by that of Josias Force's Tannery.[1]

The causes of the decline were numerous and the effect was at first gradual. New factory methods of weaving were taking over from the old hand-loom and the machines depended on coal for their power. It was cheaper to transport Devon wool to Yorkshire than Yorkshire coal to Devon. Fashions, too, began to change and Devon weavers failed to realize that serge was being replaced by lighter materials. Finally the long drawn-out Napoleonic Wars that began in 1793 and ended on the field of Waterloo in 1815 effectively closed many of the profitable continental markets.

In the boom-years there had been work for everybody and many people had come into the area in search of jobs. The chance of a steady income had tempted many small-holders to give up their meagre livelihood on the land and take employment in the wool trade. Their fields had been absorbed by the bigger farms and when the crash came there was no going back to any sort of independence. Nor could agriculture absorb the unemployed, though the shift away from sheep towards more corn and dairy produce certainly found work for a good many. They were wretchedly paid. Though a labourer's 7s. a week in 1808 was supplemented by a daily ration of cider or ale and an opportunity to buy certain farm commodities at reduced prices, many a family man still found himself below subsistence level and had to come on the parish for Poor Relief. As the years went by matters went from bad to worse. Brown's Farm account book shows that by 1829-30 a labourer, George Cross, was still being paid 1s.2d. a day, or 7s. for a 6 day week, though wheat had gone up from 3s.9d. to 9s. a bushel, potatoes were 5s. a bag and he was paying 15s.9d. per ½ year's rent for his cottage.[2]

Farmers' incomes rose sharply as food prices soared, though a great deal of it went in high rents and taxation. There was Poor Rate and Church Rate, Horse Tax and Dog Tax, Land Tax and Window Tax, and a great many more. Browns Farm paid tax on 6 windows — Nutwell Court on 131. But it was the land-owners who made fortunes, not tenant farmers, and the poor got poorer, the rich richer. One might suppose that Lord Rolle, with an income in excess of £30,000 a year,[3] could have done more for his poor tenants. In fact, he was an enterprising and generous landlord by the standards of his time. Both rich and poor were caught up in a system that only legislation could remedy and successive governments, while recognizing the need for reform, failed to grasp the nettle. The labourer did not want charity or poor relief: he wanted a living wage for his 60 hour week that would restore to him his old independence and self-esteem. But there was little he could do to help himself. Out of Woodbury's total population of around 1800 only 79 had the vote.

The plight of the unemployed was far worse. As they could not afford to pay a proper rent it was no longer profitable for private people to build or let cottages. In fact, many owners would rather allow a property to fall down than house a pauper family. Alternative accommodation was found by dividing up some of the older houses in the centre of the village, as they became vacant, into cramped and inadequate tenements. Govetts became six cottages[4], sharing a pump and water trough in the old cobbled courtyard, and many others were soon to follow.

Tales are still told among the older generation in Woodbury, who heard them from their grandparents, of how men-folk set off on the long trek northwards in search of work, leaving wives and families to fend for themselves as best they could. In 1801 three young married men, Hingston, Shepherd and Hill, disappeared in this way and Overseer Thomas Huckell Lee advertised in the Exeter Flying Post offering a reward of one guinea for their apprehension.[5]

Shepherd and Hill had both received "shirt cloth for the poor" from the Haydon Charity in the previous year.[6]

The growing crisis was reflected in Woodbury's Poor Rate which rose steadily from 4d. to 1s.2d. in the £. In 1808 Woodbury raised £597 in rates and distributed £475 directly to the poor, while other amounts were spent by the Overseers in legal actions, leaving a total of £77 for all other purposes together.[7] It is to the credit of Woodbury and its Overseers that the problem was contained without resort to the horrors of the workhouse at Heavitree.

Even so, the job of Overseer was unpopular and there were some who were known for their harshness and lack of sympathy; and the Vestry minutes contain resolutions that the poor should be paid their ready money regularly every Monday morning, which had not apparently been done in past years. What John Snow Hayman, Overseer for Salterton Quarter, did to make himself unpopular we do not know but in 1803 a rick at Cooke's Farm was deliberately set alight. While he was actually engaged in questioning two suspects, someone else set fire to the farmhouse, buildings and ricks and the whole property was burnt to the ground.[8]

An increase in crime was only one effect of the desperate conditions of the poor. In Woodbury in 1808 there were 296 families living in 263 houses, while 14 houses stood empty. Overcrowding and enforced idleness had the inevitable result of a higher rate of bastardy. The rate which had been around 1 in 60 in 1700 had risen to around 1 in 30 by 1800 for those baptisms registered in the parish church, though that figure camouflages the true state of affairs. The Gulliford Meeting register reveals a bastardy rate of 1 in 17 and a study of the names shows that not all of them were from non-conformist families. One is left to draw the conclusion that some wretched women found in Gulliford a 'soft option' where their babies could be decently baptized without the glare of publicity and shame attached to baptism in the parish church during the normal course of Sunday Matins.

In fairness to the vicar of the time, the Rev'd John Davy, it must be said that he was a deeply caring and compassionate man, much beloved in Woodbury. It was during his incumbency that the form of the words "base child of — ", used in the register for centuries, was dispensed with in favour of "son (or daughter) of — " followed by the mother's christian and surname. It makes it impossible to pick out a bastard child by casting one's eye quickly down the register.

His popularity may even have had something to do with the decline in the fortunes of Gulliford Meeting — though there were other causes.[9] By the time Thomas Huckell Lee was buried there in 1822 nearly all Woodbury names had already disappeared from the books and returned to the register in their parish church.

If Woodbury's problems seemed bad, conditions throughout the country were worse. At least we were not the victims of "dark satanic mills" nor of the enclosures of common land which caused such distress elsewhere in England, and if one had to be poor, Woodbury was not a bad place to be poor in — with the Common at hand to provide free fuel, litter and acorns. It was a very worried Board of Agriculture that commissioned a survey to be made in each county, to see how food supplies could be improved to feed an ever increasing population of city dwellers. Charles Vancouver's survey of Devon, published in 1808, shows exactly the state of farming in East Devon at that time. He is full of praise for the small farmers, describing them as honest, sober and industrious, though living in humble circumstances. It was customary, he says, for a husband to give his wife on marriage the care of the pigs, poultry and dairy for her "pin-money". On this she was expected to clothe and supply her household. Wives and daughters were singled out for special praise for their remarkable industry and neatness in marketing their farm produce in Exeter — rising early on Market Day and making the journey whatever the weather. These customs survived in Woodbury until recent years.

Even before Vancouver's survey was made Lord Rolle had initiated a scheme to help poor labourers which has left an interesting mark on land just below the Common. The old turbary, where peat had been cut since Saxon times, was worked out and had gone back to scrub. Lord Rolle now offered it to landless people, an acre at a time, to reclaim and cultivate. If one acre prospered the worker was offered another — and so on — and finally a long lease at a nominal rent. The soil of the area is still black from the remains of the peat. Many of the tiny fields thus created have lost their identities in amalgamation with their neighbours but for a century they were known by the names of the men who toiled to reclaim them — Miller's Plot, Marks's Plot, Stokes's Field, Bazeley's Plot, Skinner's Plot and many more — 24 in all totalling some 50 acres, mostly of one or two acres each, though Robert Stokes managed to get together 18 acres in two fields.[10]

Vancouver surprisingly shows that, while most people were engaged in agriculture, Woodbury still had 256 people engaged in what he calls "manufactures", though he gives no further information on the subject. Some light is shed by the register of baptisms which described the occupation of the parents. So we know that as well as butcher, baker and blacksmith people were engaged in building, brick-making, lime-burning, tailoring, barrel-making, malting, brewing, shoe-making, tanning, candle-making and lace-making. This last had taken the place of spinning amongst many women-folk and, though lace was not enjoying the popularity it later achieved, Woodbury had many lace-makers in the early years of the 19th century.

But there was another form of employment opened up by the inequalities of the time. Vancouver had noted that the excellent qualities of the East Devon villagers — politeness, gentleness, thrift and a desire to please — made them particularly good servants. Rich people were being attracted to the area by the climate and scenery, now made accessible by the turnpike roads, and because their fashionable haunts in the South of France had been closed by the Napoleonic War. Everywhere large houses were appearing. Thomas Huckell Lee built Mount Ebford on the site of his father's "Pleasure House" for his widowed mother. Along Broadway half a dozen genteel residences sprang up around the year 1800, and Oakhayes followed in about 1830. All these houses required servants, both male and female.

And for those with a spirit of adventure there were good posts to be found in London and elsewhere. It is apt to be forgotten these days that the big houses provided a real career structure where one could work one's way up to be Housekeeper or Head Butler. So it was that Hannah Pine packed her box and took the stage-coach to London. In 1814, the year before Waterloo, she wrote to her 22 year old cousin, Sarah Dagworthy. The letter is beautifully written and has all the gentle charm of a Jane Austen novel and it tells us something about life in a titled family with a town house and an estate in the country.

"My dear Sarah I suppose you have oftentimes wondered the reason of my long silence. But I flatter myself that your goodness will pardon me....I went to London, was out of a Place a fortnight — I then engaged with Sir Thomas and Lady Beauchamps Proctor and left London the same day....I have been with them about five months. I like it pretty well as yet but am all most tired out with company as usual. Where we are now is at the Country House one hundred and ten miles from London near Norwich....it is a fine county for game — the Place is very handy for the shooting season to which I am thankful to say is allmost over for we go to London the tenth of next month....My Lace-making goes on very slowly I have not made any for three months....I am much better than I have been for two years.....and am got quite fat I must let out all my gowns soon....Lady B is an odd sort of Lady. She is so flighty and thinks of nothing but gaiety. I have the care of the Linen and Everything except her Wardrobe. We are but three in our room, Butler Lady's Maid and my self — about fifteen in the servants' Hall....I hope you will Excuse all faults as I am in Haste.

from your affte cousin
H. Pine[11] "

Every now and then brief glimpses of the Napoleonic War emerge from the Vestry books as, for instance, the ringing of the church bells to celebrate what the church-wardens' accounts called "Nelsons Victuary" at Trafalgar in 1805. And nine months later the Burtons proudly carried their baby son to the font of St. Swithin's, there to receive the names Horatio Nelson. As the threat of a French invasion grew, Woodbury Common became a large army camp and artillery park under the command of General Simcoe.[12] The country was in a great state of alarm and wagons and horses were kept ready for the evacuation of women and children. A volunteer force was raised and armed with light cavalry curved swords and flint-lock pistols. Thus the Woodbury Volunteers, under their captain, Thomas Hucknell Lee, came into being and the guidon presented to them in 1794 hung until recently in the church. It seems probable that the Volunteers held target practice in the field below the Globe Inn, where dozens of lead musket balls of the period have been located by metal detection. The invasion threat remained for several years and military exercises on the Common drew large crowds of spectators. There must have been others besides John Gordon who enlisted in the forces. Gordon joined the 14th Regiment of Foot in 1804 when he was 21. After 8 years as a private he became a corporal and took part in the battle of Corunna for which he received a medal and clasp. Later, as sergeant, he served in India until his discharge in 1829 when he returned to Woodbury and entered employment at Nutwell Court as gamekeeper.[13]

The Nutwell people also took active part in the war. Sir Francis Drake's (5th Bart) brother-in-law, General Sir George Elliot, distinguished himself in the Peninsular campaign and was made 1st Lord Heathfield of Gibraltar. His son, the 2nd Lord Heathfield,

The 2nd Lord Heathfield on one of his thorough-breds against a background of the Exe estuary at Nutwell. by Agasse — c. 1810

Sir Thomas Trayton Fuller Eliott Drake, Bart.

Lady Fuller Eliott Drake

inherited Nutwell in 1794. His great passion was horses and he built the stud stable and indoor riding school at Nutwell where thoroughbreds were raised.

On Lord Heathfield's death in 1813 Nutwell passed to his sister's son, Capt. Thomas Trayton Fuller (knighted in 1821) who took the additional names Elliot Drake in deference to his uncle's family. He saw service in Spain with the 52nd Light Infantry and Nutwell became the home of war relics – among them a wooden table and intricately worked brass box made out of a "floating cannon" taken by his uncle at Gibraltar.[14]

Unlike his predecessors at Nutwell, "Sir T.T.F.E. Drake", as he is referred to in the Vestry minutes, threw himself whole-heartedly into the affairs of Woodbury, though he seems at times to have been overbearing and unpopular. But he was not the first nor last well meaning new-comer to throw his weight about and Woodbury had its own quiet way of dealing with him and getting on with life.

Changes had taken place in Woodbury as well as at Nutwell. John Holwell signed his approval of the annual accounts for the last time in 1799 and there was no member of his family to come after him. For 400 years every generation had felt the benefit of their remarkable public spirit: never a crisis but they had been there to help, never a charity but they were trustees, never a jollification but they were prepared to enter into the fun by dressing up as "Robin Hood" or whatever. A family of extraordinary vigour and buoyancy, with a deep sense of commitment to the soil of their birth-place – how fortunate Woodbury has been in families such as the Holwells!

Those same accounts for 1799 show that Gilbert Ware and John Glanvill were churchwardens for the first time. Thus as one long association finished two others began, for both families are still in Woodbury.

For the Wares it might almost be described as a home-coming for they were related by marriage to the Haydons. Earlier they had lived at Ottery St. Mary and Colaton Raleigh but Gilbert Ware's father, George, was farming at Mallocks by 1779, as the church rate list shows. Gilbert's daughter, Julianna, married James Sanders. Both the Wares and the Sanders had family connections with tanning as well as farming so it is not surprising to find William Sanders taking on the tannery at Gilbrook after the bankruptcy of Wm. Hole in 1829 and being joined in partnership with Gilbert Ware's grandson, William Walter Ware. William eventually succeeded Sanders in 1855 and Gilbrook has been their home ever since.[15]

The first Glanvill entry in the registers appears in 1775 when Peter Glanvill of Milton Farm, Payhembury, married Jane Roberts of Woodbury in St. Swithin's Church. The couple returned to Milton and no more is heard about them but it is not hard to imagine the happy family occasion with, perhaps, Peter's younger brother John acting as Best Man while Jane was attended by her younger sister Ann. At any rate, John and Ann were married at St. Swithin's three years later and settled in Woodbury, probably at Exton. Their son, Henry, married Mary Lee and it is doubtless through their relationship that the Glanvills became tenants first of Lower Bagmores and, by 1816 (church rate list), of their present home at Rydon — both farms leased to the Lees of Ebford.

For families living in isolated farms dotted about the parish life was healthy enough. They lived off the products of their own land and drank water from their own wells. In fact, Woodbury was remarkably healthy and long-lived considering the overcrowded conditions and inadequate diet of the poor. For instance, 18 deaths were recorded in the register for 1823 and of those 10 were sixty years old or more, 4 of them being over eighty and 1 ninety. Yet housing conditions in the village itself presented a health-hazard that was to go up like a time-bomb in 1832.

The bright little stream that bubbled up at Parsonage and sparkled through the Vicars' fish ponds to join the Gillbrook had been the precious commodity which had attracted the very first settlers and made the original village of Woodbury possible. But imagine that same stream in 1832. It passed the farmyard at Parsonage, skirted behind Lamb Park Farm and, after running over the road at the Pound, passed in front of Leaches Farm. It then wound its way along the backs of all the cottages from Chowns to Haydons — each having a "privy" in the back garden. Where Webbers Farm buildings now stand along Bonfire Lane there was a long row of poor cottages, after which the stream passed down the side of the Church Steps Cottages to receive the effluent from the Green Tannery. Next it ran right by the doors of the squalid cottages in the churchyard wall and dived behind the White Hart Brewery to emerge as an open stream between the rows of houses on the spot we now call the Arch. As these and the churchyard properties had no gardens whatsoever, it is obvious that the sewage was chucked straight out of the doors into the stream. And so past Teeds where the same thing happened and on to the second tannery at Gilbrook! The whole village depended on well-water and cottagers drew their daily supply from communal wells at the corner of the Green Spot, at the junction of Miry Lane and Church Street and at the Chute at the foot of Globe Hill. All were probably contaminated by sewage seeping through the ground. Never was a scene more invitingly set for disaster.

Cholera had been unknown in Europe until 1830 but by October 1831 it had made its appearance at Sunderland in north-east England, despite official quarantine regulations. By July 1832 it had made its way through England and struck first Plymouth and then Exeter. The disease was water-borne and thrived on overcrowded housing and bad sanitation. It took the form of violent diarrhoea leading to dehydration, coma and death within a few hours — though slightly more than 50% of those affected did, on average, recover.[16]

It so happened that the summer of 1832 was long, hot and very dry. The stream was sluggish and the stench was unimaginable. Between 22nd August and 27th September fourteen people died in Woodbury — though there are no helpful little notes in the margin of the register to give a clue as to which were cholera deaths. But, coming in the two healthiest months of the year that rarely showed more than one or two deaths, it can be assumed that the majority were from this cause.

The death that had the greatest impact on the village was undoubtedly that of Sarah Jarman. Sarah was the daughter of the village thatcher, Michael Howe of Broadway, and as a girl of 19 in 1817 she had married Abraham Jarman, a farm-labourer. By 1832 they had six surviving children and were finding it hard to make ends meet on 7s. a week. On 16th August Sarah applied to "the Parish" for a pair of shoes for one of the children. The request was turned down. This was normal practice in summer months, except in cases of extreme need, for children could go bare-foot in summer to help conserve the Poor Rate for the bleak days of winter and sickness, when most applications were granted. But Sarah persisted and a fortnight later she re-applied and her application was again refused. Four days later she was dead from Cholera at the age of 33, leaving her six motherless children to the mercies of the Parish.

The Parish were shocked to the core. As the hot days of

September went by deaths mounted to one a day, while those who contracted the disease but survived needed continuous care. The Select Vestry met weekly in emergency sessions. On 20th September a special meeting was called "to take into consideration an application from the Board of Health for the Sum of £20 for defraying all expenses in Cholera cases" and on 27th they voted to pay £8 for "extra attendance during the prevalence of the Cholera in the Parish."

From the records of their meetings emerge some of the unsung heroines of those fearful days. Anne Lockyer received 2s.6d. a week for taking care of the Jarmans' baby daughter, while Abraham's brother Joseph and his wife Susan received 2s.6d. a week for each of the other children — though they had five of their own! Jane Daley and Mary Venn nursed the sick, sat with the dying and laid out the dead with no thought for themselves, despite the risks they ran. As happens in a closely-knit community, the crisis was matched by the pure gold of human nature.[17]

There was gold of a more material nature too. A Cholera Fund was immediately started in the parish and subscriptions came pouring in for the relief of the sufferers. And though nothing could bring back those who had so suddenly been snatched away, at least decent bedding could be bought to replace that which had been burnt in houses the disease had visited.

The Cholera Epidemic of 1832 has left an indelible mark on the minds of Woodbury people, though with the passing of the years the facts have probably been lost in a web of myth. Robert Furse, clerk to the Parish Council in the first half of this century and a great authority on Woodbury's history, gave a talk to the Women's Institute in the 1930s in which he said "People and children died of it like flies. My grandfather lost two sons."[18] Yet the records show that not more than twelve people died of it — perhaps not so many — and it did not claim two lives in one family. Perhaps he was referring to Exeter where some 400 people died.

Another rumour handed down from that time has it that people fled from the village in droves and that the Rev. J.L. Fulford was left to dig the graves of the cholera victims himself. It is possible that large numbers of people did take flight, for there was great panic. But the epidemic occurred fourteen years before Fulford's time, and it does not sound like the actions of his predecessor the Rev. John Edsall.

What is certainly not a myth is that the whole country was badly scared by the outbreaks and schemes were immediately put in hand for the improvements of water supplies, sanitation and housing. Exeter embarked on an £80,000 scheme to put the open sewers into culverts and Woodbury stirred itself, rather more slowly, to see what could be done.

The task that faced the members of the Vestry was formidable and with all the will in the world it would be twenty years before much could be done to bring about the necessary improvements. But the priorities were clear enough – to cover parts of the open stream and to invent some means of flushing it from time to time; to improve sanitation and water supplies; and to pull down and replace the worst of the cottages. Slowly, slowly Woodbury began to grope its way towards better times.

17.
Two Victorian Giants

What came next is best understood in the light of two extraordinary, twice life-size characters who arrived in Woodbury almost at the same moment and dominated the events of the next quarter century – the parson and the doctor.

Victorian England had a way of producing giants — politicians or churchmen, businessmen or thinkers, eccentrics or social reformers — and John Fulford and Robert Brent were no more than typical of their age. They shared a relentless energy, passion and self-confidence for the things nearest to their hearts and each believed he was absolutely right. In practically all else they differed.

The Reverend John Loveband Fulford was one of a new breed of high-churchmen resolved on putting an end to the long decline in church affairs. Everywhere the life of parish churches had fallen into a sorry state of neglect and indifference.

Woodbury was luckier than most for it enjoyed the continuing care of the College of Vicars Choral. Nevertheless, when Fulford was appointed vicar in 1846 he found the church shabby, while curious customs had crept into the church services which were not in accordance with the Book of Common Prayer. Fulford, a young man of 32, found there was a great deal for him to do.

Born at North Tawton in 1814, John was the son of a serge manufacturer. He was educated at Mount Radford School in Exeter and at Trinity College, Cambridge, where he gained an M.A. in 1840. Already in 1839 Fulford had been ordained priest by Bishop Henry Phillpotts of Exeter and in 1841 he became curate at St. Thomas, Exeter under Prebendary Medley.[1] Medley was, like Phillpotts, a high-churchman and had been closely involved with Professor Pusey in the formation of the Oxford Movement. Medley influenced Fulford deeply and lastingly and the two men shared a good deal of unpopularity for what was regarded as 'popery'.

The strangest story has been associated with Fulford's high-churchmanship.[2] The winter of 1855 was hard, with deep snow and enough frost to freeze the Exe. On the night of 8th February some unknown "creature" made cloven tracks over a wide area including Woodbury, Lympstone, Topsham and across the river as far as Totnes. In all it was estimated that the tracks were continuous for over 100 miles, over walls, roofs and stacks, down garden paths and up to church doors. The phenomenon provoked widespread curiosity and made the headlines even in the Illustrated London News but was never satisfactorily explained. The Western Times went so far as to report "Some people say it is sent as a warning to the Puseyites — hence it....has visited the Puseyite parishes of Woodbury, Topsham and Littleham". That people's minds had been prepared to believe such an unlikely tale can be judged from an unsigned letter in the Exeter Flying Post for 11th January 1855 which speaks of such unthinkable outrages in Woodbury Church as Christmas carols that referred to pagan evergreens ("Wreathe the Holly, Twine the Bay") and, even worse, lines in Latin ("Ex Maria Virgine"), although as the writer says "the miserable intoning there makes it almost a matter of indifference what language is used". Clearly Woodbury was prepared to believe that the Devil himself had been to call on the vicar!

Upon his appointment to Woodbury Fulford set to work to renovate his church, build himself a vicarage and bring church worship into line with his high-church principles. At first he and Mrs. Fulford lived at Bronte House, Lympstone, but the College of Vicars Choral gave him a site at Parsonage and here Fulford built himself a new vicarage.

Changes had been going on at Parsonage. The Vicars Choral had sold their ancient manor-farm to Ulric Hemmingson of Woodbury Lodge (Springhayes) on whose behalf John Pile farmed it, and had retained only the mediaeval house with its garden and orchard and several acres of glebeland. St. Theobald's Barn had finally become redundant and the vast building had already been demolished before Fulford's time, the stone being used to build Holy Trinity Church at Woodbury Salterton in 1844. The other buildings were now also demolished and some of the material re-used in the new vicarage which Fulford built, very much in the old style, 50 yds. or so from the original site. The house cost £1000 and Fulford paid most of it out of his own pocket.[3] He was the first vicar of Woodbury to live at Parsonage since the end of the 16th century. Previous vicars had had to find their own accommodation — Gilbert

Langdon at Govetts, John Davy at Critchards (later called Izel Cottage and now gone) and John Edsall at Sidney Cottage, Broadway. Fulford's energy and the enthusiasm for the restoration of the church remained unabated throughout the 52 years of his incumbency. When nearing 80 he gave a lucid and detailed account of his work to a meeting of the Exeter Diocesan Architectural and Archaeological Society at Plymouth.[4]

Much has been written about Fulford's 'vandalism' of Woodbury Church but the Vestry Minute Book makes it clear that it was not only his architectural excesses and his high-churchmanship that exasperated the parish. It was his utter disregard for people's feelings, his failure to consult or explain, his passion for spending money (very often his own, let it be said) at a time of great poverty and hardship and the devious way he went about flouting his Church Council in order to get his own way. John Loveband Fulford was an infuriating man. But if he thought it was going to be easy, he seriously underestimated the calibre of his chief opponent, Dr. Robert Brent.

Robert Brent, a Scotsman, combined his medical practice in Woodbury with being District Medical Officer of Health for St. Thomas Union, Exeter. He took up the appointment immediately after his marriage in May 1846 to Annie Louise Fox of Sittingbourne, Kent, and arrived a few months before Fulford to reside at Sidney Cottage (now Bixley Haven) on the death of its previous occupant, the Rev'd. John Edsall. At 27 years of age Brent was a younger man than Fulford. He had become a member of the Royal College of Surgeons in 1844, M.D. of the University of St. Andrew's in 1845 and a Fellow of the Royal College of Physicians (Edinburgh) in 1846. His early practical experience had been gained in the East End of London, especially in gynaecological work,[5] and it was there that Brent's compassionate nature was deeply stirred by the plight of the poor, the sick and the homeless.

Woodbury soon began to feel the impact of his personality and energy. Both Robert and Annie were very well liked here and they threw themselves whole-heartedly into many aspects of village life, using their considerable private means for the benefit of many. Brent's interest in religion is illustrated by his membership, in 1853, of the Provincial Medical Theological Association. It is not surprising to find that such a man was of evangelical low-churchmanship and this inevitably brought him into violent conflict

▲The Rev'd. J.L. Fulford on his tricycle at Parsonage, 1895

with Fulford.

The first major struggle between the vicar and his Vestry came at his very first Annual Vestry Meeting in 1847. Fulford, obviously meaning to start as he meant to go on, challenged the right of the Vestry to appoint both Churchwardens and brought an action against them which he lost in the Bishop's Court. It cost him several hundred pounds and soured the relationship at the outset. His next encounter came in 1848 over a matter so trivial as to be almost laughable. It concerned a Wedgewood porcelain bowl given to the church by Lady Drake for use in the Communion Service. Fulford not only declined to use it in the service but pinched it for his own use and, when asked by the council to return it, made what were considered churlish remarks. A furiously indignant council threatened him with legal action and Dr. Brent, acting as clerk, was instructed to write the letter that finally returned the bowl to the council. Lady Drake was now dead and Sir Trayton felt that Fulford had insulted his wife's memory. His feelings were deeply hurt and as long as he lived he never forgave him.

Fulford was already engaged in the first of his extensive alterations to the church, by which he hoped to restore the building to something like its pre-Reformation glory and make it more suitable for his high-church rites. As work proceeded the Vestry Council had to leave its old haunts in the church and hold meetings at the Globe Inn. Thither, on 14th November 1849, they summoned the parishioners and rate-payers "to receive a Communication from the Churchwardens on the subject of certain alterations made in the Church, as is represented to them, by the order of the Rev'd. J.L. Fulford minister thereof, without their Sanction or Authority." Those present were asked to vote on the proposed removal of the screen and the result (only 4 in favour) was an overwhelming defeat for Fulford.

It is evident that Fulford was genuinely perplexed by the resolute opposition that all his new ideas encountered. His flock was outraged by such innovations as turning East for the Creed, intoning the responses and prayers, having a robed choir and, for some reason not quite clear, using the marriage service from the Prayer Book. So great was the antagonism that he decided to issue a printed "Letter to the Inhabitants of the Parish of Woodbury" in 1849.

In the letter he expressed surprise and concern that his efforts had been misunderstood and attempted to set out a carefully reasoned argument for the changes, quoting the Prayer Book. Dr. Brent immediately sprang foward and published an answer. In this pamphlet he counters Fulford point by point. Though claiming to offer cool arguments and impartial observations it was not in Brent's nature to be cool or impartial.

To Fulford's "If the days in which we live had been days of Christian quietness...."Brent hotly replies "And who was it that put an end to those days of Christian quietness in which we once lived....?

Fulford queries: "....from whence came the congregations....at Gulliford Meeting-house and at the one in the village?"

Brent counters: "Of the congregation at Gulliford I know nothing....because it has not been used by our Parishioners. But of the one in the Village I can affirm that though it had been tried by almost all classes....of Dissenters, yet none could fill it until our present Incumbent emptied the Parish Church".[6]

These are strong words and, even allowing for Brent's passionate and impulsive nature, indicate that a breakaway movement was gaining momentum, based on a small core of dissenters in Woodbury not connected with the Gulliford Meeting-house.

One thing is clear. Fulford's innovations and his autocratic disregard for others split the village and led to Brent, Drake, Henry Ware, the Rev'd Wm. Wippell, the Lees of Sparkshayes, George Edsall (son of the previous vicar) and a number of other influential parishioners setting up their own church at Christ Church in 1851 in which they continued to use the Book of Common Prayer of the Church of England. Christ Church was built by subscription amongst its supporters and William Wippell became their minister. The splinter group flourished as long as Fulford lived and largely fell out of use when his popular successor reclaimed his flock to the Parish Church.

With the removal of Brent and the others from the front pews of the parish church Fulford was better able to pursue his objectives, although Brent had become churchwarden in 1849 and remained so until 1857. The animosity between the two men was illustrated in 1853 when Fulford opposed Brent's reappointment and a crowded Annual Vestry Meeting finally voted for Brent by 25-23. An even more dramatic battle occurred in 1856 when Brent was again opposed and the Vestry Room was opened all day to receive

Christ Church in c. 1900 (built 1851)

parishioners' votes. Brent won by the handsome majority of 198-48.

The Vestry Room in which the ballot was held was something of an innovation. Since getting rid of the Church House in 1619, the Vestry had had nowhere to meet except in the church itself, now full of workmen, scaffolding and builders' materials. The cottage known as Haydon's had been church property since mediaeval times and was let out by the church on 21 year leases. When Thomas Gibbings took on the lease in 1849 he found that the 'hall' end of the cottage was not in use, so he let it to the Vestry at an annual rent of £3.10s. and they used it for the first time in May 1851 — though occasionally well-attended meetings had to be "adjourned to the Globe's covered Skittle Alley, there being insufficient room....for conducting the business of the day".

Brent's main interest now switched to the adminstration of the parish and the improvement of drainage, roads and water-supplies, still in the hands of the Vestry. Already in the 1840s a start had been made in building brick culverts over the offending brook. The first section to be so covered was from the corner shop at the entrance to Church Street down to the cross-roads and it meant the disappearance of the ford at the entrance to Church Street and the wooden footbridge used by people going to church. The road was raised 3ft. and an arch turned over the brook as it ran down between the rows of cottages, which for the time being remained. It was this "Arch" that gave the road the name by which it has ever since been known.[7]

Other sections were soon to follow. In 1849 a similar barrel-drain was built at Pound Lane Corner where before there had been a ford. This was followed in 1850 by the section from "the Green Gate" (as the minute book has it, i.e. the gate to the Green) and on behind the White Hart to join the Arch at the corner shop — "for conveying nuisances which now lodge at the bottom of the Green".

These improvements were accompanied by rigorous measures against "certain individuals....(who allow)....rubbish, timber, carts, etc. etc., to remain on the Highways, also not pruning their hedges and clearing ditches as required by Act of Parliament....The surveyors are requested to summon all parties so infringing the Act".

Much of the cost of these improvements was raised by public subscription, the balance being met from the Highway Rate. Probably the most important improvement of all was the construction of the "flood hatch", where the brook passed under Bonfire Lane. This allowed the water-level to be artifically raised and the water then released with sufficient force to flush the brook throughout its length to the Gillbrook. The tenant of Haydons Cottage was appointed at an annual salary of 10s. to operate the hatch at regular intervals. The "twice a week in dry weather" eventually became "daily from May to October".

Most of the improvements made were in an endeavour to prevent another outbreak of Cholera, which did in fact keep popping up in towns and cities all over England, though not again in Woodbury. But the possibility remained a great fear in people's minds. Isaac Critchard Wilson of Heathfield wisely noted a 'cure' in his diary, alongside cures for broken wind in horses and advice on keeping snakes away by repeating the 1st and 2nd verses of Psalm 68.

"Take equal parts of Laudanum, Tincture of Cayanne Pepper treble strength, Rhubarb, essence of Peppermint treble strength,

Spirit of Camphor, mix it in a bottle, take for a dose from 5 to 30 drops according to violence of Symptoms, to be repeated in 10 or 15 minutes if needed. A few drops of this mixture will prevent looseness of the Bowels and should be taken on the slightest effect being experienced during the prevalence of Cholera".[8]

Isaac Wilson's diary also has observations to make about another terrible enemy of the poor. The great potato blight that brought famine to Ireland in 1845 arrived in Woodbury the same year. "In August" writes Wilson "there came in a disease on the potatoes, it came upon the stalk went down to the potato and caused them to rot and perish". The disease, which continued to 1860 in varying degrees of severity, created a great shortage of potatoes and the prices went rocketing. There were riots in Exeter in 1846 and the Volunteers were called out to restore order. Potatoes had become the staple diet of the poor and so fragile was their economy that the shortage caused very severe hardship. Some help came from John Haydon's Charity and the Vestry book recorded the number of "shirt cloths" rising from an average of 12 a year to an average of 22 during the years of the potato famine. To be sure, one could not eat a shirt but the gift released a few pennies to spend on food.

One way out of the difficulties of poverty and unemployment was emigration. The Ratepayers of Woodbury met in the Vestry Room on Thursday 28th December 1848 and "it was Resolved, That the Churchwardens and Overseers shall, and they are hereby directed to raise the Sum of £10 as a fund for defraying the Expenses of the Emigration of Poor Persons, having settlement in this Parish and being willing to emigrate, to be paid out of the Rates raised or to be raised for the relief of the Poor in this Parish."

The following year Dr. Brent was paid 2 gns. for attending the magistrates sitting at the Globe Inn to testify to the settlement of two Woodbury men called Hart and Hyett. It is not clear whether these two were the first to take advantage of the scheme and choose a new life in the colonies but throughout the nineteenth century Woodbury families emigrated to every part of the world, though most of them paid their own fares and sent for their families to join them as soon as they found employment. 1859 saw the departure for America of William Phillips's eldest son, Thomas. He sailed from Liverpool on August 3rd and made his name and a small fortune building churches in both America and the Montreal district of Canada where he eventually settled. That same year 19-year-old

William White said goodbye to his family at Greendale Barton and went to New Zealand where he cleared a farm for himself at Hawks Bay. It was not long before he sent for his childhood sweetheart. Mary McLaren, daughter of the Broadmead Headmaster at Church Stile. Their descendants are farming there yet. Two members of the Rew family went to Iowa, U.S.A. in 1875 and were followed in 1888 by Samuel Rew and Samuel Payne. And Alfred Ekers set up in business in Montreal as a maltster and was joined there by others who, with Tom Phillips, created a small colony of ex-Woodbury families. Places called Woodbury are to be found in Canada, America, Australia, New Zealand and Tasmania. Some of them may have been founded by unknown Woodbury families pioneering a brave new world, just as their Saxon forefathers had done twelve hundred years earlier.

In the meantime Dr. Brent was busying himself in an extraordinary variety of pursuits He founded a Mutual Benefit Society for working people in Woodbury[9] and was the founder of the Topsham Lodge of Freemasons, known to this day as the Brent Lodge. He was a founding director and subscriber of the Exeter and Exmouth Railway Company, and he was Estate Agent to Sir Trayton Drake at Nutwell. But his most colourful contribution to village life was as commanding officer of the re-formed Volunteer Artillery. It will be remembered that at the time of Napoleon's threat of invasion a detachment had been formed in Woodbury under Capt. Thomas Huckell Lee. But the French War finished in 1815, Lee died in 1822 and the Volunteers had been allowed to lapse.

In 1859 it was considered that a new threat from France existed and when the Lord Lieutenant of the County called for officers to come forward Brent immediately volunteered. So successful was his call to arms that he very soon had a contingent of 87 men from every walk of life in Woodbury. They included Sgt. Maj. W. Ware (tanner), QMS Wm. Archer-Ellis (maltster) Sgt. Perry (baker), and Corp. Hyett (butcher). At first they met at the Globe Inn and kept the equipment in a lock-up shed, but later the Volunteers had their own drill hall behind the Brents' house in Broadway and built "Artillery Cottage" for their drill sergeant, Wm. Smitheram. With their smart uniforms and their disciplined bearing they were much in demand for public occasions. They even had a band which used to lead the procession on "Visitation Day", and their annual exercises on the Common became so popular that the schools found it wise to

Return of the 1st Field Battery of the D.C.V. Artillery to Head Quarters, Woodbury. 27th Oct. 1860

give their pupils a week's holiday. It was not long before Brent was promoted to Colonel — the title by which he was usually known until the end of his life.

This splendid body of men was soon to provide another valuable service for Woodbury. Throughout the 1860s Woodbury, and especially Woodbury Salterton, was plagued by a series of disastrous fires. It cannot be ruled out that as far as Salterton was concerned a fire-raiser was at work, for there were three big fires in April and May 1860. Salters Farm was entirely destroyed and 100 bushels of corn, 70 hogshead of cider, 2 yearlings and 5 calves went with it. Joseph Phillips was injured while rescuing his daughter from the flames. Three weeks later Bonds Farm was similarly gutted and Sam Lindsey's house adjoining it caught fire 8 times but was eventually saved. These fires were followed by another in 1864 when five cottages in Woodbury were burnt down and a further fire in Salterton the following year when 2 cottages were destroyed.[10]

Since the middle of the previous century, when Samuel Dagworthy had insured his weaving business, insurance had become much more general and most of the buildings were insured. The big insurance companies were almost the only people at that time to have fire-engines. But the process of calling out the brigade was hardly one to inspire confidence. Someone jumped on a horse and capered off as hard as he could go and knocked on the door of the Norwich Union Offices in High Street, Exeter. The insurers then, presumably, went off to catch and harness the horses and drive the appliance the 6 miles to Woodbury Salterton. No wonder the thatched buildings were gutted!

These terrible fires gave Brent the idea that Woodbury ought to have its own fire-engine which could be manned by the Volunteers. He bought it out of his own money and did not have to wait long before there was an opportunity to use it.

One day in July 1868, soon after 6 o'clock in the evening, flames were seen coming out of a barn adjoining Mr. Hyett's butcher's shop at Well Park. Soon the buildings were well alight and, fanned by a strong wind, burning thatch was blown across the road and the thatched cottages which then covered the Green Spot were ignited. The newspaper report goes on: "Praiseworthy efforts to arrest the progress of the fire were eagerly made by the Fire Brigade attached to the Woodbury Volunteer Artillery and by the inhabitants generally and the fire was well nigh extinguished by 10 p.m.". But for all their gallant efforts ten houses were destroyed and fifty people lost nearly all their possessions and were made homeless. A fund was immediately started for the sufferers.[11]

One of Brent's proudest moments and a red-letter day for Woodbury must have been 1st May, 1861 when the railway line from Exeter to Exmouth opened. As a director, Brent was privileged to make that first journey with his fellow directors. Whistles blowing, flags flying and people waving all along the route, the train chugged its way along the scenic river-side, through the new stations of Topsham, Woodbury Road and Lympstone to be met in great style by an official welcoming committee at Exmouth. The grand procession was headed by the band of Brent's own Volunteer Artillery, the Police Constables, Coast-Guards and Naval Reserves, the Royal Standard, Exmouth Brass Band, Tradesmen, School Children, and all round the town they went. During the first 5 days 10,000 people travelled on the line. From that day onward Woodbury was linked to Exeter by seven trains daily, between 7 a.m. and 9 p.m., and four trains on Sundays.[12]

Robert Brent still had one great ambition unfulfilled. Knowing full well the risk to health of polluted drinking water he wanted to bring a supply of piped water to the village. Together with John Holman of Topsham and others he formed a company to be known as "The Topsham, Woodbury & Lympstone Waterworks Company"

Woodbury Road Station c. 1930

and the long and impossible undertaking began.

The scheme envisaged building a dam across the valley between the Four Firs road and the Blackhill road and piping water from the reservoir thus formed along the line of the present road from Ford Water as far as the village. Turning at right-angles, the pipe was then to go down Gillbrook and Ham Lane and, following the stream, emerge eventually at Exton. Pipes laid along the foreshore would then supply both Topsham and Lympstone. It would be necessary to promote a Bill in Parliament and to obtain the site of the reservoir from the Rolle Estate by compulsory purchase. Nothing daunted, Brent and Holman pressed on and the Bill passed the House of Commons and came before the Lords in April 1868. Here it was strenuously opposed by the Rolle Estate Trustees. They had two main objections. One was that they considered the financial arrangements inadequate to see the scheme through (the capital was £8,000 with borrowing power to raise a futher £2,000); secondly, they had grave doubts about the effect the scheme would have on their two mills at Rydon and Exton. Already the mills were experiencing serious difficulties in dry weather,.... "the water will scarcely, through the whole night, fill the existing mill dams, and at such times the millers are put to great inconvenience and have to get their customers' corn ground elsewhere".[13]

However, the Bill went through the Lords and became law in June 1868. Brent and Holman, on behalf of the company, signed an agreement with the Rolle Estate on 9th May and it must have seemed as if they were nearly there. Little did they suspect that their troubles were only just beginning.

The Rolle Estate Trustees now embarked on a long series of delaying tactics — amendments, second opinions, conditions, compensation clauses and so on. The time set for the work to be completed was brought down from two years to within one year of the company entering on to the land. Three years later the work had still not started and in a desperate effort to put more muscle into the company Brent entered into an agreement with the Exeter Sewerage Company to extend the scope of the undertaking.

The move was fatal. A few months later, in February 1872, the following report appeared in the Exeter Flying Post. "Col. Brent has agreed to pay £10,000 in settlement of a dispute between himself and the Exeter Sewerage Co. and Mr. Hassell. The expenditure of such a large sum of money is a matter of moment to any gentleman, and the more is it to be regretted when seemingly no public advantage has accrued from the expenditure. In connecting himself with the Sewerage Co. Col. Brent's object was to benefit the City of Exeter; and the sympathy of every right-minded person is extended towards him. In many ways he has done 'good service to the State', and we heartily hope to find him soon in full enjoyment of health".[14]

That last sentence says it all. Brent was a broken man. He died suddenly ten days later, two days before his 53rd birthday. The death certificate states that he died of epilepsy and it is probable that he had always suffered from the disease, which had been greatly intensified as a result of the strain of these events. But a rumour in the village at the time, which still lingers on more than a century later, said that he committed suicide. That is a possiblity and it would not be difficult for Dr. Brent's medical friends to hide the truth, if it were so. But it can never be proved. Either way, it was a death that need not have happened and Woodbury was deprived of a great benefactor and a great source of inspiration. He was buried in Woodbury Salterton churchyard and his old enemy, Mr. Fulford, helped to officiate.

It was an impressive military funeral. As the cortege moved towards the church the bands of the Woodbury and Topsham

Artilllery played "The Dead March" from Handel's "Saul". After the bands came the firing party with arms reversed, followed by the gun-carriage with the coffin, draped with the Union Jack and surmounted by Brent's busby, sword and accoutrements. This was followed by his charger, with boots reversed in the stirrups.

The newspaper account lists almost 200 mourners, in addition to hundreds of people who silently lined the 2 mile route from Sidney Cottage to Woodbury Salterton Church. The account describes Col. Brent as "the most kind and the best beloved....whose name will long be associated with generous deeds and a loving nature".[15]

The Topsham, Woodbury and Lympstone Waterworks Company ended up in the hands of liquidators, with nothing more to show than the dam-wall built across the stream above Ford Water — still to be found crumbling in the undergrowth. The land reverted to the Rolle Estate and Woodbury had to wait another 70 years for its first piped water supply. Mrs. Brent presented the fire-engine to the Vestry and money was raised by subscription to build a shed to house it in Church Street. Mr. Abraham Berry kept the keys and became the first Captain of the Woodbury Fire Brigade.

Mrs. Brent continued to live at Sidney Cottage for another thirty years. At the age of 82 she remarried and became known as Mrs. Brent-Spencer. But it was short-lived, her husband being drowned on his way to visit his native New Zealand two years later. When she died in 1902 she was buried beside Robert at Woodbury Salterton where their headstones are still to be seen. With her death came the sale of Brent's properties and the sale catalogue reveals the very substantial purchases they had made during their 50 years in the parish. Besides Sidney Cottage, Oakhayes and Church Stile were theirs, the cottages on Globe Hill, and a great deal of Broadway and fields and farms in Woodbury and Salterton.[16]

18.
Salterton Comes of Age

During these years of the nineteenth century Woodbury Salterton had been slowly but steadily pulling away from Woodbury proper and making a life of its own. It had always been different – right from the beginning. The mass of small farms did not amalgamate as early as those in Woodbury and did not become labour-intensive to the same extent. A farmer could eke out some sort of living on six acres and employ nobody: he was his own man and could style himself "yeoman" rather than "husbandman" (labourer). Most of the houses in Salterton's straggling street were thus farmhouses and the number of labourers' cottages remained comparatively small. Nobody found it worth their while to build rows of cottages and there were few redundant farmhouses to divide. Billings Directory for 1857 shows that Salterton had twice as many farms as Woodbury and one-third the population. It was a poor, hardworking and unsophisticated community untouched by the influx of those wealthy and leisured families that shaped the life-style of Woodbury and paid for its many shops and services.

Salterton's far-flung outposts of agriculture, Hogsbrook, Coombe Park and Cannonwalls, shared the land on the edge of the Common with Scoarches, Whites, Eales, Podgers, Pinn Clay and Wotton — all gone without trace. At the other extremity of Salterton the area known as Heathfield supported Postlake, Pigeons, Buffhills, Friscoes, Heathfield Park, Maunders Hill and Butleys Heath, of which only Postlake and Heathfield Farm itself remain. The Tithe Apportionment Award shows a great many other small farms in Salterton whose names are now mostly forgotten — Bishops, Goslings, Hoppings, Dagworthys, Perrams, Johns, Gallops, Bonds, Embreys, Salters and Hills.

In earlier times life in Salterton had revolved around Bridge Farm, particularly in the 16th century when the Goves had lived there. Much of Salterton had been their freehold estate. But after the dissolution of Torre Abbey in 1539 Greendale Barton and the

Bridge Estate came briefly into the same ownership. When Bridge Farm was sold to the Force family the Salterton farms stayed with the Greendale Estate. In its hey-day Bridge had been a fine L-shaped Elizabethan house, abutting end-on to the lane immediately above the school. The line of its long frontage (looking towards where the Village Hall is now) was broken by three prominent bays that might have been huge chimney-breasts or, perhaps, two chimneys and a porch. But Bridge had fallen on hard times. It had probably been the site of Josiah Force's ill-fated tannery but by 1839 the property was in the hands of trustees and not long afterwards it was burnt to the ground. It is said that the house was unlucky and haunted and when the rubble was being cleared away a human skeleton was found in the wall under one of the window-seats.

The Putt family of Gittisham, to whom Greendale Barton belonged, increased their land-holding in Salterton at every opportunity until Bridge found itself something of an island surrounded by the Putt Estate. They were good administrators and have left to posterity an Estate Survey produced in 1796, bound in red leather and tooled in gold-leaf. In it is described every farm, every field, every hedgerow tree, every orchard and the pages are exquisitely illustrated with drawings of country scenes such as hay-making, cider-making or the tools and utensils of barley-malting.[1]

Cider was a very important part of the economy. All farms had orchards (there were 278 acres of orchards in the parish in 1839, nine of them at Bridge Farm alone) and the larger farms had pound-houses where the cider was pressed. The smaller apple-growers had access to these presses and so were able to make their own cider which was stored in 54 gallon hogsheads and sold for about £1.8s. a hogshead to the many inns and cider-houses in the district. There was also a container known as a 'firkin' — a small barrel holding only 1 gallon. A pretty little thing it was, designed to be hung by a leather thong from the hame of a horse's collar and accompany the men to the fields. There were many sad hearts in years when the apple crop failed. It was not unusual to find farmers raising their own trees by grafting cuttings on to stock grown from the pips thrown out with the 'mock' (chopped straw used as a filter in cider-making) into a trench at the bottom of the garden. 'Apple gribbles' Salterton farmers called these seedlings — a term that probably gave 'Gribble Park' its name. The Putt Estate Survey shows several apple nurseries in Salterton and it seems likely that Tom Putt, the famous apple-growing member of the family, carried out some of his experiments in Salterton.

Specialization was beginning to creep into farming and Salterton was ahead of Woodbury in its shift towards dairy-farming. The advent of root-crops had revolutionized the winter feeding of animals and the railways had arrived to make distribution feasible. Isaac Wilson's diary[2] gives a good insight into the farming of the time. He farmed some 70 acres in Heathfield and was the third generation of his family to do so. His land was an amalgamation of Butleys Heath and Pigeons Heathfield: lying mainly about or above the 150 ft. contour it was good, well-drained marl on which Wilson grew wheat, barley, potatoes and vetches with the help of one labourer and two boys. His only near neighbour was Aaron Ware who farmed Friscoes (opposite Pigeons) until the house was destroyed by fire in 1862. Aaron Ware then took over the cider-house in the village (now the Diggers Rest) and his departure meant a lonelier life for the Wilsons. The ruined walls of Friscoes can still be discovered among the dense ivy, brambles and elder which now also choke the old lane leading to Tuckers Wood. Then, as now, the larks sang and the partridges ran in the corn.

Most of Wilson's land was arable, though he had the inevitable orchard and enough grazing for his cows — some of it rented from others. Neither Wilson's nor Dagworthy's accounts give an indication that sheep were any longer important. But Wilson was greatly concerned with his dairying activities; his cows, all known by name — "Perty Cow", "Stump Horn", "Darling" and the rest — their calves, and heifers that might have to be grazed miles away in Rockham Wood Brake, and the stud bull which served cows over a wide area at a shilling a time: "that makes 114 besides my own" wrote Isaac in 1864. There were no big herds and each farmer had 5 or 6 cows that he could milk himself. It would be interesting to know the milk yield of these cows but the diary does not tell us. Cream, butter and cheese-making was woman's work. Besides the neat pounds of butter, stamped with patterns, which went regularly to market, butter was usually sold in Butter Jars. These straight-sided earthenware crocks with lids held about 12 lbs. of butter which sold for 14s.3d. They belonged to private customers and were left at the farm to be filled gradually as the butter became available. The jars had to be weighed before filling began — "8 lbs. and my

Isaac Critchard Wilson with his sons George and James.

penknife" as Wilson wrote on one occasion. Cheese-making was perhaps even more important. Devon Farmhouse Cheese was pale and crumbly, very similar to Lancashire, and delicious. At 3d. or 4d. per lb. it was the main source of protein for the working man and various sized wooden cheese-presses produced cheeses from 5 lbs. to 16 lbs. apiece.

Isaac Wilson's diary spans the period 1847 to 1887 (continued by his son and grandson to 1903) and it gives us a complete picture of the countryman's life, season by season. He records weather and weather-lore and relates it to the apple-blossom and cider-yield. We can share with him the first cuckoo in spring, the anxious sky-watching days of hay and harvest, and the tedium of having to carry buckets of water up from the Grindle Brook, half a mile away, during a time of drought. There was skilled winter work too — hedging, pollarding, coppicing, tree-felling and the gathering and tying of browse and faggots for fuel, either for the oven at home or to sell to the bakeries. We get to know the farm boys he takes on, who live in and start work at 11 or 12 years old for a shilling a week — if, by then, they are big enough "to see over the half door". He buys their clothes:- stockings 10d., smock 2s.8d., 7 yds. of unbleached calico for shirts at 8½d. a yard, new Batts (boots) 11s. and new "shining leggings" 5s.6d. Mark Marks, a Woodbury lad, was 15 when he started as a farm boy in 1866 and stayed, with a short break, until 1872. And the diary records in 1868 "Let Mark have 6d. up to Globe, soldiering" (the Volunteers) and in 1870 "Let him have 2s.6d. for likeness" (photograph). Perhaps it was for his sweetheart. In 1873 Mark married 20 year-old Jane Smeath, 'lacemaker'. Wilson's own recreations were few and far between and amounted to the Woodbury Ploughing Match, a day at Bampton Fair or a marketing spree to Bristol Fair by train, loaded with as much butter, cream and eggs as he could carry.

It was not, however, different farming methods that set Salterton apart from Woodbury. It was the vision of a frail woman with a joyous spirit who did not even live in the parish. Miss Marianne Pidsley lived just over the boundary in Clyst St. Mary, at a house called Greendale (not to be confused with Greendale Barton). She lived with her elder sister, Elizabeth, and a young girl, Charlotte Blanche Swete, whom she brought up as her daughter.[3]

The rising tide of poverty had engulfed Salterton to a greater extent than the rest of the parish and it was the wretchedness of the people, particularly the children, and the utter neglect of the place that appealed to Marianne Pidsley's loving heart. Without a family of her own and with a great deal to give, she took Salterton under her wing and adopted it as her family: it is probably true to say that she needed them as much as they needed her.

Miss Pidsley's approach to charitable works seems to have been markedly different from most of her contemporaries who were apt to scatter largesse ostentatiously about the place and lace their gifts with pious conditions about fearing God and keeping sober. Genuinely deeply religious, she was no humbug and her own life was simple and practical. Though not physically strong she was filled with an infectious enthusiasm which swept all obstacles before her. Her practical help started simply by buying clothes for the poor children of Salterton and in the course of clothing a hundred children regularly she came to know them and their families. As she became more involved she began to see how the quality of life could be raised. Her first objective was a school and soon after 1840 Salterton's first free school opened in a cottage (tradition says at Springfield, opposite the garage) under the care of a mistress. Such was the response that the building very soon proved inadequate and the adjoining cottage was added. In 1843 John Walling took over as "headmaster" at the age of just eighteen — a post he occupied for 25 years. The plan was to build a school and to this end a small orchard was purchased at a nominal price from Mr. Putt. But as the school was ticking along quite nicely in the two cottages it was decided that the first priority at that moment was a church. It was a major task to shepherd 130 or more children to Woodbury Church twice every Sunday "although" as John Walling wrote many years later "the smaller ones were not expected to go in the afternoon". So the decision was taken to build the church on the site intended for the school. An approach was made to Bishop Phillpotts and he readily acceded to the request that the patronage of the curacy should be vested in Miss Pidsley and her heirs. A fortnight later the Bishop called personally to inspect the site "and was exceedingly kind in every way".

The enthusiasm knew no bounds. Nothing was impossible. Woodbury's old tithe barn at Parsonage was bought from the College of Vicars Choral in 1843 and the eager work of demolishing the building and carting the stone to Salterton began. Nearly all the farmers assisted in drawing the stone with their horses and carts and it was confidently predicted that there was "enough for two churches". Miss Pidsley must have had visions of the vicarage and school coming out of the tithe barn. But there was inevitably a high proportion of wastage and a sandy foundation on the north side of the new building swallowed up the stone so that more had to be purchased. Some came from Exmouth, quarried at low tide, shipped to Lympstone and carted from there, more came from Babbacombe and was carted from the quay at Topsham, while the stone for the chancel arch (stuccoed and painted to look like Beer stone) came from the quarries at Heavitree. The carting became a serious problem and many farmers could not keep it up. But ways and means were found and Miss Pidsley's cheerful ingenuity and her pocket seemed bottomless.

The building, though not beautiful, is full of intimate detail and stories can be told of many features. The big lock on the south door came from Exeter Prison, complete with giant key, and the panels of the old wooden lectern came from the mediaeval pulpit of the chapel at Nutwell — a gift from Lady Drake. While the chancel was being built a pair of robins made their nest there and successfully reared their young, undisturbed by the builders. The event was commemorated in stone and the robins immortalized in the bosses of the chancel arch, carved by Mr. Stephens of London, son of an Exeter monumental mason. The embroidery on the chancel chair was worked by Caroline Anne Pearce who, while still in her teens, used to get up early to catch the best daylight. At over 1000 stitches to the square inch one wonders how many fine mornings it took her. The glass in the windows was hand-painted by the Pidsley sisters, Blanche Swete and John Walling and the work took them ten months. From the little that now remains one can be forgiven for thinking their time might have been better employed! Nevertheless, it was an extraordinary do-it-yourself exercise, sustained by a real religious fervour which must have lifted Salterton's morale to heights it never dreamed of. There are many people in Salterton today who can say with pride — and with certainty — "My great-grandfather did that!" Present-day parsons who blow in for a brief stay and want to sweep it away as impractical or irrelevant fail to understand the collective memory of a Golden Age it still represents to the village.

Finally the work was finished and on 24th September 1844 Bishop Phillpotts consecrated and dedicated the church to the Holy Trinity amid scenes of great splendour and rejoicing. All the notable nobility and gentry of the neighbourhood were there, the church was packed to capacity and a large crowd overflowed into the church-yard and street.

This was Salterton's "coming of age" for it now became an ecclesiastical parish quite separate from Woodbury, while remaining in the administrative parish. It was fitting that, after their complete dedication to the cause, John Walling and Caroline Pearce should have been the first couple to be married at Holy Trinity, in April 1845.

For most people the expenditure of £10,000 and the work and worry so far experienced would have been enough for one life-time. But the completion of the church merely freed Marianne Pidsley's hands for her next project — the provision of a school and vicarage.

Woodbury Salterton

Church *Vicarage* *School*

The new church occupied the site intended for the school but a strange sequence of events put another suitable site in Miss Pidsley's possession. While the church was being built the trustees of Bridge Farm brought a case against her for encroachment of the east chancel wall on the stream. Miss Pidsley was able to solve the difficulty by buying Bridge Farm, thereby securing the land she needed for her other projects. By the Summer of 1847 the school was nearing completion and awaiting its first pupils. It is a romantic little grey stone building, reminiscent of a Ruritanian comic opera stage-set, with white bargeboards on the gables and a sturdy and important little bell-tower surmounted by an Italianate cupola. The bell is still rung from the rope inside to call the children into school and the clock (added in 1876) still strikes the hour.

Marianne Pidsley was now physically over-wrought and the three ladies went off for a holiday to Clovelly. Thither in August 1847 they summoned John and Caroline Walling to join them for a week or two. Caroline was recuperating after the birth and death of her first child. The Pidsleys then moved on to Tintagel and the Wallings returned to Salterton to put the finishing touches to the school. Ten days later Marianne Pidsley died suddenly in Tintagel at the age of 42 and her body was brought back to be buried in the place she had loved in life. September 29th 1847 must have been a day of weeping in Salterton but one hopes the natural grief was outweighed by gratitude. Not many people achieve half so much, even in a long life. The simple stone that marks her resting place is indicative of her philosophy — if there were money to spare it was better spent where it would do some good.

The £13,000 expended on these projects covered one more edifice that stands as a memorial to that remarkable woman. There is a charming little stone conduit by the side of the village street and for just 100 years Salterton people daily descended its flight of shallow stone steps to draw the clear spring water as it bubbled up through the gravel. Until the conduit was built the only source of drinking water was the stream, for those who were not lucky enough to have a well of their own.

In 1848 Marianne's ward, Blanche Swete, was married at Holy Trinity to the Rev. John Thornycroft of Thornycroft Hall in Cheshire. Blanche inherited Bridge Farm[4] and the patronage of the living and, although she was now far away in Cheshire, she kept in touch with the parish, continuing her generosity in imaginative ways — such as fitting out the school children with scarlet cloaks and giving the school clock already mentioned.

Under the Pidsley-Thornycroft patronage vicars came and went, as vicars do, Stannus, Grey and Alford among them, the latter remarkable for his infinite wit and humanity. At the instigation of one of Mr. Alford's successors (Mr. Chase), he recalled in writing his years in Salterton, 1882-1903. He "found the church well attended. It had a strong evangelical tradition and drew some members of its congregation from Woodbury. The chief of these was Mr. Hole, an old gentleman who had once been in the Navy, and was present at the Battle of Navarino. He had attended the church ever since its consecration. He deeply resented any change in the Services, but continued to attend until failing health prevented him. He was over 90 when he died....Two ladies, Mrs. Brent and Miss Johnston, rivals in good works, and in other ways, also came regularly....John Skinner had been Sexton for many years and continued until 1884....(he) was much troubled with rheumatism, and walked with two sticks. He was very autocratic and used the sticks on the boys' heads in Church. Children's Services, when children sat in the front seats, greatly troubled him. He held the opinion of Church Warden Tavender, who said on one occasion 'Labouring men should sit with Labouring men, Farmers with Farmers, Gentle-folk with Gentle-folk, and Lords with Lords'."

After the death of Marianne and the marriage of Blanche, Miss Elizabeth Pidsley came out of her shell and did her best to fill the gap left by her more dominant younger sister. The school outings to Greendale continued, with tea and sports, as did the weekly visits to the school, the joints of beef at Christmas time and clothes for the needy. Elizabeth lived to be nearly 80 and when she died in 1879 Greendale was bought by Lord and Lady Dunboyne. It was fortunate for Salterton that the Dunboynes picked up where the Pidsleys had left off and were greatly liked in the village.

Many years later Marion Dunboyne was to recall their early days at Greendale. "My first acquaintance with Woodbury Salterton dates from the cold winter of 1879-80 – when the canal froze between Topsham and Exeter....It was a model village, only just deprived of the almost motherly care of Miss Pidsley....Many names recur to my mind of friends now gone....Harding, the blind man, who wrote poetry, and whose life of active cheefulness was a lesson to all....The choir was extremely good for a country church, thanks mainly to....Mr. Phillips who for over 25 years walked to and fro (from Woodbury)....Our first Christmas Eve is vividly imprinted on my memory. Late in the evening we were surprised by voices outside the drawingroom window and....we discovered a donkey-cart containing the lame old Sexton, with various young companions...who had come to serenade us with Christmas Carols. Of course they were invited in, to drink hot coffee and sing in the hall, among glistening holly and ever-greens, and heartily to exchange Christmas greetings".

In April 1866 the school was made a National School, John Walling and his family said goodbye to Salterton and Isaac Rees reigned in his stead. The school log-book starts from that date and tells its own story of the struggle towards literacy and against poverty, bad health, inadequate heating ("this morning was so cold....half the children were crying — in consequence little work was done"), ignorance and the constant censure of the Inspector for failing to reach set standards and the reduction in grant-aid accordingly. There were many excuses for absence; helping with the baby, hay-making, Woodbury Fair Week, lace-making, "Sarah Skinner absent this morning — the donkey tumbled into a pit and she was obliged to assist in getting it out". Often the reason for absence was that the weekly penny per child could not be found. Yet, despite all difficulties, some did well and went on to become teachers themselves; Bertha Kaine was one, Maggie Turner another.

Maggie's father, Mr. Frederick Turner, took over the headship in 1877. He came straight from training college and stayed until 1920. He is still remembered — not least for the way he used the cane on the back of the wrist at the exact spot where it hurt most. Strict he certainly was, but a good teacher and a good musician, which brought the children both pleasure and prizes at Musical Festivals. But during his time the rural population started to decline rapidly and he saw the numbers in his school dwindle from a peak of 99, when the Harrisons' private school at the Post Office closed, to 50 at the turn of the century. Working people looked to the towns for better paid jobs and the days of enormous Victorian families were over. The population of Salterton in 1861 was 498. By 1901 it had shrunk to 289. Many cottages contained single people -- elderly widows — while others were too dilapidated to be lived in at all. The butcher, the baker and the shoe-maker had gone and only the Post Office remained.

Yet Salterton had made it as a village in its own right and stoutly defended itself against Woodbury. There was keen rivalry between them and the young bloods of the day used to hurl "Woodbury Pops!" and "Salterton Pops!" against each other — terms of abuse that could be guaranteed to start a fight. Usually the battle-field was somewhere near Parsonage Pound, beyond which Salterton boys rarely advanced alone unless they were very brave or very foolish.

Lord Dunboyne died in 1909 and in his memory Lady Dunboyne placed the pre-Raphaelite-type glass in the east window — quite the best thing in the church — and built the Village Hall. She herself died suddenly at Greendale in 1919 and the vicar's description of her as "saintly" hardly seems an exaggeration. Woodbury Salterton had been extraordinarily lucky in its benefactors for three-quarters of a century. But with its leadership gone, the young people reduced by half and a slump in farming, life in the village slipped back into the grey mist from which it had come. Salterton's golden age became a memory, told to grandchildren and perhaps scarcely believed by them. Only in the last twenty years have the good times returned, the one-time farmhouses been re-thatched and repainted. Yet for all the changes there are enough of the old families left to keep the continuity going. Channons, Dagworthys, Tavenders and Wilsons were all there the best part of 200 years ago — some of them even earlier — while other families still carry the blood, if not the surnames, of Salterton's ancient past.

19.
The Wind of Change

The nineteenth century witnessed enormous change in Woodbury. The open stream that had been such a feature of the village landscape for over a thousand years, and the delight of countless generations of children, gradually disappeared into culverts. Of the many fords and footbridges by which Woodbury had gone about its daily business only the one in Miry Lane survived into the present century.

Old houses went; new houses came. Lower Venmore was built in the 1840s and was an amalgamation of two farms that are shown on the tithe map, Venmore and Cadhayes Venmore. The home of the influential Ashford family, Venmore marked the dawn of a new era in Rolle Estate agricultural policy. The huge yard surrounded by extensive farm buildings set a pattern soon to be repeated at Webbers, Rydon, Postlake, Woodmanton and Exton Barton, in most cases reflecting the amalgamation of several smaller farms. Larger-scale, labour-intensive farming was coming to Woodbury.[1] The shake-up was to mean the end of Sparkshayes, one of Woodbury's most ancient farms. Lewis Lee was the last member of his famous family to farm there. He was followed briefly by Frederick Hearn in 1857 (Billings Directory). The rest is silence.

An elegant addition to the village scene in the first half of the 19th century was Oakhayes. The name was recorded as far back as 1549 when the church bought a narrow strip of land "lying by the West Syde of the Churchyard and adjoining John Tyll ye ground named the Oakhaye." The two fields that lay between Oakhayes Lane and the Arch had remained free from development except for a farmhouse that stood where the Arch bus shelter now is — its small farmyard approached from an entrance near the bottom of Globe Hill.[2] The land formed part of Church Stile Farm when it came on the market in 1829 and was bought by the Rev'd. Francis Filmer of Crundale, near Canterbury. Oakhayes House first appeared in the Land Tax Assessment in 1832.

Oakhayes

What brought Filmer all the way from Kent to Woodbury is not known. He was a bachelor, born in 1775, and had retired early from the living at Crundale of which his titled family were the patrons.[3] His purchase of Church Stile gave him an excellent building site and he set to work with considerable energy, funds and stylistic flair to build himself a comfortable place for his retirement. His positioning of the house and the landscaping of the grounds were masterly. Making good use of the sloping ground and the mature trees already on the site, Filmer created a wooded drive, walled and terraced gardens, a miniature park with specimen trees and an idyllic private church-path through the rookery and between the primroses to the corner of the churchyard. It was a potted "stately home" all in the little space of 8 or 9 acres and one senses that Filmer loved beauty and nature and took a very personal interest in the creation of his mini-estate. In 1849 Richard Dagworthy, Official Collector of Taxes, noted in his annual return that Filmer paid tax for 23 windows, 2 resident male servants, a four-wheeled carriage, 2 hunting horses and his family armorial bearings — in all, £25.8s.2d.[4] Woodbury owes Filmer a debt of gratitude for Oakhayes and it is fortunate that subsequent owners have maintained the house, garden and grounds much as he left them when he died, aged 84, in

1859. As more recent developments have swallowed up gardens, orchards and paddocks Oakhayes has remained a green and tranquil oasis in our midst.

An early in-filling occurred at Woodbury House as a result of the financial embarrassment of its owner, Metcalfe Graham Steele. In Philip Lemprière's time the house had stood in its own grounds, with a walled garden at the side and a walled orchard at the back. By the time Steele died in 1833 some of the farm premises has been turned into three cottages and the kitchen and dairy of the house converted into William Tapscott's bakery, while parts of the walled garden and orchard had been sold off as building sites. The Tithe Map (1839) shows that the garden site had already been developed (now The Bakery) and Preston House was built soon afterwards.[5]

Woodbury was growing fast. A population of 1,280 in 1801 had mushroomed to a peak of 2,014 by 1851. Poverty was widespread but rather than "go on the parish" people thought up ingenious ways of making a living. Woodbury could boast of something like twenty shops, though the majority were no more than the front-rooms of cottages from which the occupants sold home-made sweets and cakes, or combined shopkeeping with occupations of carpentry and tailoring. There was no need to go out of Woodbury to have a

Haydon's alias The Clerk's House

saddle and bridle, a suit of clothes or a pair of boots, or a watch, or chair made specially to order. Market-gardeners sold flowers and vegetables from their plots in Flower Lane and John Burton ran a carrier service from his back yard at Haydon's to Exeter every Tuesday and Friday, later carried on by his son-in-law John Gordon from the same premises.

John Gordon — carrier, c. 1880

The 1851 Census shows that it was rare for women and children not to work. Mrs. William Stokes was a straw hat maker, Mary Hart a midwife and many women were dressmakers or took in washing. But the biggest single source of female employment was undoubtedly lace-making. The craft was an old one and had been slowly growing since the collapse of the wool trade. Westcote described it in 1630, Vancouver in 1808 and Hannah Pyne had mentioned it in her letter of 1814. The cottages in Broadway now known as Ailsa and Ivydene were called 'Necklaces' in Michael Howe's will made in 1832 and were obviously connected in some way with the manufacture of lace, as the recent discovery there of hand-carved lace bobbins (or 'sticks') goes to show. But when in 1840 Queen Victoria went to her wedding wearing a gown, veil and train of Honiton lace she started a fashion that swept England and created an enormous demand. By 1851 no less than 307 people in Woodbury were engaged in lace-making. Nearly every cottage had its lace-makers, working steadily away with their pillows (or 'peels') on their knees, often in the open doorway, often in bad light and to the detriment of their eyesight. "Farthing hearts", "½d. leaves", "shells", "fly-aways", "Woodbury Greek" and "Shepherd's Crooks" – romantic and picturesque names but it was virtually impossible to earn 3s.6d. a week as had been done by wool-spinners in the previous century

The usual age to start serious work was 10. Mrs. Quaintance was assisted by her three daughters aged 10, 13 and 15. Mrs. Cain and her five daughters (10 to 20) were all lace-makers. The youngest lace worker mentioned in the census was little Lewisa Gooding who at six years old was helping her mother and two elder sisters.

Apart from financial rewards, the Honiton lace trade followed pretty much in the pattern already established by the wool trade. Home-workers made the sprigs to patterns supplied to them, and these then went forward to be assembled and finished, and finally to the "manufacturers" who sold the lace wholesale to the dealers. The names of two of Woodbury's manufacturers are known – William Hayman 1850-57 (who also had establishments elsewhere) and Mary Ann Davey who was operating around 1866. In earlier times it is possible that even the linen thread with which the lace was made had a Woodbury connection. The 1839 Tithe Map shows a "Flax Field" at Venmore and it is known that flax was grown in the Otter Valley and the linen thread made at Axminster – though it is probable that the very finest thread was imported from Antwerp.[6]

Other traditional trades carried on as before but not without hiccups. The Hole family had succeeded the Weekes as tanners at Gilbrook and opened up a second tannery on the Green. But after William Hole's bankruptcy in 1829 the business changed hands frequently and did not get back onto its feet until the Wares of Gilbrook took over from Thos. Gibbings in the 1850s. By 1871 Thos. Ware jun. was tanning at Gilbrook, employing 9 men and 2 boys, while his son Henry was running the Green Tannery with 8 men and 3 boys. When Henry took over from his father at Gilbrook the Green Tannery closed for good. A large tan-heap rose up by the side of the road in Gilbrook yard and people used to send their children to scrabble about on the heap to gather 'tan' for fuel. (This was the used remains of the oak bark from the tan-pits). Woe betide those children who returned home with their knickers stained orange-brown through sliding down the heap! And Woodbury found another use for the tan. When a death occurred, a few wheelbarrow-loads of tan were strewn on the road in front of the houses to deaden the sound of the metal-rimmed carriage wheels on the gravel road.

With such a handy supply of good leather, Woodbury's many boot and shoe-makers carried on a flourishing trade. In 1851 there were twelve "cordwainers" (the old word comes from the Spanish town of Cordoba, home of the best boot-leather) in the parish, carrying on their own businesses and employing others. John Sellick worked from his cottage in Church Street and employed his two sons James and Eli. Also in Church Street was Samuel Francis who agreed in 1858 to take a parish apprentice, Fred Bamsey, a disabled boy. The Guardians of the Poor paid Francis £6 when the indentures were signed and a further £6 on Lady Day 1860 and the boy lived in. Eventually Fred was able to set up his own boot and shoe business and hand it on to his son.

The population explosion found work for an ever-increasing number of men in the building trades. Michael Howe, thatcher, was succeeded by his son-in-law, Thomas Skinner, working from Thorn Cottages. There was enough demand for carpenters to keep William Stokes, Robert Phillips, Thomas Smeath, William Ekers and John Stamp busy – each on his own account. William Phillips was the chief, though not the only mason, employing 12 men and 6 boys in 1861, and in 1877 Messrs. Summerfield and Jarman arrived to make their distinctive additions to Woodbury's village architecture, working from William Summerfield's premises at Brookside, Gilbrook. But till the end of the century it was the Phillips family who reigned supreme over the rebuilding of Woodbury. The Priory was one of the small-holders' cottages to be turned into a gentleman's residence. William Phillips built Rosemary Cottage in Broadway and marked it for posterity with "W.P. 1833" in white pebbles in his front path (now concreted over). Rows of cottages began to appear – Claremont Cottages before 1839 and Castle Cottages shortly after – another Phillips development. An older generation knew the latter as Bastin's Row because three generations of the Bastin family lived at the corner house where they combined a bakery and shop with their craft as basket-makers. People can still remember Blind Bastin sitting in his open doorway working at willow potato baskets and not infrequently children played truant from school to "skim willows" for Blind Bastin and earn a few coppers.

Meanwhile the work of dividing redundant farm-houses, cow-sheds, barns – anything with a roof – into cottages went on. Chowns became four dwellings and Franks (Church Steps), with some additions, became seven. At Gillbrook Cottages five dwellings emerged from an early Tudor farm-house and range of buildings and there, in No.1, James Miller kept a shop and carried on his trade as a blacksmith, leaving the tell-tale scorch-marks of dozens of horseshoes on the ceiling joists. If it seemed a very long time before the clearance of the cottages on the stream, which had borne the brunt of the cholera epidemic in 1832, it was probably because the need for housing was so great that a bad house was better than none at all. After reaching a peak in 1851 the rural population started to decline slowly and as pressure eased the demolitions began.

But the first cottages to go were in Broadway and had nothing to do with housing improvements. Since the turnpiking of the road in the previous century Broadway had carried an increasing amount of wheeled traffic and the Exeter Turnpike Trust decided to widen the road in 1858. It involved the destruction of two cottages belonging to Dr. Brent which jutted out awkwardly into the road opposite the smithy, causing a bottleneck only 13ft. 3ins. wide. At the same time the smithy, described as being in a very poor state, was demolished and rebuilt a few feet back from the road. Joseph Hitchcock was the blacksmith who gained a new smithy but lost his cottage so conveniently opposite his place of work. The plan accompanying the scheme shows that the site adjoining the smithy was a piggery belonging to Hitchcock's neighbour, Brooks, whom Brent described as "a scoundrel." Brooks had already fallen foul of the overseers for not being able to produce his marriage lines and at the baptisms of his many children he is described as "Traveller" – i.e. gypsy.[7] His "marriage" had probably consisted of no more than "jumping over the broom", as gypsies say.

The wind of change was blowing and it was not to halt until most of old Woodbury had been blown away. There are few records to tell us the order in which the demolitions occurred but it is likely that the row of cottages in Bonfire Lane were the first to go. After the fire in 1868 the cottages on the Green Spot were not rebuilt, though Butcher Hyett's new shop at Well Park rose like a Phoenix on the ashes of the old. Round about 1870 the three rows that stood on the Arch were demolished. Nothing altered the look of Woodbury more than the loss of those cottages. Suddenly the congested area of thatched houses, narrow streets and alleyways was transformed into an open square with nothing to show where a dozen families had lived except the unevenness of the surface which was soon green with grass. Almost the last of the clearances happened in 1874 when the venerable and ancient row tucked into the churchyard wall came down and "a subscription" footed the bill for a new retaining wall of brick and 'popples'. It is unlikely that anyone at the time knew the history of the building – how it had been built in 1440 as "the Church Howse called the Market Place" – later the Alms-houses.

The Arch and old Post Office c. 1890

These demolitions, taken together, add up to a loss of more than 30 houses and it is difficult to see how the poor were housed. There must have been much overcrowding and discomfort. But some help was now at hand in the form of a Rolle Estate building scheme. The first to be built in Woodbury were the cottages in Broadway, still known as "New Buildings". Initialled M.R. (Mark Rolle) and dated 1877, they occupied the site of older buildings. For excellence of standard these cottages were far ahead of their time and opened up a new chapter in social conditions. New buildings were shortly followed by similar cottages at Exton and others in Broadway and they have needed very little modernisation in the 100 years of their life. The Estate building style was very distinctive, with the fussy details of the fashionable 'Gothick' revival, while Wm. Phillips still favoured the plain neo-classical style reminiscent of the Georgian period of which the wide, overhanging eaves were a noticeable feature. Two more Phillips buildings made their appearance in the 1860s. The first was something of an historical landmark. In 1860-61 he built the Court House on Globe Hill. Very soon the Magistrate's Court would pack up its belongings at the Globe and move a hundred yards down the hill to a new home.

The first policeman was Acting Sergeant Patrick Flaherty, an

Irishman needless to say, with a large family, and his arrival in 1861 was to mean the end of the road for the Parish Constables. They were the oldest remaining representatives of village self-government. Since mediaeval times men suitably qualified by good character and property had been appointed in turn and the Parish records give us the names of many splendid men who served Woodbury in this way. Occasionally one would try to excuse himself from the onerous task but others seemed to relish the job and Richard Kenwood combined the barrel-making business he ran from Ballymans with being a zealous 'copper' for many years in the last century. His name is constantly cropping up in cases brought before the magistrates at the Globe.

Names continued to be put forward until 1871 when the Vestry nominated the following:- Abraham Berry, machinist, Edwin Perry, baker, John Marshall, blacksmith, John Cain, yeoman, Charles Pidsley, miller, Henry Hitchcock, pork butcher and James Ware and William Pile, yeomen. But they were never called upon to serve as the Court House was in full operation, complete with Sergeant Ryall in residence and lock-up cells for the drunk and wicked.

William Phillips's second important building at this time was Southcroft in Town Lane, built as a residence for the Rev'd Wm. Wippell who tended the "rebel" flock at Christ Church. It was paid for by subscription among the Free Church supporters and was first known as Ebenezer Cottage. The house has a certain genteel elegance of line and proportion but lacks many of the internal details then currently fashionable — there are no ornate plaster friezes in the best rooms, for instance, and doors and skirtings are unusually plain for their period. Obviously, the little flock did what it could to ensure the status of its minister and it was plain but adequate.

The Rolle Estate, under the enlightened guidance of the Hon. Mark Rolle, did not draw the line at improving farm buildings and providing new cottages. In 1863 they embarked upon an ambitious programme of land-reclamation and the creation of an entirely new farm at Bagmores. The area had remained wet and unproductive and although by 1839 it was roughly divided into numerous strange-shaped fields virtually none of them was arable and their names give some idea of their nature. Mirey Mead, Shamble Marsh, Alder Plot, Withy Plot, Wilderness and Rushy Moor are some of them. One can imagine them, "stogged in mud", rank and overgrown with rushes and willow, suitable only for rough grazing in dry weather. As it was necessary to involve the Inclosure Commissioners it seems probable that a small part of it still had rights of common pasture for the people of Ebford, reached by a well-banked drove-road that leads off the Ebford Lane into the heart of the area.

It was a time of high unemployment and, though a Government subsidy could be claimed, Mark Rolle was motivated as much by a desire to remedy social evils as by any gain in land-values. He engaged a London firm of land-drainage specialists and put the following announcement on the front page of the Exeter Flying Post for 27th May 1863.

> 'Rolle's Drainage & Farm Buildings Improvements. Notice is hereby given That under the powers of "The General Land Drainage & Improvement Co's Act 1849" a Provisional Contract has been entered into between the Hon. Mark Rolle....& the said Co. for the improvement of certain land....in Woodbury....by the execution of drainage works & erection of a farm house & farm buildings, as mentioned in the said contract.
>
> And notice is hereby given that application is about to be made....to the Inclosure Commissioners for England & Wales for a provisional order....declaring that it is right & proper & for the benefit of the parties having any interest in the land....to be improved....etc.'

The Company prepared a detailed and comprehensive plan for draining the entire basin from Sowhill to the Ebford Lane and right through to Lower Bagmores and Exton, and sent a team of engineers and foremen to organise and supervise a local work-force. The work fell initially into two main sections: the digging by hand of many miles of drainage channels and the making, on site, of the millions of clay drainage tiles and bricks needed for the job. The first of these was carried out by a large labour-force recruited over a wide area. The channels were up to five feet deep and arranged in rows or chevrons eleven paces apart. These, in turn, drained into 6in. main carriage drains that eventually discharged at a number of points into the stream at Exton.[8] It was a dirty and back-breaking job but since the completion of the Exeter–Exmouth Railway two years earlier men had been glad to find any sort of labouring work.

The brick and tile making was a venture of extraordinary enterprise. Clay had been dug from the hillside opposite Bagmores long before (probably for cob-building) and by 1839 there was a lime-kiln on the site, though work there had ceased by 1850. The clay -seam was now reopened and the kilns rebuilt. They were fired by brushwood and no doubt the scrub cleared from the land to be drained was used for the purpose. From the temporary works came all the tiles needed for the drainage and the bricks to build the house and farm-buildings — so says the tradition which also says it was Mr. Phillips who ran the brickyard. Nor did they have to go very far for their building sand. Generations of Woodburians had known just where to find good quality sand near the top of Rydon Lane, for the road cut through the sandstone leaving red cliffs some twelve feet high on either side. In the days of cob-building there had been little call for sand but with the arrival of brick-building a sandpit had been opened up on one side of the lane and this was now excavated for the building at Bagmores. Though the sand-pit continued to serve Woodbury builders into the early years of this century it is likely that the brickworks were abandoned soon after the Bagmores scheme was completed. The remains of the kilns were visible until a few years ago when the clay-pit was filled in with surplus soil excavated from the flood-relief channel in the village.

So finally emerged the last new farm to be created in Woodbury: Henry Pile was farming Higher Bagmores by 1870 and the ripples were felt throughout the parish. In June 1870 a special Vestry Meeting was called "to consult whether it would not be desirable to have the present Land Tax Assessment equalized, as the said Assessment is very unequal and also on account of such vast change in the Hon. M. Rolle's property."

Certainly the parish could do with the higher rateable value. Roads were the biggest headache left in the hands of the Vestry and one can imagine the problems facing the Way-wardens. "Muddy Lane", as the road to Bagmores was aptly called, had been acknowledged as a Parish Road back in 1849 and repairs undertaken then. But it was only one of many.

After the introduction of the penny-post it was not long before Abraham Green's corner shop on the Arch became Woodbury's first Post Office. Mr. Green had the assistance of an official "messenger" who carried the mail bags twice a day, at 7 a.m. and 7 p.m. from the Post Office to catch the Royal Mail coach at Pink House Corner —

then called Ash Trees. James Simons was the Messenger and as he was also the Schoolmaster he was able to write a well-worded letter of complaint to the Way-warden.

"January 10th, 1860. Sir, Having met with great inconvenience in passing up and down the road leading from Woodbury Post Office to Ashen Trees on the Exmouth road to meet the mail with the letter bag, I found it necessary to write to the Post ofice authorities complaining of the obstructions and I am requested....to ask you.... to kindly see to the removal of the obstructions complained of and that nothing impede the free passage of the Mail Bags on the above road. The obstructions complained of are the occasional overflow of water at Gilbrook, at Scotsmoor Gate, at and near Lower Venmore and other obstructive matter at Lower Venmore making the road dangerous to pass up and down in the dark. By taking such measures as may prevent their future occurrence you will oblige and prevent further proceedings on the part of the Post Office.

I am, sir, yours most truly,

James Simons"

The Vestry found itself faced with a painful course of action, raising a 6d. way-rate. Part of the trouble stemmed from the bridge recently built over the Gilbrook at the entrance to Ham Lane. The arch was not in accordance with the specification, being too small for the flood-water to run through, while the retaining wall on the roadside prevented the surface-water from draining off into the brook. A new bridge had to be built (the present one) and 8ft. of wall removed at a cost of £12, of which Mr. Ashford, the principal user and Mr. Ware, the Way-warden at fault, paid £6 between them to try to appease the very disgruntled rate-payers.

Meanwhile the coming of the Exeter—Exmouth Railway meant that Woodbury people needed a road to get to the station at Exton — called Woodbury Road Station. Most people would be walking and for them Ham Lane and the "pathfields" were good enough and remained so for almost a hundred years. But a carriage road was also needed and its provision fell to the lot of the Way-wardens. Rydon Lane was the "direct route" chosen and it had to be "thoroughly repaired." The lane had first come into existence in the 13th century, to carry corn from the village to the mill at Exton. But after the making of Rydon Mill in the 17th century there was less need for trafic to go further than Rydon and the lower end of the road had fallen into a deplorable state — water-logged underfoot with a thick canopy of branches overhead to concentrate the drips in wet weather and keep out the sun at other times.

The great flurry of activity on the roads was reflected in Isaac Wilson's diary. Throughout the years 1860-63 he was kept busy by the Way-wardens and typical entries read:- "1862 Sept. 20 Drawed 2 loads of stone upon the Highways, for John Coles, Surveyor.

Sept. 23 Drawed 4 loads more

Oct. 30 Drawed 4 loads more

Feby. 24 (1863) Drawed 5 loads more

The Parish Drs. to I. Wilson by order of Mr. Pile for a cart, man and two horses drawing stone upon the Highway, labour 5/-, for six loads at 9d. per load 4/6."

Wilson was paid for labour and materials out of the way-rate but not for the use of the horse and cart. Multiply these entries by the number of farmers in Woodbury and one gets some idea of the scale of the task.

It is astonishing how doggedly Woodbury rate-payers clung to this last vestige of parochial independence. The maintenance of the 32 miles of Parish Roads was enough to tax the genius of a full-blown engineer, yet here were the doctor and the tanner, farmers and shopkeepers all taking their turns. There was very little reward in terms of satisfaction and none at all in money. It is hardly surprising that when Sir Trayton Drake's son Sir Francis tried, in 1871, to make them a present of the "New Road" from Nutwell to Lympstone the Vestry would have none of it.

For a while, in the 1870s, they seemed content to relinquish the roads to the new Highways Board but the results were even less satisfactory. The money still had to be found in Woodbury but did not go nearly so far as it had done in the hands of the Way-wardens. It was for this reason that the Vestry bitterly opposed the reorganisation of the parish boundaries in 1876 because they would have lost Houndbeare which had no parish roads and no paupers, so that the rates were all clear gain to the parish. But when in 1878 the Highways Board proposed to put a bridge over the stream in Honey Lane, Salterton, at an estimated cost of £81, the whole Vestry unanimously rejected the estimate and called the rate-payers to meet on site and examine ways of reducing the cost. Mr. Phillips's estimate of £45 was eventually pared down to £30, with the assistance of Salterton's farmers with their horses and carts. (Mr.

Phillips had already built the bridge at Greendale in 1852 for £74.)

But it could not go on much longer. The railways were an instant success and most long-distance traffic was soon transferred from the Turnpike roads, causing their revenue to fall drastically. One by one the main roads were disturnpiked. The first to feel the keen competition was the Exeter—Exmouth road and the Courtlands Cross gate was removed in 1872. The Clyst St. George — Woodbury road hung on till 1884 when the Exeter Turnpike Trust wound up and the road was taken over by the Highways Board. Despite parish opposition, Woodbury lost Houndbeare in the same year, which also marked the new system of parish road maintenance by contracting out the work for so much a mile. Competition was keen and small firms sprang up calling themselves "Road Contractors." One such was Josiah Down of Higher Venmore who undertook many jobs on the roads of Woodbury — though it is hard to imagine how anybody could make a profit at £5.10s. a mile. The last Way-wardens were appointed in 1893 and with the passing of the Local Government Act 1893/4 the mediaeval Vestry was replaced by an elected Parish Council.

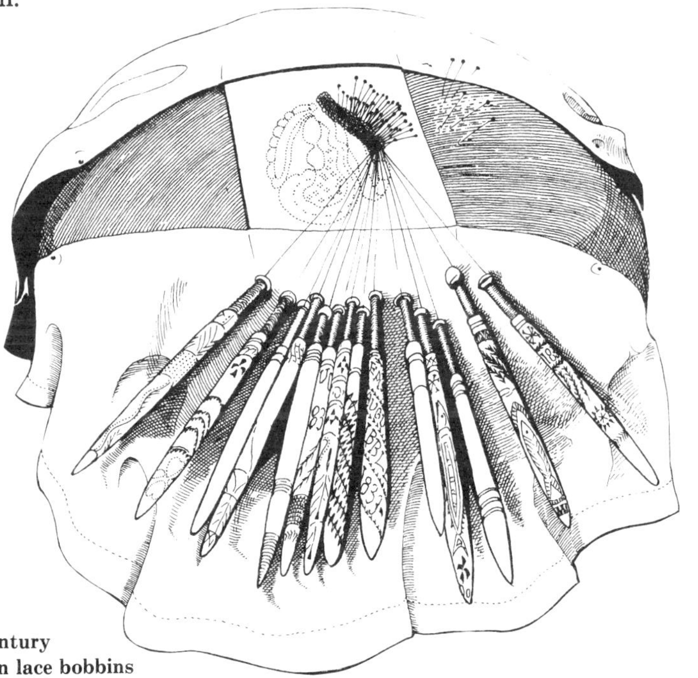

19th century Honiton lace bobbins

20.
The End of an Era

The desire for universal education was quite spontaneous in the 19th century and Acts of Parliament merely underlined what was already happening in most areas. The great increase in the number of "scholars" between the 1851 and 1861 censuses had nothing to do with compulsion. The ability to read, write and do simple calculations was seen as the only chance to rise above the semi-serfdom of land-work into the world of shopkeeping and small business. Yet education was still considered a luxury by some parents who were only too ready to keep their elder children at home to help them or to earn a few pennies. And, indeed, so many jobs were traditionally considered children's work that schooling must have placed a severe strain on large families. Older children were up before 6 a.m. to fetch water, chop and carry firewood, clean boots and feed the hens before going to school and as many tasks awaited them on return. It was usual for employers to approach the school-teacher to recommend likely lads for farm-work or girls for domestic work and the children would be excused school to "live-in" from the age of 11 or 12. In many cases homes were so overcrowded that there was no question of all the children living at home. Little Pat Stoneman lived-in with the Langdon Fulfords at The Priory from the time she was 13 until she married William Hitchcock seven years later. Even after her marriage, and with a large family of her own, she continued to do the Fulfords' washing.

The Broadmead Charity School tottered on from crisis to crisis, mainly brought about by inadequate funds and unsatisfactory trusteeship. Back in 1783 new trustees were appointed and they included two Stogdons, two Lees, two Heathfields and John Holwell. But it was not long before the Charity was in deep trouble again.

After the Napoleonic Wars ended land values slumped and the rent from the Trust's land, Edmonds, had to be reduced from £39 to £26 annually and poor management had allowed the farm cottage to

The Priory (Garden Front) c. 1890

fall down. To try to offset the fall in income the trustees felled and sold some of the hedgerow timber at Edmonds for £110. But the money was soon more than swallowed up in a scandal that brought the Charity to the brink of disaster. In 1814 serious complaints of "misconduct" were laid against the Master, John Hill Wright. We are not told what his offence was but the trustees felt they had no other course open to them but to give him a quarter's notice. His salary was stopped and his replacement appointed. But Wright absolutely refused to quit the school-house and brought an action for wrongful dismissal and misappropriation of funds. The Master of the Rolls declined to make an order; the case cost the trustess £87 and they were no nearer to getting Wright out. The matter was further complicated by the bankruptcy of Thomas Heathfield, one of the Trustees, in whose property the school was housed. Mr. Heathfield's assigns now sold the property and the new owner, being stuck with Wright (who still refused to budge) and no income, claimed loss of rent from the trustees, who had to fork out £60 in compensation and costs. Finally, and not before time, an ejectment order was successfully sought and Wright was thrown out — at a cost of another £48. The whole wretched business dragged on for six years and cost £196, equal to nearly 8 years' income, and only the sale of the remaining timber at Edmonds (for £80) saved the trust. The hopelessly unbusinesslike muddle is all the harder to understand since that remarkable man Thomas Huckell Lee was treasurer to the trust and had had the principal management of it until shortly before his death in 1822. But as he had not attended the annual Vestry Meetings since 1812 it is probable that he was latterly a very sick man. His place on the board of Trustees was taken by his son, George, who was with the East India Company, and by 1823 not one of Esaias Broadmead's Trustees lived in Woodbury. [1]

Up to this point the school had not been at Church Stile, where it was to spend the last 50 years of its life, but evidence of its whereabouts is hard to come by. It had probably had several homes during its lifetime but there is reason to believe that at the time of these upheavals it was being held in part of Woodbury House which Thomas Heathfield had bought from the Lemprières in 1808. A tradition handed down in the Stamp family says that there was once a school at Woodbury House. It may well have been Broadmead.

What is more certain is that this was the moment (1823) when it finally came to rest at Church Stile, then the property of Thomas Huckell Lee's eldest daughter, Mrs. Rebecca Huckell Pennell, and it was the Pennells who took Broadmead under their wing and cared for it steadfastly to the end of its days, just as the Pidsleys had done at Salterton. But though Broadmead settled down to resume its proper function of teaching children there was never enough money to pay staff properly, therefore the difficulty of attracting certificated teachers and keeping them was acute. In 1823 the Master received £13 a year to teach 13 boys the Three Rs and an additional £2.10s. from the Holwell Charity for teaching another 8 children in the same school, while two Mistresses shared the princely sum of £7.8s. for teaching 12 girls apiece — less than 1s.6d. a week! By 1850 the income from Edmonds had been further reduced to £16 and the deficit was being largely met by Miss Pennell.

In 1863 the school was recognized by the Board of Education and the Log-Book begins.[2] Mr. Angus James McLaren was the Master

Church Stile

and a dreary martinet he seems to have been. His wife, Mary, was Mistress and their eldest daughter, Elizabeth, a pupil-teacher who struggled for her certificate against the continual criticism of the Inspector: "E. McLaren's paper is very unsatisfactory throughout. My Lords had great hesitation in passing her and will not do so again without marked improvement."

McLaren was replaced by William Arthur Philpotts in 1867 — an uncertificated teacher who only managed to stay the course for six months. Yet he is memorable for actually giving us the names of the children. Remembering the aim of the charity was the education of *poor* children it comes as a surprise to find that most of the pupils were the sons and daughters of farmers, tradesmen and shopkeepers. Kenwoods, Skinners, Stamps, Phillips, Hearns, Clapps, Chapmans and Annings were all at Broadmead.

During James Gardener's brief reign (he found the children "very dull") things looked like improving. There were 54 names on the register and the Log-Book becomes almost human. "February 5th

1868 took the upper class to Woodbury Salterton for a game of Football with the scholars of that village." But, alas, on March 4th Mr. Gardener had an accident with a gun. Mrs. Gardener looked after him, taught in the school and tried to keep the children quiet, but he died on 27th March: he was only 24. For another three months his widow carried on as best she could until Mr. A.L. Sparkes took over in June 1868. Sparkes was a holy terror and the Log-Book is full of punishments. Attendance fell to 26 and "Mrs. Chapman came to make a disturbance about her boy (William) being kept in. She took him away and I requested her not to send him again."

Throughout these comings and goings Miss Pennell and Miss Ann Lee (Thos. Huckell's youngest daughter) continued their weekly visits and were always ready to step in and teach if the school were short-handed — which was often! But the days at Church Stile were numbered. With the building of Woodbury Church School in 1871 it was decided to close Broadmead, sell the land at Edmonds and use the money to build a new school at Exton. The Hon. Mark Rolle gave the trustees a site and Sir Francis Drake of Nutwell gave £1000 for Edmonds. There may be some people still alive who were pupils of that devoted head-mistress Mrs. Mary Anne Randall who gave over 30 years of her life to the children of Exton.

Broadmead was not the only school in Woodbury. From White's Directory 1850 we learn that there was also a National School and Billings in 1857 adds that it had 140 pupils and a small endowment — otherwise supported by public subscription and "the children's pence." Obviously a school does not acquire 140 pupils overnight and it seems a fair guess that it had been there for some time. Further evidence is of an architectural nature, for the school was housed in the long building behind The Beals which has remained largely unaltered since 1871 when the new school was built. Though the thatch has been replaced with corrugated iron and the inside stored with everything from chicken feed and apples to old bicycles, scaffolding and ladders, it still requires little imagination to see those 140 children streaming through the pointed Regency/Gothick double doors and taking their places in the great hall. Plastered, ceilinged and whitewashed, it is 42 x 16 ft. and the full height of the building, with a gallery at one end. High up in the walls are square windows whose glazing bars are finely moulded. An inner door leads through into the Master's house — two up, two down, with staircase, kitchen range and cupboards in the thickness of the walls. The front door is six-panelled in the best Regency manner.

From 1848 the school was under the headship of that same James Simons who carried the Mail Bags to Pink House Corner and he may have been the first Headmaster. He was assisted by his wife Mary Ann. It was in that school-house that their daughter Jane Elizabeth (Bessie) was born in 1850 to be followed by seven other children. In 1860 their eldest son, James, died at the age of 8 in an epidemic which carried away ten Woodbury children between February and May. Four years more and the Headmaster himself went to an early grave. He was 45 and in the margin of the register Fulford noted that he had been Schoolmaster and Parish Clerk for 16 years. For a while Mary Ann stayed on to help his successor, George Payne, until he found his own assistant by marrying Emma Stokes on Christmas Day 1867. Even so, the Simons family did not sever their connections with the school, for Bessie became Sewing Mistress and Infant Teacher, moved to the new building with the school in 1871 and stayed until her marriage to James Livermore in 1877.

With the arrival of Tom Edward Lear at The Beals in 1869 the Log Book begins.[3] He was not an imaginative man and his entries in the log are unrevealing, yet one entry for The Beals period is worth quoting, "10th Oct. 1870. Made enquiries as to bad attendance the preceding week and found it arose principally through the children picking *acorns* which were worth 1s.4d. per bushel."

Already plans were well advanced for the building of a new school. Whatever may have been said about the Rev'd John Loveband Fulford, he certainly knew what he was doing in building the school. He was the driving force behind it. It was he who engendered the enthusiasm which raised the £1000 needed and pursuaded the Hon. Mark Rolle to give the site. Fulford's well-known architect son, the Rev'd Robert Medley Fulford F.R.I.B.A. drew up the plans, Wm. Phillips was the builder and Lady Drake laid the foundation stone. But if anyone thought that time had mellowed Fulford he would be wrong, for the old man had learnt nothing about handling his Vestry in all the 24 years he had been in Woodbury.

A special meeting was called for October 17th, 1870 "to discuss the propriety of forming a School Board for the Parish of Woodbury under the new Education Act." Owing to Fulford's latest outrages in church, however, the meeting boiled over and the school came near to not being discussed at all. It was the old story — alterations without a faculty, high-church "ornaments" without consulting the church-wardens: and the old solutions — representations to the Bishop and a fighting fund set up to defray all legal expense incurred by the Churchwardens in resisting the Innovations of the Incumbent." Fulford wisely absented himself from the meeting but feelings ran so high that it was all the incumbent's son, the Rev'd John Langdon Fulford, mild and gentle soul that he was, could do to calm the meeting down sufficiently to propose that "a Voluntary School is preferable to a School supported by the Local Board." In this way Woodbury remained a Church School while qualifying for grant-aid.[4]

And so 20th October 1871 dawned. The 145 children assembled at The Beals for the last time and, carrying their slates and accompanied by their teachers, walked in excited procession past the Green and Abraham Berry's Machinery Works, past Woodbury House, past William Stokes's bell-hanger's yard at Fernlea, past Webbers Farm, past Mrs. Clapp's grocery and sweet shop to enter their new school for the first time.

Built of brick the school had a large hall divided into two classes

The Village School in c. 1900

by a curtain, and with a small gallery above one end for the younger children. Heating was provided by two large open fires, one either side of the main door, and it was Sarah Stamp's job to light the fires early each morning and keep the school clean — for £4 a year. Two architectural features well-remembered (and now much-lamented) were the bell-turret with its narrow spire and the large sunny porch to the main door, with seats on either side, where little bunches of children used to gather and chat.

The Schoolmaster's house adjoined the school and here Tom Lear lived until 1886 when after 17 years he decided that £100 a year was no longer enough. He moved to Copplestone Cottage in Broadway where he kept a grocery and sweet shop and ran a small private school while, ironically, the School Managers advertised for a new Headmaster at £120 a year.

Although the decline in the rural population which Frederick Turner had noted in Salterton equally applied to Woodbury itself (between 1851 and 1901 the population dropped from 2014 to 1527) yet the village was full of children. Six or seven was still considered a normal family. A large proportion of them knew what it was like to be cold and hungry, to go barefoot, to work hard on the land or in the house, to receive harsh punishment both at home and at school,

Mrs. Clapp's sweet shop

and to have to mind younger brothers and sisters. Yet there was inevitably another side to the coin. Children had amongst themselves a tremendous bonhomie, a zest for life which triumphed over hardships. The streets were their play-ground and with little traffic to impede them children amused themselves with skipping ropes, hoops, tops, marbles, chestnuts, hop-scotch and a game like 'jacks' which they played with pork knuckle bones. Wooden hoops could be bought at the village shop, though many boys preferred, and saved up for, iron ones made by the blacksmith, because they were faster and made an impressive noise on the gravel road surface. These were mostly winter activities. In the summer the children fished in the Gilbrook, built 'houses' in the hedge-bottoms, went birdnesting and swarmed up to the Common to fly home-made kites with long tails, or to fight mock battles inspired by those of the Volunteers they had watched so often.

The joy of living was sharpened by the ever-present possibility of dying. Few families managed to rear all their children. Many babies died in the first few weeks of life and over-crowding had greatly increased the incidence of tuberculosis, while every winter produced epidemics of one sort or another. Thanks to Fulford's passion for recording and annotating everything, the burial register tells us that in 1864 no fewer than 24 children died from Scarlet Fever. Woodbury's last serious outbreak of Smallpox occurred in 1871 when there were seven deaths — all young people — including Walter Skinner who had been a bearer at the funeral of Louis Parsons a month previously — a fact that Fulford obviously thought significant. Fulford was a pro-vaccination man and remarked disapprovingly in the margin that all the fatalities were unvaccinated. Readers will remember that Matthew Lee had been the first in the field with some sort of experimental immunization for his children in 1748. In the winter of 1791/2 this was taken a step further when that kind and philanthropic man, Thomas Heathfield of Upper Nutwell, paid for 200 people in Woodbury to be immunized against Smallpox.[5] Throughout the first half of the nineteenth century the parish was paying Dr. Butter and his successor 5s.3d. a time for the innoculation of poor children and by the 1860s vaccination had been made compulsory. It remained a highly controversial subject, however, and so many people availed themselves of the "conscience" clause that a substantial portion of the population remained at risk. Perhaps that was soon to be altered, for when Dr. Henry Wallace Furnival arrived at Sunnyside, Broadway, in the early 1880s (later he moved to Southcroft in Town Lane where his dispensary under the stairs is preserved) he was specifically described as a public vaccinator.

The doctor had a horse and carriage in which he made his rounds but as he grew older he liked to call upon the services of Mr. Walter Skinner who kept a waggonette behind his premises in Gilbrook. Mr. Skinner's two-horse vehicle was in regular use between the village and the station but many a long night did he spend waiting for the doctor attending a difficult confinement. Most of the leading families in Woodbury had carriages and, of course, coachmen but the smartest was undoubtedly the shiny, black, closed carriage with coats-of-arms on the doors in which Lady Drake came to church. Everyone was expected to bow or curtsey as she passed and her arrival was timed to make the maximum effect. The congregation stood respectfully as she swished by in her black silk bustle and train, down the aisle and into the Drake chapel, followed by her little retinue.

Of the commercial vehicles, pride of place went to Robert Glanvill's beautiful pair of shire horses and the brewer's dray in which he delivered malt and beer from his premises (now the

Glanvill's brewery and malthouse

Looking up Gillbrook towards the Arch. Eli Bamsey's shop, right.

Maltsters Arms) to his customers in Exeter. John Gordon's carrier's cart was a kind of covered waggon, four wheeled and drawn by a powerful shire, which he kept in the yard at Haydons. Butchers, bakers and farmers mostly had high two-wheeled traps for delivering their goods and going into Exeter on a market-day. Farm waggons were gaily painted and once a year they were cleaned up and decked out to carry the school-children on their summer outing to Nutwell. And for poorer folk the humble donkey was as popular as ever, carrying furze and firewood from the Common.

This amount of horse-drawn traffic produced a great deal of work in Woodbury which today's traffic does not. Thomas Smeath kept his carpentry and wheel-wright's business at Chowns, making carts and waggons for the farmers, while Robert and John Furse carried on a similar trade in Flower Lane, and Ebford and Salterton each had its own wheelwright. Blacksmiths were numerous. Woodbury had four at the end of the century including Herman Crook who moved from Salterton in the 1890s and took over the smithy in Broadway built for Joseph Hitchcock 35 years earlier. Besides the shoeing of horses Crook used to put the iron hoops on cart-wheels — rolling the white-hot hoops out of the fire with tongs and flinging them over the wheels which immediately burst into flames and had to be doused — an exciting occupation that attracted an audience of children. Crook also made iron fences and gates and his name is still to be seen on the railings round the Green.

Somehow one would expect the Rev'd J.L. Fulford to be different in his mode of transport as in all else and, while his family had a pony and governess cart, he in his latter years took to a tricycle on which he could regularly be seen, black hat pulled on firmly, white beard jutting and frock-coat tails flying wildly behind him as he careered down the village street. What a man!

With the last years of the 19th century slipping by great changes were taking place in local government. In October 1894, in accordance with their instructions from central government, the Vestry met for the last time and appointed a small sub-committee to draw up a list of persons considered suitable to fill the office of Parish Councillor. Some thirty names were put forward and the first-ever Parish Council election was held at the school on 24th November. Then, as now, twelve councillors were elected, the successful candidates being:-

Harry Stokes	Town	104 votes	Bell hanger
Henry Glanvill	Webbers	86	Farmer & Registrar
Robert Mitchell	Broadway	86	Mason
George Thorn	Nutwell	86	Farmer
Luke Browning	Town	85	–
Tom Lear	Broadway	83	Schoolmaster
John Passmore	Myrtle Cottage	82	Gent. Ret.
Arthur Phillips	Brookleigh	81	Builder
Frederick Cumes	Salterton	80	Cooper
Harold Ware	Gilbrook	80	Tanner
Samuel Marks	Town	76	–
Uriah Pearce	Town	76	–

It was a brave new start — quite unlike the Vestry. Yet there must have been feelings of "I've been here before" when Fulford, now aged 80, turned up at the first meeting obviously expecting to be appointed Chairman. Equally obviously others had expected that Harry Stokes would fill the post, and Stokes had in fact, chaired the preliminary meeting. The matter was hotly debated, Fulford was proposed and squeezed in by a narrow majority. Harry Stokes accepted the alternative of Vice-Chairman and the Council went on to discuss the state of the Green — its uses and abuses. It has been discussing it ever since.[6]

There was one more important event over which Fulford was to preside — Queen Victoria's Diamond Jubilee in 1897. Unfortunately the records are very stingey with their accounts of how Woodbury celebrated the occasion. The Parish Council minute book is silent on the subject but as the schoolmaster grudgingly records in the Log Book that the children had a week's holiday one may suppose that events of various sorts were spread over several days. All we know, from newspaper accounts of Exeter's celebrations, is that the weather was perfect and that a great bonfire on Woodbury Common was the first in a chain of signals to be set alight.

A more permanent memento of the event was 'Jubilee Stores' — a house in Gillbrook bought by Mr. Walter Skinner that year and extended and converted into a grocery shop. But meanwhile the Church Vestry was not missing the opportunity of making its own permanent memorial and the six bells in the tower of St. Swithin's were rehung to mark the Jubilee. A subscription was raised and 158 people donated a total of £107.6s.2d. with individual contributions ranging from £10 to 2d.

Mr. Harry Stokes, already a bell-hanger widely renowned, carried out the work which took six months to complete and the bells were once again in place ready for a service of rededication on 16th January 1898. The Bishop of Crediton performed the ceremony and a band of ringers from St. Sidwell's rang changes — "and were much pleased with the swing and go of the bells". The whole proceedings must have pleased Fulford mightily, for he was an expert bell-ringer himself and a past President of the Devon Guild of Ringers.

It was just in time. Eight weeks later Fulford died at the age of 84. He had been vicar of Woodbury for 52 years and was buried in the churchyard on the left-hand side of the main path, under the tall cross that also marks the resting place of his loving and patient wife. Their eldest son, John Langdon Fulford, had predeceased him by nearly 20 years and in the next century they were to be joined by other children and grandchildren. The Parish Council mourned his loss and paid tribute to his inestimable services to the parish, and the Vestry raised yet another subscription to add two bells to the tower in his memory, bringing them up to a full peal of eight. That would have pleased him too. The Rev'd Henry Alford of Salterton remembered him thus: "He was a most kind-hearted man but injudicious. He contrived to set the Parish against him from the first....He was liked personally but his influence (in church affairs) was not very great and the Church was poorly attended." A Quixotian character, tilting at windmills! Subsequent writers have been unkind to Fulford but his eccentricity belonged to the spacious Victorian age which was big enough to accommodate individuals of every shape and size.

On 22nd January 1901 the old Queen died and on 2nd February Woodbury paid its own tribute to her memory. A muffled peal of bells called people to a service in the church. They came in their hundreds to hear the vicar, the Rev'd Robert Neely, preach a sermon in his strong and attractive Irish brogue and afterwards the great crowd posed in brilliant winter sunshine for a group photograph as a souvenir of the occasion. And there we can see them, ladies in their best black, men in top hats, bowlers or flat caps, the vicar in his mortarboard, the choir in their surplices (which had so shocked the parish when Fulford introduced them), the Volunteers in their uniforms and busbies, the postman, the policeman, and children hoisted on to shoulders so that the camera should not miss them.

It was more than the end of a reign, more than the end of a century. It was the end of an era.

Woodbury mourns the death of Queen Victoria

21.
Epilogue

The Coronation of King Edward VII was a double celebration for it also marked the end of the Boer War. Marshalled by Mr. Wm. Abbott, ironmonger and captain of the Fire Brigade, Woodbury got out its flags and bunting, its carnival floats, bands and choirs and went round the town. A float depicting 'Britannia', attended by Canada, India, Australia and S. Africa was followed by 'Peace', showing a British soldier shaking hands with a Boer.

The war had been unpopular, though several Woodbury men took part in it. John Edwin Hitchcock had no choice for he was a Colour-Sergeant in the Coldstream Guards. But there was no happy home-coming for him — he was invalided out and died shortly after. Bill Summerfield, on the other hand, made a triumphant return. His train was met at Woodbury Road Station by George Berry and Woodbury's new Merryweather Fire Engine and he rode home at the gallop with bells ringing.

George Berry and his brothers carried on the family business started by their father, making agricultural machinery at their works on the Green (formerly the Tannery). It was Berrys who made and installed the horse-driven mill machinery at Gilbrook Tannery for the grinding of Myrobalan — a type of Indian acorn used in dyeing leather. Three sons of Henry Ware ran their businesses from the same premises — Harold was the tanner, Edgar farmed and Gordon, the youngest, ran the mill. When the tannery had to close down in 1913, due to heavy importation of hides from Argentina, Harold Ware built up a leather-wholesaling business and Gordon's mill went over to cattle feed-stuffs.

The Wares had been a driving force in Woodbury for over a century — and not only on the business front. A strong evangelical streak had put them into Dr. Brent's break-away from the parish church in 1851. But following the death of Brent in 1872 and the Rev'd Wm. Wippell in 1881 much of the impetus had gone out of Christ Church. Then, following a 'tent campaign' in Flower Lane by

Gilbrook House

two Brethren Assembly evangelists, Henry Ware spear-headed a new break-away movement and soon a band of followers, the Gibbings, Annings, Bamseys, and 'Drishy' Troake among them, were being baptised by immersion in the 'Baptising Pond' in the Wares' orchard at Gilbrook. The meetings gathered momentum and graduated from members' houses to a part of the old National School behind the Beals and later to the old Artillery Drill Hall in Broadway — their permanent home until they moved back to Christ Church in the 1960s.[1]

The Wares and the Berrys were by no means the only old-established businesses still flourishing in the village. Harry Stokes, son of Robert, and his son, also Harry, were still at Fernlea where their carpenter's shop had expanded into a bell-hanging business second to none in the South West. The premises were larger then than now and included not only the carpenter's shop but also stalls for 5 cows and the draught-horses, and a forge where the iron-work of the bell-frames was made and the horses were shod. Delivering the frames and installing them in their towers, maybe a hundred miles from home, was a major operation — the journey alone taking several days. Emmanuel Hawkins was carter and it was customary for farmers living near steep hills to keep trace-horses which could be hired cheaply to assist with heavy loads. A trace horse was always kept at Ford Farm to help loads up to the top of the Common and the Stokeses were often glad to make use of the facility. Messrs Summerfield and Jarman, who had arrived in the 1870s to challenge the supremacy of the Phillipses, at first ran their building firm from Brookside in Gilbrook. But they produced between them so many sons who wanted to join the firm that the two families separated amicably and ran their own businesses, Summerfields from the Beals, specializing in maintenance and repair work, and Jarmans from Chowns, building many of Woodbury's new houses in the first half of this century.

But another family firm was faltering. The Phillipses can only be described as a dynasty. Founded in the 18th century, the firm had reigned supreme over Woodbury's great expansion of the 19th century. Now the 20th century found only Arthur Edward Phillips carrying on in the 4th generation. 'Artie' lived with his sister Sarah in the house their father, Robert, had built — Brookleigh. He was a bachelor, unlike his lusty grandfather, Abraham, who sired nine legitimate children and left a number of little legacies to otherwise respectable village maidens, as the Register reveals! Choir-master, church-warden, parish councillor and school manager, Artie was a respected figure and is still remembered by his ex-choristers ('Artie Phillips's white mice' as they were nicknamed) for the cream teas he used to stand them. As he lay dying a slow and painful death in 1921, some of the last of the tan from the dwindling tan-heap at Gilbrook was spread over the road outside Brookleigh, and the village was hushed.

Opposite Brookleigh, on 'the Brewery bank', the last of Woodbury's mediaeval malt-houses had ceased malting by the time Artie Phillips died. Jack Hitchcock recalled the horse-wheel by which water was drawn up from a well at the corner of the Green, the old malting-floor where the curved shovels turned and turned the grain, the kilns and the homely smell of roasting barley wafting out over the village.

Rydon Mill had already stopped production (1909) and Exton Mill

The Choir of St. Swithin's. Artie Phillips and his "white mice", c.1919. (left to right) boys: Robert Bamsey, Bill Summerfield, Bill Newberry, Jack Crook, Frank Parr, Wilfred Marks, Percy Newberry, Roland Curtis, Fred Parr and Gussie Marks.

was soon to follow in the early 1920s.

John Gordon's carrier business was taken over by William Chapman and moved from Haydons to Prospect House: William Daley succeeded his father as sub-postmaster at the corner shop and built himself a new Post Office in Broadway (1912) on the site of a Tudor farmhouse. Into the old Post Office moved James Hall who turned it into a bakery while George Goss, baker, replaced Halls at Claremont, later to move to the corner of Flower Lane. 'Donkey' Stamp harvested furze on the Common to keep the bakery ovens going and housed his donkeys behind Gadd Square. Other traditional skills lingered on. Frank Radford made rush mats and sold them from his donkey cart. 'Blind' Bastin had gone but blind Jack Searle made baskets in Broadway and grew his 'withies' by the Polly Brook as Bastin had grown his by the stream at Pound Corner. And Sidney Marks was the last of a long line of highly skilled shoe-makers for which Woodbury had been renowned.

The Fulfords stayed on at the Priory. They were an institution and few people could remember, or imagine, Woodbury without them. When old Fulford's eldest son and curate, John Langdon, died at the early age of 37 he left his young widow, Blanche, with five children and expecting a sixth. They lived in greatly impoverished circumstances and practised every kind of economy — teaching, patching and turning 'sides-to-middle' — yet could always find the wherewithall to be generous. In hard winters Mrs. Fulford ran a soup-kitchen for the poor from a shed behind No. 1 Gillbrook Cottages. Jane Toulmin devoted her life to the Fulfords, looking after the children in return for nothing but her keep. For forty-five years the Priory was her home and she lies buried with the Fulfords in the churchyard. Young Jock was only nine when his father died but from that time he read the family prayers. He was a bright boy, going from Exeter School to Exeter College Oxford where he gained a D.D. in 1913. Being a bachelor, he lived with his sisters, Kitty and Blanche, at the Priory, and finally became vicar of Woodbury in 1939. Jock died in 1945, almost exactly 100 years after the arrival of his eccentric grandfather but, unlike his grandfather, he was a greatly loved parish priest, humorous and compassionate, always on the spot where there was need or sorrow. Kitty and Blanche (they died in the 1950s) ran their well-remembered Bible Classes from

Looking up the Broadway c.1900 — from the right; Broadway House, the Tudor house demolished 1911 for present Post Office, Perry's Bakery, Crook's Smithy. Left: The Lawn.

Threshing time at Cornishes Farm, Gillbrook c.1912.

1909, tirelessly organizing activities for the young and interesting themselves deeply in the Girl Guide Movement and the Women's Institute. In later years the family came into money and were able to employ staff, many of whom still remember their time in service at the Priory — the family prayers, the uniforms they wore and the beautiful garden which was John Down's pride and joy.[2]

The young people enjoyed a lot of simple fun. The building of the school had provided a room large enough for social functions. But the restrictions were irksome and people began to talk about the need for a 'Public Hall' — egged on, no doubt, by a twinge of envy for Salterton's new Public Hall, then nearing completion. The idea really got off the ground on Bonfire Night 1909 when Tom Lear had a whip-round and obtained promises of loans totalling £250. A private company was formed and an old tin chapel at Topsham became available at just the right moment and was moved to Flower Lane. Tom Lear was the moving spirit of the enterprise and his fellow-directors were the Rev'd. Dr. Jock Fulford, Harry Stokes sen. and jun., Artie Phillips and Wm. Abbott. Very soon Flower Lane was resounding to the strains of the Valeta, the Lancers, Quadrilles and Polkas, as George Berry's '6d. Saturday Night Hops' got into their stride. "If you didn't dance all night there was something wrong with you" remembers Mollie Skinner (nee Hitchcock).

The most glittering occasion for which one might angle an invitation was the annual staff ball at Nutwell. The Drakes kept an indoor staff of about 20 and the staff from other big houses, Bicton, Winslade, Courtlands and others, came to make up a party of well over 100 dancers. The girls pinched and scraped and with a little borrowing, altering and ingenuity always managed to make themselves ball gowns for the occasion.

As the numbers of young people in Woodbury declined, attendance at the school dropped from a peak of 240 to 161 at the beginning of this century. Not that it concerned the children themselves: the street-games continued and life went on for the most part uneventfully. But there was an event that no child at school in 1911 will forget. May 10th seemed just like any other day until late in the afternoon when the sky became very black. As daylight was inadequate the headmaster, fearing a storm, decided to send the children home early and the main door was open when the storm broke. Almost immediately the school was struck by lightning. The bell-turret was destroyed and tiles and masonry came hurtling through the roof, showering the children with rubble. At the same time a thunderbolt ('electric fluid' was how Mr. Pyne described it in the log-book) tore in the open doorway and through the crowded classroom, destroying the boots of two children. For a brief moment the children were paralysed with terror and then panic broke out. Their screams could be heard half a mile away at Venmore but as they rushed for the open door their flight-path was barred by the strong arm of Mrs. Down who roared above the tumult "Where is your presence of mind?" Miraculously no-one was seriously hurt, though Annie Crook had a dent in her skull for the rest of her life and Mrs. Hearn was away from school for a week, suffering from shock. Mollie Skinner recalls the strong smell of sulphur and the great reluctance with which she accompanied her mother that evening to inspect the damage — her heart sinking and her steps growing slower and slower as the school came in sight.

A steady trickle of Woodbury's younger generation was still finding its way to the colonies, where prospects seemed so much brighter than at home. Cyril Abbott went to Australia, Tom Wills and James Vickery to Canada. Alfred Stokes went to Saskatchewan in 1910 and was joined there four years later by his brother Harry, sisters Ivy and Mary, and his sweetheart Elsie Phillips from Ford Farm. Elsie took with her a wedding dress carefully packed in a box.

Goss's Hygienic Steam Bakery 1902

A Cottage Interior
Mr. & Mrs. Sid Gooding at home at No. 5 Gillbrook

Ham Lane c.1910

Mrs. Fox & Mrs. Brewer
in their Forestry Commission uniform, 1915.

Woodbury men in the Devonshire Regiment in India 1914.
George Crump George Cook
Walt Chapman, Sam Hawkins, Mark Marks, Edgar Wright,
Sid Stamp, Fred Searle, Walt Godfrey, George Carter,

But the ship's captain insisted on conducting the wedding ceremony on board ship before allowing her to land, and Elsie's wedding dress was never unpacked.

But it was still a predicatable world and nobody suspected that the clouds were gathering — certainly not Jack Coles when in July 1914 he wrote a postcard to his school-chum Reggie Skinner, then languishing in Whipton Sanatorium. The photo showed an idyllic and leafy Ham Lane by the side of the sparkling Gilbrook and on the back Jack wished Reggie a speedy recovery "in time for the corn-harvesting so we can go up the hill shouting to the rabbits".

The First World War seemed to come from nowhere. August 4th was the day chosen for Salterton's annual choir-outing and Maggie Turner put on her best ankle-length frilly skirt and went with the rest in an open motor charabanc to Haytor. It was a brilliant, happy day and from the top of the tor they could see a tiny Woodbury Beacon standing up on the distant horizon. Passing through Exeter on the way home they were astonished to see a large crowd gathered in Bedford Circus. On making enquiries they were told war had been declared. "I shall always remember the awful shock" wrote Maggie fifty years later, "it was as if my innocent, carefree childhood ended on that day".[3] Several Woodbury men were already in the 4th Devon (Territorial) Regiment and were holding their annual summer camp on Woodbury Common. Reg Berry, Reg Newton, Charlie Morrish, Jack Skinner and Jack Sellick were among them, and Bert Smeath was bugler-boy. By 1915 133 men had enlisted and church-warden Artie Phillips entered their names in the account book. But the task of keeping the entries up to date became too great and was abandoned. More were to serve in those four horrendous years from which 37 of Woodbury's sons did not return.

Meanwhile the womenfolk had to play an ever-increasing role in what had been a man's world. Several served with the Forestry Commission, manning the large cross-cut saws that produced thousands of pit-props for the mines at home and the trenches in France. Soldiers camped and trained on the Common, as they had done in the Napoleonic War, and their lives were made less harsh by the constant supply of fresh bread and doughnuts from Woodbury's four bakeries — Perry's in Broadway, Hall's at the old Post Office, Wheaton's next to the Maltsters and Goss's. Vera Perry had to set to, after school, and help her widowed mother to run the bakehouse and deliver bread as far afield as Exton, Salterton and the camp on the Common with the pony and trap (these four bakeries survived until after the 2nd World War). It was hard and unglamorous work only occasionally enlivened by home-grown excitements. Early one morning in April 1916 the old Globe Inn caught fire and was burnt to the ground. The blaze from the thatch could be seen for miles and Sam Carter was one of the hundreds of helpers and spectators who were fascinated to see the window glass melt and bottles take on strange, twisted shapes — so great was the heat. But Ned Miller, spending his first night in bed after a spell in the trenches, said "I've seen better fires than that" — turned over and went to sleep again. It was a sad end to an honourable piece of village history. The corner of 'Globe Field' still yields up its souvenirs — broken glass, fragments of blue and white cider mugs, donkey shoes and bits of clay pipe by the bucketful.

The Builders of the War Memorial 1920.
Back Row: H. Summerfield, Chas. Summerfield, Harry Lock, Bob Havill, Walter Godfrey, Wm. Crook, Herbert Leach, Harry Sellick, Harry Stokes, Bert Stamp, Walt Veal, A. Kilmaster.
Front Row: Sam Hawkins, Chas. Morrish, Jim Davey, Walter Chapman, Chas. Norton, Chas. Lang, Reg Summerfield.

The war came to an end but the rejoicing was tinged with sadness. So many families suffered bereavement. Young Maj. Robert Masefield had been killed in action at Armentières when the war was barely eight weeks old and the Davey family had lost four of their number. The 37 Woodbury names are written in gold on the memorial organ screen in St. Swithin's and on a more public War Memorial Cross erected by voluntary labour at the cross-roads (now moved to the Green). It was unveiled on Saturday 10th June 1920 by Maj. Morrison Bell M.P., assisted by the vicar, Robert Neely, and on May 1921 the cross-roads was the scene of a great gathering of flag-waving people when the Prince of Wales stopped momentarily at the War Memorial on his way from Bicton to Exeter.

Salterton remembered its own dead with the erection of a lychgate.

Old Dr. Furnival retired (not before time) and his place was taken by young Dr. Darbyshire 'of blessed memory'. Darbyshire had been gassed in the war and was recommended to lead a country life. He and his wife lived first at Thornlea and later at the Grange which they had built for them. Tall, good-looking and always immaculately smart; kind, comforting and generous, Dr. Darbyshire was everybody's idol. Maggie Turner remembered "The sound of his voice — his hand on one's shoulder — did more than all the modern tablets". The doctor entered energetically into village life. He had Woodbury's first loft of racing pigeons and it was he who pioneered the first two public tennis courts in Woodbury, behind Southcroft where now there are council houses. He also had a car — a solid-tyred Trojan — though it was not the first car in the village.

The first motor-traffic had already appeared before the war. Apart from 'Charas' for joy-riding there were two cars to be seen regularly in Woodbury in 1914 — Lady Dunboyne's chauffeur-driven limou-

The Prince of Wales pauses at the War Memorial 17th May 1921.

sine in Salterton and Harold Ware's T-model Ford at Gilbrook. At the sound of their horns children came running to their doors to look. The long cloud of dust raised on the roads before the days of tarmac is well remembered. Woodbury Council was still contracting its parish road repairs out in the old way. 'Dobbins' Miller was the last of Woodbury's stone-crackers — expertly breaking stones with a hammer and protecting his eyes from flying chips with a special shield. "Cor, the smeech!" recalls Vera Stediford (nee Perry). In dry weather a water cart toured the village, laying the dust. But with the use of tarmac in the 1920s the old methods gave way to the new.

Woodbury was picking itself up. Modernization schemes, shelved during the war years, kept the Parish Council busy. The first council houses appeared. In 1925/26 electricity arrived in the village. It was a private undertaking installed by Mr. Clifford Gould of Topsham and generated by a diesel engine located behind the Maltsters Arms. The Rev'd Robert Neely, chairman of the Council, was always a progressive man and the scheme was his brainchild. He was asked to switch on the first electric street lights and Mr. Gould recalled the transparent and childlike delight with which he did so. A proper sewerage scheme finally made its appearance in 1926/7, ninety-five years after the cholera epidemic. Until then the White Hart's toilet facilities had consisted of a small 'privy' perched precariously over the open stream in the garden and naughty boys had a disconcerting habit of waiting till someone was in there to throw stones and create a well-directed splash! The Council was still talking about a main water supply but the project got no nearer. With most houses now connected to the sewer the risk of polluting Woodbury's many wells was much less. In 1929 the village said goodbye to its Fire Engine after sixty-years and the team of voluntary firemen under their captain George Berry was disbanded. From then on Woodbury came under the Topsham Fire Brigade. No more would Walter Skinner blow the bugle to summon the firemen from their work: no more would 'Darkie' Stamp down tools in his butcher's shop at the Teeds to catch and harness the horses.

Farming, which had enjoyed a brief boost during the war, fell back into a state of abject neglect in peace-time. The simple cause of the depression was a deliberate governmental policy of "Empire Preference". Whatever political candidates might tell their farming audiences at election times England was committed to this policy for decades. Large quantities of farm produce were imported into this country from the Dominions — wheat from Canada, butter and lamb from New Zealand, wool from Australia and so on — at greatly subsidized prices in return for the export of manufactured goods from city factories — textiles, coal and steel. While British engineers were making fortunes building dams in India or railways in S. Africa the standard of living among Woodbury farmers was falling to an all-time low. Between 1920 and 1938 arable acreage dropped by a quarter while the area of rough grazing almost doubled. It is easy to see why so many men left the land — less easy to put one's finger on the reason that still tied so many to it.

Percy Sharland was a farm labourer all his working life. "It was the only life we knew and though we never had any money we were happy — *and healthy.* Nowadays folk think too much about money but it isn't everything. I started when I was 12, living-in at Venmore. I had 1s.2d. a week and my keep. I gave Mother the bob and kept the tuppence for myself. It's surprising how much you could buy with it. Then I went up to Bridge Farm with Mr. Henry Sage and worked with the horses. Those were the happiest days. Mr. Sage used to breed big shires for timber-hauling at Bicton. A good horseman he was. If you were eating your lunch and the horse had nothing he'd say 'Hasn't the horse done any work?' I used to plough with a single-furrow plough and two horses and I'd talk to them all the time. And I'd sing and listen to the birds. You can't do any of that with a tractor. Mind, I thought the tractor was a fine thing at first but if I had my time over again it 'ud be horses. Then there were Cart Horse Parades at Exmouth and Ploughing Matches on Mr. Hallett's farm at Gulliford and I used to turn the horses out smartly, with polished brasses and their manes plaited with ribbon and reed. Manes were easy but I never could get the tails quite right. When we married, Sarah and me, in 1925, we had thirty-two-and-a-tanner a week and a tied cottage for 3s. a week. We had pump water and cooked on a black range and if we wanted an evening out it meant walking to Exmouth and back. But I wouldn't want it any different".

For young Harry Stokes it was much the same tale — no bell-hanging for him! He went from school to work on a farm at Cullompton and when Henry Glanvill died at Webbers in 1933 farming was at such a low ebb that the Rolle Estate found great difficulty in reletting it. Out of the blue Stokes senior received a letter from the Estate offering Webbers and father and son were soon in partnership.

Harry Stokes casts his mind back nearly fifty years. "It was a shocking state of affairs. People only just lived. The fields behind Hands Barn ran out to nothing — gorse and scrub almost back to the Common. But there was never any alternative for me. I'm part of the land: it's built in. You can't explain it to anybody but there is a whole life in the countryside. To be with your sheep at lambing time, to get your crops just right, or pigs perfect for the market: to see a deer break cover or a fox run, or birds rising above the wood — it's lovely. It's different for the women. They go to work in the town, behind a typewriter from nine to five, and they don't want a hard life on the land; and I don't blame them. But *they* were the reason a lot of men left farming".

The setting up of the Milk Marketing Board in 1933 was to be a turning point and gradually Woodbury farmers moved more and more towards dairying, herds became bigger and healthier and milking parlours slowly replaced the old hand-milking in the stalls. The advent of the Woodbury Young Farmers Club in 1937 also served to improve standards, widen outlook and draw Woodbury and Salterton together — to say nothing of providing a remarkably successful marriage bureau. George Daw was the first Chairman and Harry Stokes the first leader of the club which is still providing a lively outlet for Woodbury's young farming community.

Throughout the doldrum years Lord Clinton, who had succeeded the Hon. Mark Rolle to the Estate, remained a father-figure. The farm buildings were immaculately maintained and his lordship liked to see things for himself, knowing his tenant farmers personally, remembering the names of their children and the chief events of their lives.

By 1938 there were again rumblings of war and the Admiralty opened up a brand new camp for the training of Royal Marines at Nutwell. To supply the camp with main water a deep bore-hole was sunk at the top of Globe Hill and a pumping station and storage tank constructed. Until then Woodbury had enjoyed a plentiful supply of well-water, though wells were, on average, only about 14 ft. deep and apt to run low in dry summers. But now one by one the wells began to peter out. At first it was thought to be caused by the unusually dry summer, though there were plenty who shook their heads and said "What did I say?" As matters went from bad to worse petitions were got up and the Parish Council found itself with the most pressing problem of its career.

When the Second World War broke out on 3rd September 1939 it did not take people by surprise as 4th August 1914 had done. Already there was a nucleus of self-help in the village and volunteers in large numbers, both men and women, were training to be Air Raid Wardens, First Aid workers, Billeting Officers and Fire Fighters. A strict blackout was imposed necessitating hasty improvisations with any dark material that came to hand. Sunday Evensong moved to the Village Hall, as the church could not be blacked-out. Some twenty-three Woodbury men already in the Territorial Army had been called up on Friday 1st September — Sgt. Frank Miller was slashing hedges at Postlake when he received his telegram — and were on church parade in Exeter Cathedral when the Bishop announced that war had been declared. Evacuees arrived from London, labelled with luggage labels and carrying gas-masks in little cardboard boxes slung over their shoulders, and were billeted by Mrs. Chattock's committee.[4]

Wilf Hooper was recalled to the Royal Navy and was serving as a stoker in the Destroyer HMS Hardy when she was sunk at Narvik in April 1940. Flo Hooper received a telegram to say her husband was 'missing presumed dead' and all Woodbury shared her delight when Wilf turned up, proudly sporting a fancy Norwegian sweater and knitted woolly cap, to a great reception of neighbours with flags and banners proclaiming "Welcome Home Hardy Hero".

It was to be a war quite unlike the one so many people still remembered all too well — "OUR war", as they liked to call it. There was, mercifully, to be no mass-slaughter in the trenches, no sitting at home waiting for news from the front, no jingoism. The total involvement of the civilian population, the privations and dangers they faced and the part they were able to play put them on a much more even footing with the fighting forces and recreated over the whole nation something of the comradeship which the men who survived the trenches remembered.

With the collapse of France in May 1940 an invasion seemed imminent. Anthony Eden, War Secretary, came on the air on 14th May to appeal for volunteers to come forward for the defence of the homeland. Before Eden had finished speaking Norman Bowles and Charlie Middleton had jumped on their bicycles and belted down from Woodmanton to the Police Station, where they took the bobby by surprise, he not having heard the broadcast. So the Home Guard

WOODBURY PLATOON

Back Row, Left to Right – L/Cpl. Gooding, Pte. Morrish, Pte. Baker, Pte. Down, Pte. Bowles, Pte. Blackmore, Pte. Miller, Pte. Brewer, Pte. Goss, Pte.Skinner, Pte. Yeo, L/Cpl. Jarman.
Ladies attached to Back Row – Mrs. Wright (left), Mrs. Lowman (right)
2nd Row, Left to Right – Pte. Palmer, Pte. Stamp, Pte. Baker, Pte. Tucker, Pte. Stubbs, Pte. Auton, Pte. Edworthy, Pte. Hawkins, Pte. Ridler, L/Cpl. Middleton, Pte. Williams, Pte. Sharland.
Ladies attached to 2nd Row, Standing – Mrs. Brewer (left), Mrs. Morrish, Mrs. Daw, Mr. Daw (Signals Master), (right), Miss Fulford, Mrs. Grey,
3rd Row, Seated – L/Cpl Boyland, Cpl. Wilson, Sgt. Smith (G), Sgt. Gallienne, Sgt. Loman, Lt. Rickeard, Lt. Pavey, Q.M.S. Chattock, Sgt. Tapley, Sgt. Hollet, Cpl. Smith (A), Cpl. Marks, Pte. Reeves (D.R.), Pte. Armstrong, Pte. Sellick, Pte. Marks, Pte. Newton, Pte. Hitchcock, Pte. Bamsey, Pte. Chapman, Pte. Radford, Pte. Hawkins (G), Pte. Davey (D.R.).

was born. At first distinguished only by an arm-band with the letters L.D.V. (Local Defence Volunteers) and equipped with any weapons they could lay their hands on, Woodbury's Home Guard, under Major Rickeard, soon numbered some fifty men. Their headquarters were at the White Hart Skittle Alley and target practices were held in Rydon Lane sand-pit. While the threat of invasion remained the Home Guard patrolled nightly in pairs, manned checkpoints (Ford Water was one) and guarded the water-tank on Globe Hill. As uniforms and equipment became available the Home Guard grew into a very reputable fighting force — composed as it was of the too old, the too young, the unfit and the 'reserved occupation' men — and their remarkable good-humour had an effect on morale at home which was of the greatest value in the dark and dangerous years 1940-42. This was Woodbury's private war against Hitler.[5]

Women played a role undreamed of in the First World War — not just as cooks, nurses, clerks and drivers — and volunteers who rushed to join the services found themselves in an exciting and emancipated world. Esmé Ware was accepted by the W.A.A.F. and sent for training as a Radar Operator. Conditions were very spartan — bitterly cold nissen huts, scrubbed boards and peas that defied knife and fork! For many girls it was their first time away from home and not everyone could see the funny side. "If my mother could see me now!" wailed one girl and burst into tears. But they settled down and, training over, Esmé found herself at the highly secret Radar Station on the cliffs at Branscombe, plotting the approach of enemy bombers during the blitzes on Exeter, Plymouth and Bristol.

For Woodbury the Exeter blitz of May 1942 was uncomfortably near at hand. As the sirens at the Marine Camp and Topsham sent out their doleful warning and the shaft of light from the search-light battery up Castle Lane joined countless others probing the blackness, and the drone of distant engines came nearer, Woodbury resigned itself to another night under the kitchen table. Many homeless and terrified people walked the seven miles from Exeter to friends, relatives, or even complete strangers in Woodbury.

More evacuees arrived from the London area and happily settled in with families in the village. The school was overflowing and makeshift arrangements included the use of the Vestry Room, and a staggered time-table for the main school by which some children attended in the morning and some in the afternoon.

In the midst of these diversions Woodbury at last got its main water — a far from satisfactory supply hastily put in by St. Thomas Rural District Council. The year was 1942 and children were fascinated by the first mechanical digger they had ever seen. Standpipes appeared at strategic intervals, one against the school wall, another down Gilbrook and so on, and Woodbury had to make do till the supply could be extended and piped to every house.

Woodbury gives evacuee children from Croydon a taste of hay-making. 1942.

The war saw a sharp upturn in the fortunes of the farmers as, belatedly, the government recognised the deplorable state to which agriculture had sunk and the utter dependence of a near-starving nation on the produce of the land. George Smith of Higher Hogsbrook, a thoroughly go-ahead farmer, had had the first tractor in Woodbury in 1935. But it was not until the war that tractors became general. As men were called up for the forces and 'ploughing orders' served on farmers by the Ministry of Agriculture, tractors became indispensable. As so often happens, war had hastened a social revolution which would have come in time. The days of the big shire-horses, their waggoners with special expertise and secret cures, the blacksmiths who shod them, were over. So too were the hosts of farm-workers hand-milking cows, stooking and threshing the corn, skilfully hedging and ditching, and peopling their little tied cottages with large families. The necessities of war changed all that and when it was over there was no going back.

Throughout the six long years of the war a countrywide ban was placed on the ringing of church bells — they were reserved as a warning that the Germans had landed. Only once was the ban lifted and that was to celebrate the victory of El Alamein in 1942. Bert Skinner managed with some difficulty to scrounge up a band of six ringers and Woodbury momentarily rejoiced. It was to be another three years before the tower of St. Swithin's again rocked to the sound of bells — this time for total victory — and the ringers were able to re-form under their captain John C. Glanvill of Rydon.

In 1944 occurred the death of Robert Furse. He had given a lifetime of service to Woodbury and had been Parish Clerk for 42 years. Always keenly interested in parish history, he had over the years amassed a large collection of letters, accounts, wills, leases and documents of all kinds. Harry Stokes senior, himself no mean historian, thought of these papers and a day or two after the funeral went to call on Mrs. Furse with a view to begging them for himself. As he rounded the corner of Flower Lane he was greeted by the sight of an enormous bonfire in the garden of Myrtle Cottage. "I've just been turning out the attic", said Mrs. Furse.

Woodbury emerged from the war relatively unscathed, though ten families knew the heartache of losing husbands and sons. No bombs which fell on the parish caused loss of life and a heroes' return awaited the men and women from the fighting services who packed into the Village Hall for a Victory Supper. And civilian life returned. Improved transport brought jobs in Exeter and Exmouth within reach of people living in Woodbury and rebuilding programmes meant more work for the sand and gravel quarry at Blackhill. The drain of population from village to town, which had gone on for a hundred years, was halted and reversed.

There were always Woodbury men ready to step into empty shoes. William Hallett succeeded Dr. Jock Fulford as chairman of the Parish Council and Harry Jarman replaced Robert Furse as clerk. Many people — too many to name — came forward to shoulder the duties and pleasures of village life; charity trustees, School managers, church-wardens or organizers of the Cricket Club, the Flower Show and the Carnival. A new Queen was crowned in 1953 and the many hands that made light work of the flags and bunting, the tea parties and children's sports were the grandchildren of those who had performed the same happy tasks in 1902. What is village life but a collection of the joys and griefs of its people, a caring and a sharing, and the renewal of all things living?

The Silver Jubilee of King George V and Queen Mary 6th May 1935.

c.1900 Panoramic View from the Church Tower.

The same view in 1981

Engraving of Woodbury Church c.1850.

From Miry Lane, the Church (c.1900) seen across the ford and foot bridge, (right) the Bird Cage.

Part II

The Church

St. Swithin

St. Swithin (various spellings), to whom Woodbury Church is dedicated, was reputed to be a Devon man – a kinsman of St. Boniface of Crediton.[1] Personal friend and adviser to Egbert, King of Wessex, and tutor to his sons, Swithin was subsequently made Bishop of Winchester and died in 863 AD. More than a hundred years later, about 973, his body was removed from its first humble grave and reburied in a sumptuous shrine in the New Minster at Winchester. Many miracles were reported and the Cathedral added St. Swithin to its dedication.

Swithin was never formally canonized by the Pope but was made a saint by popular acclaim and on a great wave of enthusiasm dedications to him began to appear in Wessex at that time. It is interesting, though perhaps not surprising, to find the majority of churches dedicated to that humble and kindly man are to be found in the manors of the Saxon kings who knew and loved him. Sandford, near Crediton, was one and Woodbury another. Our first church may have been built by King Alfred's grandson, King Athelstan (925-940) for until the Reformation prayers were said annually here for "King Athelstan our Benefactor". It may well have been Athelstan who personally chose the dedication to St. Swithin for family reasons. The alteration of the spelling to "Swithun" was made by the Rev'd. J.L. Fulford in the 19th century.

The Fabric

We have no idea what Woodbury's earliest church was like for no remains of it have been traced. But it is evident that soon after the Vicars Choral of Exeter Cathedral were given Woodbury church in 1205/6 they set to work to rebuild it completely. The work was probably financed to a large extent by Geoffrey Albemarle and a crypt or vault constructed under the chancel especially to house the Albemarle burials. When Fulford was renewing the chancel roof in 1849 a section of the floor under the altar caved in to reveal a vault with evidence of burials and wax candles in brackets. Unfortunately he does not seem to have explored further.[2a]

Fulford stated that in his opinion the nave, chancel, porch and S. chantry chapel all date from the first half of the 13th c.,[2b] and there may well have been a matching chantry on the N. side, making it a church of cruciform shape so popular in Devon at that time. He discovered evidence of a "squint" in the S. chancel arch to match the one in the N. arch, and if these squints were contemporary with the earliest building they were obviously designed to give a view of the altar from each of the two transepts. None of the windows fit happily with an early 13th c. date but Fulford found indications of an original triple lancet window at the E. end and double lancets in the S. chancel. The priest's door (now blocked), by which the vicars entered their church, and the nearby piscina are both early 13th c. in date. The original building would have been extremely plain — almost severe — with emphasis on good

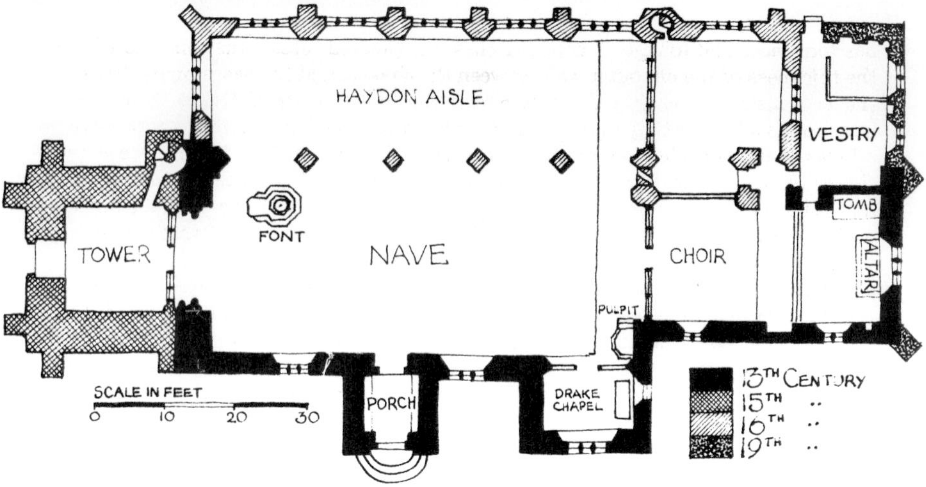

Plan of St. Swithin's Church, Woodbury.

proportions, sharply-pointed arches and a minimum of detail on door jambs or window dripstones.

When the tower was added in the first decade of the 15th century architecture was in a very different frame of mind. Here we have an altogether noble structure, eighty-four feet high and built mainly of Salcombe Regis sandstone, full of beautiful detail which deserves to be studied at leisure through a pair of binoculars. The corners are interestingly double-buttressed in the Somerset style and pedestals have been left on the buttress-steps in readiness for pinnacles which were never added. The crenellated parapet also was intended to be finished with eight pinnacles and a marvellous sight it would have been. As it is, there is plenty of good carving: the stone panels which form the crenellations themselves are decorated with quatrefoil reliefs and the gargoyles (by which rain-water from the roof of the tower was shot out clear of the stonework) are suitably grotesque! The West window is in the best style of the Decorated Period with good tracery, in sharp contrast to the lancets which would then have lighted the body of the church. The builders could not restrain their desire to beautify the outside moulding of the Tower door-arch, though it was but secondary and the principal (south) door-arch was plain.

The next addition was the N. aisle, completed about 1533. It was a time when the country was rich and much money was being channelled into church building in a last great flowering before the Reformation. Richard Haydon of Ebford Barton, whose gift tradition says it was, was not a man of fabulous wealth[3] and there are some signs that the money began to run out before the work was completed. Once again the building started with a vault under the E. end in which there are numerous Haydon burials. The walls of the aisle are of a soft local sandstone pierced by good Perpendicular windows. The really tremendous task facing the builders was the entire removal of the main N. wall of the original building and the insertion of pillars and arcades to hold the full thrust of the roof. The best Beer stone was used to excellent effect, particularly in the capital of the pillar opposite the S. door which has four faces and foliage. A double-arched and pillared recess was constructed in the thickness of the old outer wall between the chancel and the easternmost bay of the new aisle, the capital decorated with the Haydon arms. Evidently it was intended as a last resting place for the founder, a canopied table-tomb, maybe, with effigies of Richard Haydon and his wife, on the right-hand side of their aisle-altar and with a view through to the sanctuary. It would have been an imposing memorial. At the same time the chancel arch was greatly enlarged to unify the whole of the interior and make room for the addition of a rood-screen. Finally the new aisle was roofed with a fine wooden wagon roof. It is the only original roof to survive in the church, though the carved bosses on the intersections were replaced in 1799.

But something went wrong. The new pillars began to lean ominously out of the true and when Richard Haydon died in 1533 he was buried under a slab in the floor of his new aisle. What happened and why was he not buried in the handsome place prepared for him? The church-wardens' accounts (starting 1537) show that the parapet of the aisle roof was completed after Haydon's death and paid for by the parish. Within a very few years (1540/41) the whole nave had to be completely reroofed and two centuries later iron tie-beams had to be inserted across the nave. It looks as though the builders hit a major structural snag and that the whole work cost more than the family was prepared (or able?) to pay, that Haydon died before it was completed and was buried temporarily in the floor. But the family had to revise

The Parish Church of St. Swithin's before the alterations to the roof in 1893.

his grandiose plans and the Haydon aisle was never properly completed. It seems likely, however, that the founder was commemorated in a memorial window. When Fulford arrived in 1846 he was told that old people could remember fragments of ancient painted glass in one of the aisle windows, protected on the outside by an iron grille — all that the Reformation vandals left.

In 1806 the E. end of Haydon's aisle was converted into a vestry and the stair turret became a chimney and fireplace. No more actual building took place until the addition of the present vestry in 1842/43 but by the time of Fulford's arrival the church was badly dilapidated and a great deal of restoration work was put in hand. The biggest job was the entire replacement of the 1541 wagon roof of the nave by the present hammerbeam roof which is sadly out of character and has drastically affected the accoustics of the church, though the chance was taken to straighten the pillars and dispense with the tie-beams. Fulford 'discovered' and enthusiastically 'restored' the three-step sedilia, credence table and the attractive and unusual 'squint' or Hagioscope in the N. chancel arch but it is difficult now to tell how much is original work and how much restoration.

Interior Fittings

The Font is a good example of Decorated work of the early 15th century in Beer stone, octagonal in shape and supported by a nicely carved and vaulted pillar. The wooden cover, recently restored, is Jacobean, one of several excellent examples of the period in the church.

The Screen has been the subject of endless controversy since Fulford altered it in 1862. The original was almost certainly conceived as part of the Haydon aisle for it ran right across the church and linked up with the specially constructed stair-turret in the N. wall which gave access to the walk-way along the top — the rood-loft. The screen was surmounted by a 'Calvary' — wooden figures representing Christ on the Cross flanked by the Virgin Mary and St. John. It is doubtful whether it was ever in the first flight of carved wooden screens for which Devon is so famous but in its entire length, with figures and candlesticks above, supported by a richly carved cornice, and the spandrels below filled with fine tracery, the whole painted and gilded, it must have been a magnificent sight on the eve of the Reformation. It is sad to think that, supposing it was finished about 1535, there were only 14 brief years before the first wave of mutilations began. From 1549 onward the screen suffered much damage, alteration and neglect and by Fulford's time the N. aisle section had disappeared, as had also the cornice, and the rest had been moved back, botched and mended with plain deal. Much of the tracery was missing. Fulford left the spandrels open, raised the screen some 18 ins. and restored the paint. He also re-opened the chancel arch which had been blocked above the screen with lath and plaster. He has been ruthlessly attacked for his vandalism but it is unfair to blame him for damage done before his time. The present screen is no disgrace to the church.

Pews. The church has been reseated several times. In Pre-Reformation days the congregation stood for the Mass but there were benches for the elderly and infirm. Seats became necessary after the Reformation when congregations sat for long sermons and the "newe seages" made in 1571 were probably the first proper pews in the church. They had the carved, square-headed bench-ends so especially 'Devon' in style – a type still seen to perfection in neighbouring E. Budleigh – but at Woodbury just one of them now remains in use at the N.E. end of the choir stalls.

From 1639 these pews were being rented, "and for such as Clayme any right to the same seats by their tenements must pay to the next Wardens for ye planckinge of them as it cometh to". Free benches were provided at the back of the church for the poor. In 1795 they were replaced by box-pews at the cost of over £60 and these remained until Fulford unfortunately removed them in 1893. Then for a while chairs sufficed. The present pews date from 1911 — a memorial to Mrs. Blanche Fulford.

In 1660 a gallery was constructed across the W. end of the nave and occupied by the choir and musicians. Oak panelling was added in 1740 and when Fulford removed the gallery in 1893 he saved the panelling and used it as wainscotting round the church. Meanwhile, neglect had reduced the old choir-stalls to little more than firewood but Fulford had them reconstructed, using as much as possible of the old linenfold panelling and the 1571 bench-end, and carving the rest himself. Although he chose an inappropriate East-Anglian style of 'poppy-heads', it is a remarkable achievement for a man of eighty.

The Altar Rails are of exceptional quality and have been described as amongst the finest pieces of Jacobean wood-carving in England. But the date of their installation (1678) and the price paid for them (£3.6s.) makes it quite clear that they were bought second-hand. The design and workmanship bear striking similarities to furniture being produced by a school of Exeter craftsmen working about 1600 and our rails are very probably the work of Nicholas Garrett or James Ward. Comparisons with carvings at Tuckers Hall, Exeter, Powderham Castle, Cadhay, and Montacute House show that the basic repeating patterns came out of the same pattern book.[4] The rails have been altered many times. They once stretched right across the church but Fulford removed those in the N. aisle and rearranged them round the font.

The Pulpit is the work of Woodbury's own Thomas Crutchard (or Critchard), made in 1635 at a cost of £5.10s. It originally stood half way down the nave against the S. wall. In 1717 a sounding board was suspended over it and in 1777 the Trumpeting Angel (now on the organ screen) was added.

The Trumpeting Angel.

The Royal Arms were presented to the church in 1799 by Thomas Huckell Lee. In the tower are painted boards giving details of some of the *Charities* in the parish. The South transept, or "Drake Aisle" as it is known, contains an elaborately quartered *Drake Hatchment.*

Cranmer's Great Bible can be seen in a case at the W. end. It is one of the first five editions, printed in 1549. Originally it was chained to its wooden lectern. For years it mouldered away in the Parish Chest, unrecognised, and was finally identified and repaired by the British Museum in 1960.

The Embroidered Kneelers are a memorial to the Rev'd. Dr. William Keble Martin, the famous botanist, who chose to spend his last years in Woodbury and died in 1969, much loved and respected. The designs depict wild flowers from his "Concise British Flora".

The Church-wardens' Staves were given in 1963 in memory of Harry Stokes II, bell-hanger, and church-warden for 17 years.

Monuments

There is nothing particularly remarkable about the monuments in the church but as we wander round we meet many of our old friends who have appeared in this book and their quiet resting places and simple floor slabs mean all the more because we have come to know them. George and Robert Venn and their sister Mrs. Matthew Lee lie in front of the memorial organ screen. The Lees, of course, are mostly buried at Gulliford but wall plaques behind the organ pipes recall their family life and their services to the parish — and rightly so. Several generations of those splendid Holwells and one of the Goves sleep under the floor of the Haydon aisle. Richard Haydon's stone has to be searched out. It is between the Venns and the lectern, much damaged and stripped of its original brasses which were no doubt melted down for munitions during the Commonwealth. The Glanvills are commemorated on a tablet by the S. door, Philip Lemprière and his poor Mary on the N. wall. On the floor of the N. aisle, by the screen gate, is one of the most quoted epitaphs in England. It remembers Wm. Cooke and his wife of Cooke's Farm:-

"Hee first decesed
Shee for a little tryed
To live without him
Liked it not and Dyed".

The chancel has witnessed many burials from Nutwell. We have already noted several Dinham burials in the 15th c. and until 1840 there was still a Dinham floor-slab in front of the Communion rails, dated 1483[5] but there is no trace of it now. The handsome black marble stone with armorial bearings covers all that remains of Sir Henry Pollexfen of Nutwell, M.P. for Exeter in 1688 and Lord Chief Justice of the Common Pleas. He died in 1691. *Sic transit gloria mundi!*

A monument on the S. wall commemorates Thomas Heathfield of Upper Nutwell and his wife Mary. One of the four generations of Heathfields there, they rendered sterling service to the parish in their quiet and unassuming way in the late 18th century. A Broadmead Trustee and a generous benefactor, Heathfield always had the good of his fellows at heart. There is often confusion between Thos. Heathfield of Upper Nutwell and Lord Heathfield of Nutwell Court but they were in no way related.

Mystery surrounds the identity of the effigies which lie on their table tomb on the N. side of the high altar. It has been said that they represent Sir Thomas Prideaux (died 1640) and his wife Joan Cole, and that they were transferred to St. Swithin's from the private chapel at Nutwell when the property was sold in 1647. But there are considerable difficulties about the theory. The figures have been quite badly damaged while the table tomb on which they repose has not. If they had been newly made in the private chapel at the time of the Civil War at what point in history were they damaged? Nutwell was garrisoned for Parliament while the Prideaux were in residence and was not sacked.

A plaque behind their heads bears the date 1610 but no member of the family was buried between 1605 and 1619. Furthermore, the straight gown and small ruff of the lady and the full, gathered trunks of the man are more typical of the 16th c. than the 17th. More important, perhaps, is the stone behind their feet with a badly-damaged heraldic device showing three shadowy long bows and what are known as bowyers' knots. As far as can be made out these arms are similar to those granted to John Prideaux in 1558, the year of his death. In 1594 his son changed them and had the bowyers' knots omitted.[6] If the arms are really part of the effigies (they are not attached) they can only possibly relate of John Prideaux and the probability is that the figures represent John and his wife, Mary Stukeley. All the Prideaux are buried in Woodbury church, not at Nutwell, but the effigies may well have been in the chapel there, damaged by time and removal, and put on a new table tomb specially made for them in 1647. The date 1610 on the wall at their head is in that case unrelated. There was considerable reshuffling in that area when the Vestry was built and again later when Fulford altered the position of the vestry door.

The Bells (by the Rev'd J.G.M. Scott)[7]

There is no ring of eight in the county with such an interesting and well-documented history as the bells in the tower of St. Swithin's. There are bells here by six different founders and the church-wardens' accounts give much fascinating information about them. The Commissioners who made an inventory of the church goods in 1553 recorded:- "Wodebery V belles yn the towre their". The only mediaeval survivor is the sixth bell cast in Bristol in the early 16th century and inscribed "Sancta Maria ora pro T". But it is possible that two other bells recast in 1557 dated from the previous century when the tower was built.

The church-wardens have left us a graphic description of the recasting, from their "striking" and the "drinking for them that went forth that carried the bells to Aishe Priors at Richard Bussell's" through the three-day journey via Larkbeare, Milverton and Halse to the foundry of Roger Semson at Aishe Priors and the five-day stay there while the bells were cast, to the two-day return trip and the triumphant entry, "It'm pd. att Jane Bussell's homeward for drinking . . . iiijd". Presumably the Bussells kept an inn on the way. Fourteen oxen drew the bells there and back, and five men and a church-warden went with them. Roger Semson was paid £23.18s.2d. in four instalments.

In 1605 the second of the five (now the sixth) was recast by Thomas Byrdall II of Exeter whose son, John, recast the present fourth in 1624, putting his initials on his bell in his usual very ornate letters. Thomas Pennington II of Exeter recast the 24 cwt. tenor in 1629. She bears the inscription "Drawe neare unto God". When the bell-founder came to see the bells, when they took down and loaded the tenor and at

Rehanging of the Bells of St. Swithins — June 1960
Back Row: J. Briggs, A. Gooding, J. Gooding, H. Miller, V. Fox, K. Dawe, J.L.S. Glanvill (Ringing Master), J.H. Glanville.
Front Row: J. Sellick (Sexton), A.E. Osmond (Vicar), A.G. Betts, C. Morrish, A. Stamp, B. Stamp, W. Reeves (Ch. W.), H. Stokes (Ch. W.) W. Theobold (Bell-hanger).

every other stage of the operation there was an item for beer and bread — mostly beer. The total comes to 10s.2d., a formidable gallonage in 1629. When this tenor bell became crazed during the late 19th century Harry Stokes shrank an iron band over her shoulders and she remained in use until the last restoration in 1956 when she was recast.

In 1677 the great Thomas Purdue of Somerset, who recast Exeter Cathedral's celebrated 'Peter' bell, recast Woodbury's present seventh. This is a very fine bell, like most of his, finely decorated and full of music. That remarkable man died in 1711 at the age of 90 and on his grave-stone at Closworth is the epitaph:

"Here lies the bell founder honest and true
Till ye resurrection — named Purdue".

The former treble bell (now the 3rd) was bought in 1720 but proved unsatisfactory and had to be recast twice. The present Treble and 2nd were added in 1898 as a memorial to the Rev'd J.L. Fulford, thus making the full octave for the first time. Unfortunately the foundation timbers of the splendid frame put in by Harry Stokes in 1897 were allowed to become infected with rot and had to be replaced in 1956. The work was carried out and the bells rehung in a steel frame by Mears and Stainbank of the famous Whitechapel Foundry. At the same time it was decided to bring the bells down lower in the tower to reduce the tower sway which made this sizeable eight somewhat heavy to ring.

Woodbury has a good tradition of change-ringing and the bells are still kept going, while touring bands always find them well worth a visit.

The Church Clock (by the Rev'd J.G.M. Scott)

The Church had a clock as early as 1538, when it is referred to in the Churchwardens' Accounts. Like most early church clocks, it probably then had no outside dial and only struck the hours. By 1696 the development of the pendulum had brought a new standard of accuracy to clockmaking, and the parishioners spent two shillings on "beare" at a meeting "to talk with the man about the Clock". "The man" was a local clockmaker named Gould or Gold, and in 1697 he made a new clock and dial and a "quarter clock", a separate movement to chime the quarters. He was paid £7 for the clock and dial and 10s.6d. for the quarter-clock, which was so cheap at this time that one suspects that he may have used much of the old mechanism. When the clock was finally scrapped its iron weighed 506 lb, which would have been an unusual figure for a late 17th-century clock even if it included the chime-barrel.

The chime-barrel, playing tunes on the bells after the striking of the hour at intervals during the day, was a popular device in the 18th century, though few survive in use today. A chime-barrel is mentioned in the accounts at various times during the 18th and early 19th centuries, but Woodbury's seems to have vanished in 1846. The tunes were altered more than once, to conform with musical fashion.

The clock of 1697 was given an overhaul in Topsham in 1782, and a new "dile" was made by William Pannell of Lympstone for £5.5s. In 1815 repairs cost £12, and by 1846 the old movement must have been past its useful life. To replace it a public subscription raised £125 and a new clock was bought from E.J. Dent of London. Dr. Brent was the instigator and Sir Thomas Trayton Drake the chief subscriber.

This was one of Dent's very earliest turret-clocks, and was designed on the "flat-bed" principle which had been developed in France. The movement, which includes a quarter-chiming train with the timekeeping and striking in one frame, is rather small for the work it has to do. Later Dent was to make Big Ben for the Houses of Parliament.

The quarters are chimed on the 3rd and 5th bells, and the hours struck on the Tenor. One problem with which the clock has to cope is the sway of the tower when the bells are ringing. Though this is less severe since the bells were rehung, it is still noticeable, and there was one occasion when the clock had been stopped deliberately to set it back five minutes, and the tower-sway was enough to make it start again unaided.

Music

Music has always played an important part in the life of Woodbury church on account of the close connection with the College of Vicars Choral. In pre-Reformation days particularly, the Vicars who served the church as curates were professional musicians providing the Cathedral with choral music of the highest order at a time when English church music led the world. There are plenty of indications that they did their best to ensure a good standard here also. 1540 has an entry:- "Brede and wyne for John to syng mass wt. all", and references to the children's "rochetts" (surplices) point to a choir of boy trebles. They were accompanied by what was quaintly known as "a peire of Organs", renewed in 1539 by Richard Chapendon for £5.13s.4d., "the olde Organs geven wt. all yn exchange". New "pyppes" and bellows were supplied in 1585.

During the Cromwellian Commonwealth music in church was considered profane but with the Restoration in 1660 Woodbury immediately built a gallery across the west end of the nave for the singers, accompanied by viol, bass-viol and hautboy (oboe). For 200 years the music for the services came from this gallery, behind the congregation, and the choir-stalls fell out of use. In 1802 a barrel-organ was purchased in London and Thomas Huckell Lee was paid £11.72. for arranging the transport and obtaining a faculty for its installation. From these descriptions and from the many items in the accounts for anthem books, manuscript paper, repair of "ten tunes on the organ", candles for the singers and "Singers Salery £5" it seems that fairly strenuous efforts were being made, at a time of great laxity in church affairs, to keep the music going.

Fulford completely restored the chancel and returned the choir to their choir-stalls in 1862 — though not without terrible eruptions in the Vestry meeting which tried hard to prevent him. It shows the depths to which the standard of worship had fallen that a trained, robed choir in the chancel was considered "popery". Fulford himself was a fine musician and he trained the choir for many years. The next rumpus was caused by the purchase of a pipe-organ which he installed, without a faculty, in the E. end of the Haydon aisle. But matters came to a head when he appointed an organist from Topsham without consulting his church-wardens. A furious Vestry meeting discussed this latest outrage and countered Fulford's high-handedness by locking the organ and confiscating the key. As usual, Fulford professed amazement at their wrath and a compromise was found when the post was advertised and only the organist from Topsham applied![8]

"The Green Organ", as it was known on account of the colour of the pipes, served until 1920 when a subscription was raised for a War Memorial and the £1000 collected bought an instrument by Brindley and Foster and a War Memorial screen to enclose it. In 1964 it was rebuilt and enlarged by Hill, Norman and Beard and now has electro-pneumatic action, two manuals, 34 drawstops and a detached console. Dare one look forward to the day when church organs no longer make such colossal demands on space? How fine the church would look if the Haydon Aisle's E. end and the canopied recess could be restored to something like Richard Haydon's original vision!

The Churchyard

Like all ancient churchyards Woodbury's is raised high above its surrounding lane by many centuries of burials. Though there are no gravestones older than the 18th century the ground must have been buried over many times. In early times it was used for grazing and the animals were kept in by a fence of brushwood.

"1540 for Caryeng of Thornys and Frethyng of the haygge of the church yerde. 2s.
1593 To Dennis Splatte for geathringe upp of Donge in the churchyeard — 4d."

Entry to the churchyard was gained by four stiles, presumably one at Church Stile, one at each of the steps and one alongside the main South gate. "1544 to John Baggewyll and his man for making the four Church Styles in the churchyard —

17s.6d." Hardly a year went by but a new lock for the gate was bought.

There were elm trees in the churchyard and in 1648 some were felled, the ground levelled and more trees planted. There were also, of course, yew trees for the provision of long bows of which the two great trees, one on the North side, the other on the South, are almost certainly offspring, though the tree on the North side is very much older and could possibly have provided the twenty-three archers with their bows in 1569. The tree on the South side was planted in 1775. The Vestry book notes that in that year it was prised out of the North wall of the tower, about 9ft. down from the top. It was 4ft. high, reputed to be nine years old and replaced an old yew tree blown down in a gale. The first mention of building the churchyard wall comes in 1660 and that was probably the wall seen in the 19th c. engraving. The present wall is of three different dates, the main part of it built in 1871 and the church-wardens for that year, Thos. Ware and John Cole, left their names to posterity on one of the steps. The demolition of the cottages which had been the Church House on the southern edge of the churchyard necessitated the filling and levelling of the space and a new wall in 1874.

The Hon. Mark Rolle gave an extension of the churchyard on the west side in 1904 – the line of the old boundary wall can still be seen. And the lychgate was built in 1903, a memorial to Mr. Charles Fulford.

Nutwell Court

Nutwell Court, a small estate in the south of the parish bordering the River Exe, has had a long and well-documented history. First mention of it appears in Domesday Book 1086:- "Donne has a manor called Noteswilla which he himself held on the day that King Edward was alive and dead and it paid geld for 1½ hides. This 6 ploughs can till. Thereof D has 1 hide and 1 plough in demesne, and the villeins ½ hide and two ploughs. There D has 7 villeins, 4 borders, 2 serfs, 100 sheep all but 7. Four acres of meadow and 5 acres of pasture. Worth 20 shillings".

So Donne, Nutwell's Saxon owner, was able to keep it after the conquest — as he also kept his other manor at Newton St. Cyres. Nutwell (Nota's Well?) comprised nearly 500 acres on which were seven villeins' farms and 4 bordars' smallholdings — eleven housholds with a total population of 50 or 60 people. With only 200 acres of ploughland, the manor was mainly given over to sheep. No mill was required. When we next see Nutwell, 250 years later, there are still eleven householders listed. This is in the Devon Lay Subsidy for 1332 — a tax levied on certain types of personal possessions (not property). Peter Dovedale, John Le Rede and Thomas Poye were each assessed at 2/-, two others at 12p and the remaining six at 8d. — the minimum. Presuming that there were some householders below taxable level, it looks as if Nutwell had grown a little since Domesday — but not much — and the level of taxation makes it clear that there was no 'big house' in occupation at Nutwell in 1332. There is little doubt that at this time Nutwell was a village and there would have been a cluster of houses in the area that is now the Park.

In 1316 we find a brief reference to the fact that Geoffrey de Albemarle owned Nutwell, along with Woodbury and Lympstone,[1] but as it does not appear to have been his at the time of his death in 1321 he probably sold it to the Dinhams between the two dates. The Dinhams had come over with William the Conqueror in 1066 from Dinant in Brittany and their principal seat was at Hartland in N. Devon. But in 1371 they successfully applied to the Bishop of Exeter for a licence to build a chapel at

Nutwell and this, though drastically altered, is the oldest surviving building now remaining. Their "castle", as Risdon called it, presumably dated from the same time, together with the two-storeyed gatehouse which stood until 1755.[2] Sir John Dinham, who came to fame in the reign of Edward IV (1461-83) was born at Nutwell. He was created a baron for his loyalty to the king. (See p.62).

Throughout the 15th century there are frequent references to Nutwell and the Dinhams in the Accounts of the College of Vicars Choral. The Vicars sometimes had difficulty in keeping track of their dues in Woodbury and in 1426 an entry in the accounts reads:-

"Expenses of John Fowlere (vicar) in going to Notwell to bring the body of Robert Daldyche to the parish church of Woodbury, but before he got there the body was taken to another place assigned by John Denham."

This entry followed in 1440:- "Mortuaries after the deaths of . . . and William Werde, esquire, a stranger who died at Notewyll: the mortuary of William Werde was a gown and this was accepted on condition that it should be proved that William had no better goods there, but if he had something better it should not be withheld in deception of our mother church, because it was said by trustworthy people that he had a horse which ought to be given as a mortuary . . ." However, the horse failed to materialize and the Vicars reluctantly accepted the gown.[3]

It was during Edward IV's reign that Dinham pulled down the castle and built an elegant manor-house into which the chapel of 1371 was incorporated. Risdon writing in 1630 described it as a "fair and stately dwelling house. It standeth very low by an arm of the sea, so that the high floods rise almost to the house". It is known to have had a "great hall" and a "little chamber over the porch".

The first Lord Dinham was also the last. He had no son and when he died in 1501 one of his four daughters sold Nutwell to John Prideaux, Sergeant at Law, and a relative by marriage. The Prideaux family held it for four generations and were followed by a nephew, Sir Henry Ford. In 1685 Nutwell became the property of Sir Henry Pollexfen, a barrister of the Inner Temple. That was the year of Monmouth's Rebellion and Pollexfen sat with the notorious Judge Jeffrys at the Bloody Assizes when the wretched survivors of that ill-conceived rising were convicted and barbarously dealt with. Later Pollexfen became Member of Parliament for Exeter and Lord Chief Justice of the Common Pleas. He is buried in Woodbury church.

"The fair dwelling house" had fallen into a sad state of decay when young Henry Pollexfen (the last of his line) and his bride, Gertrude Drake of Buckland Abbey, inherited it in 1699. It was not until £500 had been spent and three years had elapsed that the young Pollexfens could finally make Nutwell their home. From this time onwards until 1938 members of the Drake family lived at Nutwell. Henry Pollexfen's sister, Elizabeth, married Gertrude's brother Francis, so the families were doubly linked. When Henry and Gertrude died childless it was natural that Nutwell should go to the Drakes.

At this point confusion often arises and it must be made quite clear that Nutwell was never the home of the famous admiral, nor of his direct descendants. Sir Francis had no children and the line descended from his brother Thomas. But the Drake family were very much aware and proud of their famous relative and over the years an enormous collection of Drake relics was built up and housed at Nutwell. It included portraits, gifts from Queen Elizabeth, mementos of his journeys and

Sir Henry Pollexfen, Knt. M.P.
Chief Justice of the Common Pleas
1689 – artist unknown.

Anne Pollexfen Drake
(Grand-daughter of the Chief Justice)
c.1710 — artist unknown.

A Section of Benjamin Donn's Map.

victories, letters, maps and the world famous "Drake's Drum". Most of them are now at Buckland Abbey where they can be seen by the public, and where all the Nutwell Drakes are buried.

In 1754 the fifth baronet, yet another Sir Francis, inherited Nutwell and began a long and disastrous series of alterations and "improvements". It is evident that by this time the humble dwellings of ordinary mortals had been banished from the vicinity of the big house and had re-appeared round the edges of what was to become the Park — at Upper Nutwell, Ash Trees and Gulliford. At first the new work at Nutwell was hampered by the great fears the carpenters and other labourers had of the press-gang, and the agent, writing his progress-reports to Sir Francis in London, described how the men would go into hiding for days on end when the press-gang was rumoured to be operating in the nearby ports of Topsham and Lympstone. Unfortunately for Nutwell, work finally proceeded and as Sir Francis's enthusiasm mounted and eventually ran away with him the house was practically rebuilt, the chapel gutted and turned into a library. He took out the Gothic windows, which contained beautiful mediaeval painted glass (accidently smashed in the process) and replaced them with the square-headed mock-Tudor ones. The original wagon roof was cut through and a new plaster ceiling suspended, while the chapel was divided in two, to provide more wall-space for his books. The ancient gatehouse was razed to the ground with the greatest difficulty — an "improvement" about which his agent had the gravest doubts.

Nutwell Court from the Exe before the coming of the railway in 1860-1.

Sir Francis was a bachelor and in his will he left Nutwell to his brother-in-law, Col. the Hon. Francis Augustus Eliot, afterwards the 1st Lord Heathfield of Gibraltar; but Heathfield died four years before Drake and it was his son, the 2nd Lord Heathfield who inherited Nutwell in 1796. Heathfield, also a bachelor, had his own ideas about Nutwell and converted the entrance hall into a 'Greek Temple', with chequered marble floor, classical columns and carved marble plaques round the wall. But horses were the great love of his life and for them he built the stud-stable and the great indoor riding school in about 1800. He also created the Park, building the long brick wall and diverting the Exton—Lympstone road in order to do so — to the intense annoyance and inconvenience of the locals. The early 19th century saw a great flowering of county estates such as Nutwell, with imaginative tree-planting of parkland, the landscaping of lakes and 'vistas'', and the provision of covers for game and fox-hunting.

When Lord Heathfield died in 1813 the brood-mares were sold[4] and Nutwell passed to his sister's son, Maj. Thomas Trayton Fuller. The Drake baronetcy had lapsed but Thomas added the names Eliot-Drake to Fuller and, after considerable effort and expenditure, managed to get the title revived in his favour.[5] It was during Sir Thomas's time at Nutwell that the Exeter—Exmouth branch railway arrived. There was no question of diverting the line — it runs along the river-bank in full view of the house — but it may have been a help that Dr. Robert Brent (a director of the railway) was acting as estate agent for Sir Thomas at that time.[6] Besides handsome compensation, he obtained concessions by which the embankment was landscaped and planted with rhododendrons, and a sluice-gate installed to control the water from the lake into the estuary, for which the railway was (and still is) responsible.

Sir Trayton Eliot-Drake lived to a good age and died in 1871. He was succeeded by his son Sir Francis George Augustus Fuller-Eliot-Drake who stayed curiously out of the lime-light and disappeared from view long before his death. His estate was managed by Mr. John Hallett of Gulliford Farm.[7] and his share of the lime-light was amply occupied by his formidable wife, Lady Drake, still well remembered in Woodbury. She died in 1925.

During the Second World War Nutwell again fell on evil days. It was commandeered by the army and the grounds became a lorry park. Some of the fine timber was felled; other trees, marked for felling, survived. In 1941 the estate was bought by Mr. George Northcott, the well-known Devon philanthropist, who spent the rest of his life bringing both house and land back from yet another sorry state of neglect.

DINHAM

PRIDEAUX

POLLEXFEN

DRAKE

The Great Field

There have been references in earlier chapters to the Open Field system of agriculture. So vast are the differences between that system and any sort of farming practised in Woodbury within living memory that it is worth attempting to explain it and taking a look at the evidence for its existence here in Woodbury.

Nowadays a few farmers produce food for the great majority who grow nothing and our needs are supplemented by imports from abroad. Ease of transport has meant that areas can specialize in what they can best produce and Woodbury now produces very little corn but something like 750,000 gallons of milk annually, against actual consumption of about 50,000 gallons — though that takes no account of butter and cheese.

It was not always so. When the first Saxons arrived to make a settlement in Woodbury some 1,300 years ago they probably brought with them a system of agriculture with which they were familiar. Until recent years it was thought that Open Field farming did not reach mediaeval Devon. Now, thanks to the work of the late Prof. H.P.R. Finberg, Prof. W.G. Hoskins, Dr. Harold Fox and others[1] it is recognized as having been fairly widespread in Devon, wherever the terrain was suitable, up to the 15th century. But evidence is hard to find — visual evidence especially. There are no great sweeps of ridge and furrow so characteristic of the Midland landscape — perhaps because Open Field farming died a natural death here in the late middle-ages, whereas elsewhere in England much of it survived until the Enclosure Acts. In some places small areas of it survive yet.[2]

It is due to these later survivals that we know something about how it worked.[3] It was based very largely on self-sufficiency and communal effort. In early times a form of communal farming was likely to be the most economical use of both land and man-power and there was neither incentive nor labour to produce more than the village community required for its own needs. As ground was cleared in the immediate vicinity of the settlement it was cultivated in long, narrow strips each representing a day's ploughing. Starting with a central ridge formed by turning the second furrow back on top of the first ("gathering it together" as Woodbury ploughmen say), the 8-ox team would plough up one side and down the other, getting further from the ridge with each journey, till the day's work was done and a strip approximately 220 x 22 yds (an acre) had been ploughed. Woodbury farmers call this a "pitch" — a word closely related to the Saxon "pyght", used to describe a strip in the Open Field.

Not every farmer in Woodbury farmed in the Open Field. From the early days of the settlement there were surely some individual farms and the two systems co-existed. But whereas the freeholder would be likely to have his own plough and ox-team, the farmer in the Open Field shared on a communal basis. In 1086 Woodbury's 30 farmers and 22 small-holders had 20 ploughs between them, so communal ploughing was certainly going on; as one might say, today Tom's strip because Tom owns the plough, tomorrow Dick's strip alongside Tom's because Dick owns the leading pair of oxen, and afterwards Harry's alongside Dick's — and so on until it was Tom's turn again. So, though one farmer might have many strips in one 'field', it is unlikely that he would have two strips side by side. The strips were divided from one another by some means of which we cannot be sure: just a "vore" as Woodbury farmers say? A balk of earth or grass? Stakes or stones? The nature of these "landmarks" has been lost to us but there is no doubt that our early farmers knew precisely the meaning of the Bible words "Cursed be he who removeth his neighbour's landmark".

The strips in one 'field' were sown with one season's crops — say, winter wheat — so that work could be done together and the land, after harvest, used for communal grazing. The work of the fields was supervised by a 'jury' of farmers who decided when a crop should be harvested and when the animals could be depastured on the stubble. It was also their job to sort out any disputes that arose (moving 'landmarks', for instance) and to make sure that fields containing growing crops had stock-proof boundaries. In Woodbury it is probable that some of these boundaries were of a temporary nature, erected between, say, beans or peas and depastured fallow-land or drove-road, and made of stakes and brushwood — "freythyng", as Woodbury churchwardens called such a fence made to contain animals grazing the churchyard in the 16th century.

From the small beginnings in the Parsonage, Pound Lane, Long Meadow and Town Lane areas, the great expanse of communal ploughland may well have reached 1000 acres by the 13th century and was still pushing out towards Salterton and Heathfield. The landlord himself had two ploughs representing possibly 120 acres,[5] and his gift of grazing rights for the Parsonage animals in c. 1225[6] mentions 16 oxen (two plough teams) from which it can be inferred that Parsonage had a similar amount of arable. The tenant also had rights to pass to and fro over the landlord's fields to carry crops and marl the land; so to some extent, at any rate, Parsonage arable was intermixed with the landlord's strips in the Open Fields. When Geoffrey Albemarle died in 1321 he had "24 tenants holding a ferling (20 acres?) apiece". Such an equal division of land could only be achieved in communal strips and this is confirmed when, at Wm. Albermarle's death in 1363, his arable land was described as "worth nought when it is sown because the land lies in common"[7] – in other words, his land was interspersed with the strips of his tenants and subject to common grazing after harvest, so that it could not be profitably let. These references alone account for nearly 800 acres; but there may have been more. Geoffrey Albemarle sold land in Woodbury to Phillip Oakbeare – possibly Bridge Farm, Salterton – so the Oakbeare family were freeholders. Yet when the Vicars Choral accounts begin in the 15th century we find William Oakbeare holding "parcels" (i.e. strips) of land in "the Great Field called Windmyllfeld". Other freeholders, besides the Oakbeares, may have done the same.

It is in the Vicars Choral accounts that we actually find the names of some of Woodbury's 'Great Fields', as they were called.[8] Windmillfield rose up behind Parsonage and probably embraced all the land from the top of Windmill Hill to Watery Lane. A second Great Field was called Clayhill Park, probably adjoining Windmillfield and stretching almost to Salterton and from Deepway to Bonds Lane. The area still contains a field called Clayhill. A close look at the 1809 O.S. map tells us where the old boundaries of these huge fields may have been. A third area is identified as "the Great Field called Brodpark". This might have been the name given to a broad but shallow 'field', perhaps only one strip deep, occupying the E. side of Town Lane, where the name Broadpark still survives. As the land slopes uphill it soon meets the spring-line of the Common and would not have been attractive ploughland while there was better to be had elsewhere.

It is tempting to identify another 'field', of which we do not know the name, as occupying the area bounded by Exeter Road, Oakhayes Road, Watery Lane and Bonds Lane. It is still neatly divided down the middle into two rows of fields, approximately 220 yds long. An inspection of the boundary hedges, particularly in Oakhayes Road and Bonds Lane, reveals a large amount of holly — that tenacious and persistent relic of the original ground cover — which sought refuge from the plough in the ancient boundaries and is not to be found in any of the much later, intersecting hedges. Here and there these large arable fields had to accommodate small woods, ponds and wet lands. Occasionally two blocks of strips would meet at an awkward angle, leaving a triangular piece that could not easily be ploughed. Woodbury's Great Field had such a piece, referred to as "Konynnger (i.e. rabbit warren) *alias* the Gore"[4] — the name by which it is still known.

Watery Lane was much more than a division between two Great Fields. It was perfectly placed (and deeply sunk) to serve as the principal drove road along which livestock could safely be driven from the heart of the village, through growing crops, to the distant grazing grounds at 'le Hethfyld'.[9]

It goes without saying that such an intricate pattern of strips and fields presented enormous problems of access if work were to be done in the furthest fields without damaging crops nearer home. Even the headland required to manoeuvre and turn a plough with 4 pairs of oxen must have been considerable if neighbours' strips were not to be trampled. Yet most of the access roads are still there on the 6″ map — the lanes already mentioned together with Moor Lane, Higher and Lower Roads at Salterton and a maze of footpaths, to which might be added some interesting continuous lines of hedges that possibly indicate the positions of old greenways and headlands. All these would be perfectly known and understood by the farmers who had the regular use of them. They were kept open by the continual passage of the plough teams in spring, and the laden carts at harvest bringing the corn home to the stack-yards in the village. Only as the Great Fields broke up would some of these ways fall out of use and becomes forgotten.

The process of 'marling' was important. Mediaeval farm implements did little more than scuffle the soil to a depth of 2 or 3 inches and seed was broadcast by hand. The weather in the first half of the 13th century (when the marling rights were given) was drier and warmer than now and there was serious risk of the corn drying out. So marl (clay with small stones) was liberally spread in an attempt to conserve moisture and cover the seed. The best marl was to be found near Pilehayes, where there was a large marl-pit from which Woodbury farmers obtained marl for centuries.

Animals fared less well in the Open Field system. They were of secondary importance and the impossibility of controlling disease or of practising selective breeding tended to perpetuate a generally low standard. Requirements were few: sheep for wool; cattle for dairy produce, meat and leather; pigs for meat; draught oxen and a few fowl. In the early days, when the supply of land seemed endless, animals could be grazed without restriction in the wastes and woods. As the population grew and pressure for more corn-land mounted, the utmost ingenuity was needed to wring every possibility out of the land. Besides the small paddocks attached to the farms in the village, there was controlled grazing, not only on the wastes and fallow, but even on the greenways, verges, headlands and any odd unploughable corner where animals could be tethered.

With little winter feed, hay was the all-important fodder crop and the rent for meadow was three times that of arable. At least some of Woodbury's meadows would be shared out in plots, each equal to a day's mowing with a scythe, and each farmer cut and gathered his stint of hay before turning out his quota of livestock. The 'common grazing' of meadows was strictly limited in time to prevent the meadows being damaged by over-cropping. Common sense suggests that much of the 30 acres of meadow mentioned in Domesday was along the Gillbrook between the village and Venmore. This is borne out by the significant name "Ham Lane". The "hams" were stinted (i.e. allotted) pasture.[10]

Why and when the Open Field system in Woodbury came to an end we shall never know. It was a gradual process. Perhaps the growing demand for sheep's wool upset the old balance: perhaps the Fields became too big to be practical, for documentary evidence suggests that the area finally stretched as far as Heathfield and Salterton. Imagine the long trek farmers in Woodbury village must have had! The sudden appearance of new farms at Salterton in the first half of the 14th century may mean that the Great Fields were being worked from a new and more convenient starting point. In the middle of this large area was the curious anomaly of Pilehayes. As the name suggests, Pilehayes was an enclosed farm from the start, for 'hayes' means enclosure. And though the Great Field advanced and finally enveloped Pilehayes, it remained aloof. First noted in 1306[11], Pilehayes might be much older. An aerial photograph taken in 1946[12] reveals the old marks of a great many sub-divisions of the present fields into very small square fields, quite unlike anything in the Great Field. It is a good example of how the two types of farming existed side by side.

By the end of the 15th century documentary evidence gives us a few glimpses of the Great Field as it neared the end of its days. In 1473 the Vicars Choral were renting out "parcels", sometimes described as "closes" (i.e. enclosures) in the Great Field for as much as 40s. Such substantial rents represented large holdings of strips and it sounds as if strips were being reorganized and consolidated until enough could be got together to warrant enclosure. Further light is shed on this swopping process by an entry in the accounts for 1481. It concerns a dispute between the Vicars and Cecily Bonville's husband, the Marquis of Dorset, about the ownership of strips in the Pilehayes area. Reference is made to "odd parcels of land" belonging to the Marquis "lying interspersed with the land of the Custos and College of the Vicars Choral . . . and the Custos etc. are seized of other parcels of land in the said closes and places interspersed with the land of the said Lord . . . for the greater peace and quietness of their respective tenants it is agreed that the said Custos etc. shall have all the parcels of land belonging to the said Lord . . . lying to the east of the ditch upon Pile Down, newly made with the consent both of the said Lord and Custos etc. leading from north to south, in exchange for all those parcels of the Custos on the west side of the said new ditch".[13] The ditch is still there. It runs, due north/south from Higher Pilehayes to Lower Pilehayes and along its edge is an ancient footpath. It still divides ownerships of land.

Cecily Bonville long outlived her Marquis and when an inventory was made of her lands in Woodbury in c. 1525 we find that one of her tenants in Salterton held 32 acres of which "26 lie in the Common Field". This does not necessarily mean that only 26 acres of the Great Fields were left. It is more likely that Salterton had its own Great Field still surviving of which Cecily Bonville had 26 acres which could not be (or had not been) extracted. Some of Salterton's "fossilized" strips are still plainly to be seen and continued to be held in a complicated alternating ownership into modern times. There is also strong evidence in maps, fields and lanes that the manor of Ebford had its own Great Field, but we know nothing of it.

It had been a remarkably democratic system. Tenants had a far greater authority for the running of the village than they have now. Drawbacks there obviously were. It provided little scope for improvement, no incentive for the energetic and progressive. In recent years we have seen many failures of collective farming methods imposed for reasons of political ideology. Yet we can all share a twinge of nostalgia with C.S. Orwin when he writes:— "Instead of sharing, turn and turn about with his neighbours in the administration of the affairs of the village, the reponsibilities of the individual today extend no further than holding up a hand at a meeting or making a cross on a ballot paper."[14]

Building Materials

Any special qualities the old buildings of Woodbury may possess are due more to the materials of which they are made than to any other single factor. In an area not particularly blessed with good building materials Woodbury has, over the centuries, made very adequate use of those that came immediately to hand – sometimes imaginative and pleasing use. Nowadays transport is no problem and bricks, blocks, tiles, windows and doors come from all over the country; but until the coming of the railways necessity compelled all but the wealthiest to use purely local materials and it is such homely substances as cob, thatch, pebbles, sandstone, home-grown oak and elm and (later) bricks, allied to the skills and idiosyncracies of village craftsmen, that ensure the uniqueness of Woodbury's buildings. They are part of the landscape and their subtle blend of colour and texture creates a harmony always easy on the eye.

Stone

This not being a good building-stone parish, it was necessary to import most of the stone of which St. Swithin's church was made. The oldest parts (13thc.) show a great variety of stones none of which journeyed more than a few miles. Of these Pocombe trap rock is the most easily identifiable. It is a plum-red-brown volcanic stone characterised by narrow veins of whitish marble running through it. Killerton and Thorverton trap, also used, are much the same colour but have minute holes formed while the lava was in a molten state. These volcanic rocks are immensely strong, and together with the much softer local sandstones and limestones, manage to give a pleasantly warm grey appearance.

The tower, added in 1407-9 is of squared, dressed stone, closely pointed. Though here again several types were used most of the stone is Salcombe Regis sandstone, one of the finest building stones in the South West and much used in Exeter Cathedral. The N. aisle, added in 1530-3 is mainly of a soft, local red sandstone which has not weathered well. Oral tradition has it that the stone came from a small quarry beyond Venmore, now filled in. Pillars, arches and other details of the interior are of Beer stone, that most beautiful of all limestones which adorns so many churches in East Devon and makes them always worth a visit.

It is probable that the great tithe barn at Parsonage was built partly or mainly of Salcombe Regis stone, for such of it as could be re-used can be seen in Woodbury Salterton church, particularly in the west end and north-west wall of the nave. The

Parsonage House
(as rebuilt by Fulford in 1849) Drawn by Fergus Kyle.

present Parsonage House built in 1849, incorporates much of the rest of the stone salvaged from the old complex of buildings, together with Killerton and Thorverton trap and local red sandstone. Since the bill for stone was £30 it is obvious that very little transport was involved and the Salcombe stone was reused.[1]

Most of the red sandstone at Parsonage and in the church was probably quarried in the parish. Written evidence of quarries exists in the 15th century[2] and old field-names mark their location. Quarry Park, north of Parsonage, is a case in point and before the pit was filled in recently (1980) the old sandstone face could be seen which probably produced the stone not only for the buildings mentioned above but also for Parsonage Pound in mediaeval times. The quarry and the pound both belonged to the College of Vicars Choral and scarcely 300 yards separate the two sites. Why should the Vicars look further afield? When the pound was demolished in 1922 the best stones were re-used in the plinth of Parsonage Cross where they can still be seen. Local sandstone also found its way into the foundations of the best cob houses and large blocks of it form the footings and fireplace at Lower Bagmores at Exton. Salterton buildings tended to favour Heavitree breccia, as can be seen at Greendale Barton and the roadside barn at Butleys Heath. It is more usual, however, to find the largest-sized 'popples' from the Common pebble beds used in this way and the bulge of their shoulders often protrudes slightly under a disguise of pitch — as is clearly seen at 'Ridges' in Salterton.

The Victorians had an unfortunate passion for the cold, hard, blue-grey limestone from the Torquay-Newton Abbott area which was shipped into Exmouth in large quantities. While it may look clean and bright in the glare of sea-side sunshine it is less at home in red earth country and the difficulty of cutting and dressing it led to a random use that can never produce anything but second-rate architecture. It is to be seen in Woodbury in many places — the east churchyard wall, the roadside wall at

Christ Church and the wall which divides the Arch from Oakhayes Lawn. Where the stones are placed up on end along the top they suggest nothing so much as those forbidding walls set with broken bottles to deter small boys from climbing them. The Rolle Estate made better use of the stone for farm-building at Rydon, Exton Barton and elsewhere, by using it in conjunction with wide red-brick edging. But though the lines are more pleasing the colour-scheme is unsympathetic and since the stone plays an unwilling host to lichen it never mellows to look thoroughly comfortable.

A far more individual and amusing use of stone concerns the 'popples' — either from the Common or from Budleigh Salterton beach whence they were drawn by horse and cart. Nowhere else in England has the humble cobble-stone reached greater imaginative heights than in Woodbury. In some cases whole buildings were made of them (i.e. the workshops at Prior Units and the barn at Cannonwalls), sometimes they were the companions of other kinds of stone, as in the farm-buildings at Webbers. But it was in their use for floors and garden walls that they were seen at their best. Woodbury still abounds in good popple walls and the first prize must certainly go to the front garden wall at Webbers — a marvellous piece of work with Budleigh pebbles built by Mr. Charles Summerfield at the turn of the present century. Another use can be seen in the south churchyard wall — the work of Mr. Wm. Phillips — where they form infill panels in a surround of brickwork, much as flint is used with brickwork in Wiltshire and Dorset.

Although most of these examples are no more than 19th century in date the craft is certainly very old. Rydon Farm had, until the 1960s, a popple floor once described as "the finest piece of secular craftsmanship in Woodbury"[3] and the church still preserves its old popple floor beneath the present floor, laid in 1621. There must have been many floors like Rydon's but when farmers' wives graduated from boots or clogs to heeled shoes popple floors were doomed, and the beautiful popple floor recently discovered and restored at Lower Bagmores may now be the only one left in the parish. The popples are small, carefully selected and matched, and laid in fan-shaped patterns, so tightly packed together that the stones support each other. They are bedded in earth with only the tips of the small ends showing — a remarkable sight. Sometimes an old popple floor or yard will be turned up by the plough, as has happened at Sparkshayes and Scotsmore. Sometimes a little nod of recognition is given by incorporating popples found on an old site in the concrete of a new path, as at Gillbrook Cottages and Ballymans.

Woodbury can boast a single example of Coade Stone — an artificial stone cast in moulds to a secret formula by Mr. Wm. Coade of Lambeth. His excellent products became very popular and were extensively used for architectural ornamentation between about 1780 and 1840. Springhayes was rebuilt in 1810 in a style very similar to the houses in Southernhay, Exeter, and, like them, a Coade key-stone with a smiling face looks down on visitors to the front-door.

Cob

The absence of good building-stone in the parish, coupled with a plentiful supply of suitable clay led quite naturally to the use of cob as the main building material. The fact that Woodbury, like other East Devon villages, has dozens of good cob houses still giving satisfactory service after 400 years gives the lie to those who regard it as a sub-standard material. Well-built and well-maintained, cob endures as long as stone and there is great charm in its irregularities, its round corners, bread-ovens, deep window-seats and odd nooks.

Nobody knows how long cob has been used as a building material but it is so basic a commodity that it could well stretch back to prehistoric times. In Woodbury no surviving building is likely to be more than 500 years old, though Church Stile, Gillbrook Cottages and Brooklands Farm (Higher Greendale) all come near to it and much of the Haydons' old house at Ebford Barton may be older still. Many later buildings, e.g. Gilbrook House and the Priory, incorporate cob walls of a much earlier period.

To some extent cob was always a "do-it-yourself" material and some of Woodbury's earliest cob houses would have been made by the families who first lived in them. Early cob houses were essentially timber-framed and the timber components, ready cut, jointed and numbered, could be bought at the saw-pit in 'kit' form ready for assembly on site. The timber frame, complete with roof-crucks, was erected on the stone foundation wall much like the skeleton of a modern Dutch barn. Clay was then dug out of a pit nearby and carted to the site where it was mixed with chopped straw, or other vegetable matter, water added, and trodden to the right consistency by a tethered horse. The mixture was then shovelled up on the walls to a height of 2 or 3 feet and left to harden before a second layer was added. So the building slowly grew, the timber frame being encased in the cob and wooden lintels being put in where doors and windows would later be cut out. The openings were made when the walls were complete and the cob fairly dry. At that point the irregular features associated with cob made their appearance: the wide-angled door splays, often rounded on the fall-post side to ease entry through the yard-thick wall, the window-seats, shelves and wall cupboards. The house was now ready for its rafters and thatch — and maybe for the cat's skeleton which would keep evil spirits away! Finally the outside walls were rendered with a smooth plaster known as 'putty-lime' — softer and more pliable than rough-cast — and the plinth pitched to keep out the wet.

After the introduction of brick, which was relatively expensive, cob continued to be used for unseen parts of the house, for extensions, outbuildings and garden walls. It ceased to be used seriously as a building material about 100 years ago. Isaac Wilson's diary describes the building of the cob barn at Butleighs Heath in 1866 and the late Mr. Reg Summerfield learned how to make it from his father and was still using it for the repair of existing cob until after the First World War.

The last cob house to be built in this district was Furze Close at the Common end of Sanctuary Lane. Here the Hill family built themselves a cob house in about 1920. The site was cleared of trees which were used in the construction and the clay was dug from the bottom of the garden, mixed with heather from the Common and trodden by the family pony. The work was assisted and supervised by old Mr. Salter from Woodbury Salterton who had been a cob builder in the days of his youth.[4] But by the 1920s the process had so far gone from people's memories that Furze Close was irreverently nicknamed "the mud house" by people who would not have dreamed of describing their own cob houses in such uncomplimentary terms!

Brick

With the vernacular style well-geared to cob it was hardly surprising that brick was a long time establishing itself. The first bricks to be used in these parts were probably the pretty little Dutch bricks which are so well-known in Topsham. They were a curious spin-off of the wool-trade, being brought back as ballast in the wool ships returning to Topsham from Holland and were used mainly for chimney stacks. The best example in Woodbury is undoubtedly at Rydon Farm: but as the house dates from about 1540 and the bricks (so far as is known) were not imported before 1680, it shows how long Rydon made do with a hole in the roof!

Matthew Lee's uncle, George Venn, built Ebford Manor in 1710 and it was almost certainly the first brick house in Woodbury parish. Venn was a wool merchant and had probably fallen in love with the brick architecture of such places as Amsterdam. The bricks for Ebford, however, were not Dutch but were made locally — as the colour denotes. It may even be that they were made on the spot, for vestiges of old workings can be seen 200 yds down the hill in a field called the Brick Field in 1839. The method employed in their making did not require a kiln. The clay would be dug in autumn and winter, the bricks hand-formed and burnt by being built into a stack — the layers of bricks sandwiched with layers of combustible material. The fire burnt slowly through, taking several weeks. This rather chancy procedure produced bricks of uneven colour and it was common to find that the ends of those bricks nearest the centre of heat had acquired a bluish tinge.[5] Architects found that by playing around with the colour and the bonding they could make pleasing patterns and this has been done very successfully at Ebford where Flemish bond has been used in conjunction with blue headers to produce a diaper pattern. But then Woodbury forgot about bricks and they were not used again until Philip Lemprière built Woodbury House in 1781.

The 19th century saw the arrival of brick building in Woodbury in a big way, with brick-works springing up at White Cross, Higher Bagmores, the Cat and Fiddle, Withycombe and elsewhere within easy reach of Woodbury. The brick technique must have revolutionized the building industry in Woodbury and have provided a great deal of work requiring new skills. Although the brick-works at White Cross were actually on the Colaton Raleigh side of the road they were owned and worked by Woodbury men; the clay was cut from clay seams in Woodbury and carted to the works. One such seam was at the top of Cottles Lane in a field called 'the Brick Field': in certain lights, when the sun is low, it is possible to see the surface of the field stepped where the clay has been excavated. But White Cross brick-works were always in trouble, changing hands at frequent intervals (several owners went bankrupt) and the emphasis placed in their advertisements on the high quality of their products probably indicates that the quality was nothing to write home about![6] By 1890 the works had closed, though the brick wall and gate piers remain to mark the spot. The coming of the railways brought bricks from further afield and the Rolle Estate used Staffordshire cream bricks as banding and decoration on the estate cottages in Broadway — the rest of the bricks being from Withycombe, which was owned by the Estate.

From 1784 brick building was bedevilled by a Brick Tax and this gave rise to a curious manufacture known as "brick-tiles". Brick-tiles carried no tax and were designed to look exactly like bricks. They were no more than about ¼in. thick at the base and were fixed by means of a nail through the hole in the flange at the back. The give-away is at the corner of the building where the thin edges of the tiles are exposed. Brick-tiles were made in S.E. England and never became very widely used,[7] but Woodbury has a notable example. When Nutwell Court was being extensively remodelled by Lord Heathfield in 1796 the whole face of the main house was clad in cream-coloured brick-tiles. They are extremely ugly but with the final repeal of the brick tax in 1850 their manufacture died a natural death.

Roofing Materials

The natural companion of cob is thatch and Woodbury is lucky to have some excellent examples of thatch in all parts of the parish, especially in Salterton. It is a country craft that has not changed in centuries and, despite the high cost of the work and the staggering insurance premiums it attracts, thatchers are still very much in demand and family firms are still taking on and training apprentices.

The usual material here in East Devon is 'combed wheat-reed'. It is not, of course, a reed at all but a wheat straw specially prepared. Changes in the type of wheat grown by farmers and the use of the combine harvester have made it difficult for thatchers to get enough suitable straw. But such is the price of wheat-reed that farmers can be persuaded to grow taller varieties and to take a great deal of extra trouble in thrashing it. In recent years increasing quantities of "Norfolk Reed" (Phragmites communis) have been imported into this country from Holland, Germany and Poland and are finding their way to the West Country — though Woodbury still has to wait for its first Norfolk reed thatch. A good wheat-reed thatch should last 25 years.[8]

In the first half of the present century the depressed state of the rural economy saw many thatched roofs covered over with unsightly corrugated iron or asbestos sheets but better times have brought new thatches to many and now only a few corrugated roofs remain. Many more roofs were replaced by tiles or slates earlier this century, as at Nos. 1 & 2 the Green, Brooklands Farm (Higher Greendale) and the Vestry Room (1960s).

Unlike cob, thatching was always the work of highly skilled craftsmen. The earliest thatchers whose names we know were Thomas Lusher and William Moyse who, with their apprentices John Yalmere and John Scutt rethatched the Parsonage buildings and tithe barn between 1402/8, so Woodbury had work for two thatchers.[9] From 1536 we know the names of a great many Woodbury thatchers, right down to the 19th century when Thomas and Joseph Skinner were employed to rethatch Haydons Cottages. Woodbury's last resident thatcher was Mr. Tom Wood of Bridge Pit Farm who had served his apprenticeship with Mr. Mair of Clyst St. Mary — famous as a master-thatcher in the early years of this century. Since Tom Wood's time Woodbury's thatching has been mainly undertaken by Mr. Coombs of Clyst St. Mary and the late Mr. Jack Turbitt and his sons from Sidmouth.

Woodbury also contains a rare example of modern synthetic thatch. This is at Cleve Cottage in Flower Lane which in the early 1970s acquired a roof made of glass-fibre rolled on in vertical sections. It looks like thatch, at a quick glance, and so far has proved entirely satisfactory but the idea did not catch on and the firm who produced it has now gone out of business.

Brick building demanded the more sophisticated covering of slate and places within easy reach of sea-ports could make use of roofing slates from the Kingsbridge region of S. Devon. They are full of subtle shades of colouring and readily accept lichens that add to their beauty.[10] There are many examples in Woodbury — Gilbrook House and Bixley Haven are two that spring to mind — but the slate is very thick and heavy and becomes porous after a time, a fault that has led to many roofs being 'turnerised' with canvas and bitumen covering during the last few years. Delabole became popular in the mid 19th century and continued to make a stand against its competitors as late as the 1930s when Foxhayes (Rydon Lane) was roofed with it. But the real rival was Welsh slate which began to flood the country with an inexhaustible supply once the railway network got going. Welsh slate is extremely durable and can be riven so wafer-thin that a little goes a long way. It became the hall-mark of good building standards and when Fulford built Parsonage 'Welsh Duchess slates of 3½″ gauge' were specified. But for all it is a sound material there is not much beauty in Welsh slate. The uniformity of its texture and colour make it monotonous and gloomy — as if it were always a rainy day. In recent years so many good imitations have come on the market that it is now quite difficult to tell which is genuine (Well Park) and which is simulated slate (Preston House).

Red clay tiles came from the brick-works and White Cross produced large quantities of the flattish, double-roll 'pan-tiles' to be seen about the village. But the same soft qualities that affected White Cross bricks made the tiles suitable only for sheds, outhouses and humble buildings. Withycombe, on the other hand, produced good tiles of several types, such as those on Woodbury School and the Rolle Estate cottages in Broadway.

Woodwork

Woodbury had no difficulty in supplying itself with hard-wood in historical times. Throughout the centuries the parish has remained thickly wooded and until the last 100 years woods, plantations and hedgerows were cropped to give a never-ending supply of timber for all building needs. While most of it was oak there was also elm, ash, beech and pine. Field names indicate that there were saw-pits at Woodmanton, Cannonwalls and Ebford, though they would move from time to time to be near the site of felling.

In 1540/1 the church was entirely reroofed and the oak timbers, interestingly enough, came from Greendale Barton. Such was their size that the road at Deepway Hill had to be specially altered to get them through. Normally one might have expected this timber to come from Woodbury Wood but 1539 had seen the dissolution of Torre Abbey and its manor of Greendale came briefly into the hands of that 'entrepreneur', Lord John Russell, who was taking a quick profit off the land before selling it on again — 'asset-stripping' we would call it today![11]

Oak was plentiful when Nos. 1 & 2 Gillbrook were built as a hall-type farmhouse in the closing years of the 15th century. As was usual at the time, the house was built without a chimney, the fire being on the floor and the smoke finding its way out through a hole in the thatch. The result was smoke-blackened roof timbers, made rock-hard and shiny by the carbon from the wood-smoke. Many houses besides Gillbrook Cottages have these blackened oak roof timbers but most have been ceiled, painted or papered and their age is not easy to judge. When alterations took place at Gillbrook Cottages in about 1600 oak was already scarce and expensive (on account of the great ship-building programme to meet the threat of the Armada) so elm was used for the beams which supported the inserted upper floors. Plank-and-muntin partitioning between parlour and chamber was also made of elm. Elm plank-and-muntin tended to be very plain, the planks wide and the muntins simply chamfered. Unfortunately when Gillbrook Cottages were restored in 1965 the elm

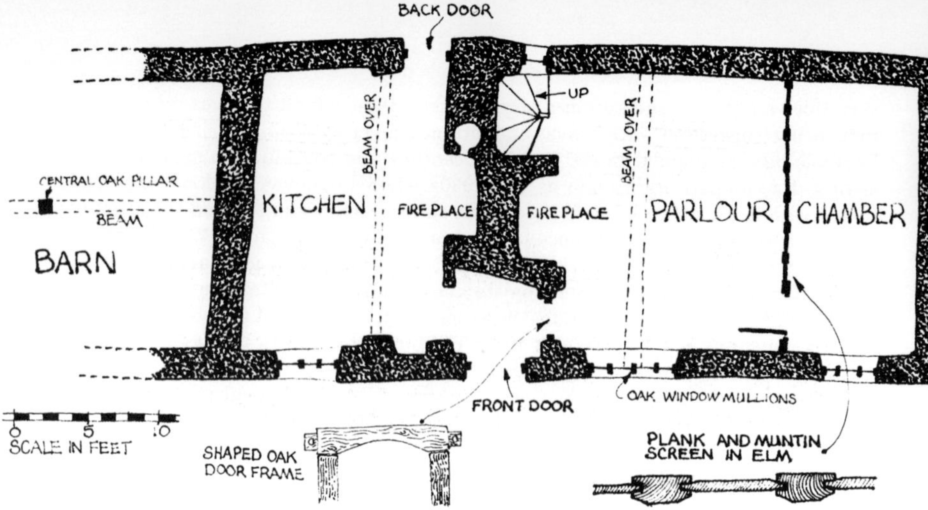

Sketch plan showing original layout of Gillbrook Cottages.

screen was found to be in state of utter decay and was removed, though the wide-planked elm door remains.

The beautifully moulded oak screen which took its place was saved from the demolition of Govetts in 1965 and is a lesson in good craftsmanship. The mouldings are so perfectly matched and the sections fit so well together that it is difficult to see where the joints are: yet when it was being dismantled for removal it was only necessary to drill out the 'trennels' (wooden pegs — or 'tree-nails') and the sections could be easily tapped apart — after nearly 400 years of wear and tear, use and misuse, to say nothing of rising damp. After cleaning and repairing they went together again just as easily and were refastened with trennels.[12]

When Govetts was built between 1580 and 1600 Richard Gove could afford oak throughout: not only the timber frame and the screen partitioning in the best room, but well-moulded beams, stairs, floor boards and panelled bedroom doors were all of oak and at the time of demolition there remained one complete four-light oak mullioned window which shared a hefty lintel with the front door adjoining it.

With the start of the Church-wardens' accounts we begin to get to know the carpenter-joiners who regularly did work in the church.In 1540 John Bagwyll was in charge of renewing the roof and it was probably he who carved the square bench-ends a few years later. By the 17th century the Crutchard, or Critchard, family had started to make their long and distinguished contribution to the church — and doubtless to many other buildings if only we knew. They lived at, and gave their name to, the house called 'Critchards', opposite the Green, later known as 'Izel Cottage' and demolished in 1902. The house stood end-on to the road and the long building at right-angles to it, on the site now occupied by West Thorpe, was no doubt the joiners' shop in which at least three generations of Critchards, with their workmen and apprentices, produced their fine work.

It was Thomas Crutchard who made the Jacobean oak pulpit in Woodbury church, in 1635, at a cost of £5.10s. and in 1717 his grandson, Henry Critchard,

Izel Cottage (formerly 'Critchards') in c.1860.

renewed the surrounding board over it (now gone). But the charming little angel with golden clarion (1777) which surmounted it and now looks down at us from the top of the War Memorial screen, was the work of Critchard's successor, Peter Daley.

Peter Daley had his joinery shop at Chowns and he and his sons continued to work there until well into the 19th century. He was in full spate when Philip Lemprière had Woodbury House built in 1781 and Thomas Weekes was rebuilding Gilbrook House and it is tempting to think that, as Woodbury's leading wood-worker at that time, it might have been Peter Daley who made the triple-light sash windows, panelled front doors and decorated door-jambs of the two houses, and the richly detailed door-head canopy of the former.

As the 19th century got into its stride the Daleys sought other occupations and the building scene was taken over by the Phillips and the Stokes families. Robert and William Stokes ran their small business from Flower Lane, occupying Fernlea and its neighbour (now gone) and the sharing the builders' yard at the back (now Prior Units). It was probably here that Robert Stokes made his own very distinctive front door at Fernlea. It will be noticed that the corners of the four top panels are cut out, giving an expressive and individual pattern to the door. And it is interesting to note that at Springhayes a slightly bigger and grander version of that same pattern appears in the front door – surely the work of the same hand.

Rosemary Cottage in Broadway, built by Wm. Phillips in 1833, is remarkable for its extraordinary door-head canopy. The two dolphins are of wood and nobody knows the history of them. The story goes that they came from a ship and that seems entirely likely as they are considerably older than other components of the porch.

Nothing in building is easier to change than windows. Nowadays we are assailed on all sides by advertisements for double-glazing. Only a few years ago it was 'the picture window'. Fashions are changing all the time and it has always been so. Few houses in Woodbury over 200 years old now have their original windows, though many show where the old Tudor oak mullions have been replaced with later casements, for the appertures are wider than they are high — Church Steps, for example, the Beals, Lower Woodmanton, Greendale Barton and many others. It was in the 17th century that windows started to be longer than wide and Gulliford Farmhouse is perhaps an early example, though the window frames themselves are replacements. Even Matthew Lee's house, Ebford Manor, has had its Queen Anne windows replaced by Georgian frames of a similar size but lighter style. Generally speaking, the earlier the window, the thicker and plainer the glazing-bars. By 1800 glazing-bars were moulded and sometimes seem to be as thin as a knife-edge. The village is full of windows of this period, Broadway House, Higher Venmore etc. There followed a craze for round-headed 'Venetian' windows, first seen at Springhayes in 1810 and soon copied at the Vestry Room (1837), Brixley Haven, and Knowle Cottage (c. 1845?) Christ Church (1851) and the Court House (1861). When the Priory was turned from a small cottage into a 'gentleman's residence' in the first half of the 19th century the new owner indulged in a flight of fancy by installing 'gothic' windows with pointed tops. An old watercolour of 'Izel Cottage' next door shows it to have had windows of similar design. They may have been genuine 15th century and the Priory windows made to match, or the two sets may have come from the same workshop and been installed at the same time.

Greendale Barton in 1900

The Rolle Estate had their own estate workshops at Bicton where they mass-produced window frames for their properties. No attempt was made to match the new frame to the existing apperture but the apperture was altered to fit one of the several standard frames, as at Ford Farm, Rydon and Webbers.

A word about glass. In Tudor times very few houses had glass — perhaps not even Govetts. Windows were set high and a variety of devices used to exclude the worst of the weather, such as movable frames stretched with bladder-skins or oiled cloth. But all windows had wooden shutters which kept out thieves as well as weather.[14] England and few farmhouses in Woodbury would have had glass before about 1700. There is a very revealing reference to window glass in one of Springhayes' deeds, There is a very revealing reference to window glass in one of Springhayes deeds, dated 1728, when Charity Hanley (nee Broadmead) leased the old house (not the present one) to Elias Sandford. The lease goes on and on about the 'Glass Windows', their care and repair. The wording suggests movable glazed panels and it is quite obvious that glass was very unusual indeed and very valuable. That one deed says more about the dearth of window glass in Woodbury than any historian could! But crown glass (cut from a large, flattened bubble of blown glass) was already on its way. It was of very superior quality and could be cut into larger panes: there is much of it still about — recognisable by its slightly curving lines and a tendency to distort.

The Window Tax, first imposed in 1696, was responsible for a strange quirk of architectural design. To save tax many houses had windows blocked up and this led to the fashion of incorporating 'blind windows' as part of the design. 'Blind windows' at Darby's Cottages, Jubilee Stores, Preston House and Well Park have nothing to do with window tax.

Plaster and Paint

Lime was the vital ingredient of mortar and plaster and before the days when cement arrived neatly packed in bags every builder carted his lime from a local lime-kiln and slaked it in a pit in his yard.[15] The limestone, mainly quarried at Berry Head, came by boat to the many coastal lime-kilns. Topsham, Ebford, Lympstone, Exmouth and Budleigh all had them.

Woodbury possesses at least two highly unusual examples of painted plaster. At Gulliford Farm an open fireplace was uncovered in 1973 which was lined with coloured and painted plaster. The side jambs are decorated with a floral design of white poppy heads and foliage, the pattern having been first cut into the blue-black plaster with a trowel. A very few other such fireplaces are known in the Exeter area and are thought to be the work of one man, possibly a Dutchman, working about 1600.[16]

The second example is at Ebford Manor where the drawingroom walls are entirely covered with 'trompe l'oeil' painted panelling. The effect is an extraordinarily convincing deception and one has to touch the walls to be sure the panelling is not real. It is painted in soft duck-egg green directly on to the original plaster and thus is contemporary with the house (1710). Discovered in the late 1960s under layers of wallpaper it was beautifully restored on the advice of the British Museum who pronounced it to be the work of itinerant Italian painters.

Moulded and sculptured plaster ceilings have since Tudor times been a feature of Devon houses and there is one example in Woodbury. No. 2 the Green has both its upstairs ceilings decorated in raised plaster. The main roof trusses are plastered and studded with large rosettes, or Tudor roses, and the smallish area of flat ceiling below the apex has geometrical patterns with central motifs of stylised flowers and leaves. Experts agree that a date of around 1630 is probable. It means, interestingly, that before the bay-windowed extension was built the main reception rooms of the house were *upstairs* — perhaps because, as part of the Manor Barton, the ground floor rooms had originally housed the court house and administrative offices of the manor.

Victorians loved to decorate their main rooms with elaborate cornices and central ceiling roses from which hung glass chandeliers. William Phillips excelled in this type of work and much of it is to be seen in the 19th century houses of Woodbury. He used a number of moulds which he could skilfully combine in different ways to produce variations, so that ceiling roses could appear to be individual while being made from the same components. Oakhayes and Bixley Haven display excellent examples of his work and there are many more. He made casts of the dolphins at Rosemary Cottage, obviously thinking they might come in useful, but he is not known to have used them.[17]

All in all, Woodbury is a parish of very unusual and diverse building materials and one cannot do more than scratch the surface of the subject here. But it is to be hoped that readers will make their own discoveries and will get pleasure from doing so.

Wildlife Neighbours and Friends?
by Margaret Parkinson

Man has made some sort of impact on his surroundings from earliest times. As he cleared the woodland for his dwellings and arable fields, made pastures and drove roads for his stock and lined them with hedges, drained some wet areas and created others, so habitats for the wildlife which shares the parish with us have changed. Some results of that long process are summarised in this chapter.

WOODLANDS

In spite of an onslaught on the all-enveloping woodland to obtain land for other purposes, man soon realised that he must *retain* woods for their valuable products. Large timber was needed for all major construction — we read of deliveries for two important buildings in 1440, of payments for felling trees for houses in 1481[1] and of Woodbury church being completely re-roofed in 1540 — and coppice poles were used for smaller-scale work like cart shafts, tool handles and hurdles. Tan bark was required for preserving leather, rope and sails, loppings were fed to stalled beasts and brushwood had a great variety of uses.[2] The fuel for specialised crafts like forging was charcoal, obtained from coppice poles; that for ordinary needs was anything gathered "by hook or by crook", under the common right of estover. Pigs were allowed to forage for acorns and beech mast during the winter (the common right of pannage) and cattle could browse selected areas.[3] The disturbance to wildlife while all this was going on must have been considerable!

Reference has been made in Chapter 4 to the need for woodland management in order to achieve these diverse aims. Ideally, the best-shaped trees and the most promising saplings were "reserved" as "standards", to be the seed parents for the next generation and to provide for future large timber needs. All the rest of the underwood was cut to about ground level — coppiced — every 15-25 years, to provide small timber for the purposes mentioned. This has been the traditional method of woodland management for at least 1000 years and it is rather sad that it has no meaning in today's economy.

Sometimes this tradition was varied. If larger timber was likely to be required more quickly, one coppice pole was "singled" when the rest were cut down — that is, the shoot which had grown tallest was allowed to grow to timber size on the coppice "stool". This practice was continued until quite recent times and some of the oaks in Rockham Wood are of this type. If felling had been too drastic and there were not enough mature trees to provide acorns for natural regeneration — the "barren woodland" mentioned in Chapter 4 — trees were then actually planted, and there are several records of this.[4]

The amount of woodland recorded for Woodbury Manor in Domesday has been estimated at 600 acres (Ch. 4). No woodland is mentioned for Nutwell Manor, but this is not necessarily significant, as there are many omissions. Coombe is traditionally associated with Nutwell, so its woods may have been where the Coombe woods are today. The main Domesday woodland probably occupied much of the west-facing slopes below the Common, where our largest woods are still to be found, and totalled at least 700 acres. It is not certain whether it was all in one piece, as the Domesday measurements implied but, as clearing proceeded, separate woods were inevitably formed.

We do not know exactly when names began to be used for individual woods, but we do have a record of one which has changed its name. A mid-13th century charter[5] describes "ffoxleghe" wood, which is identifiable as Hogsbrook Wood — this has the original bank and ditch still intact along one side. An ancient wood like this, although small (7 acres), is unobtrusively rich in wildlife. In spring, it is full of wood anemones, primroses, bluebells, yellow archangel, moschatel and other typical woodland flowers. The old oaks are covered with lichens and mosses and provide ideal feeding grounds for tree-creeper and nuthatch. Four species of tit and two species of woodpecker are there all the year round, augmented in spring by several species of warbler; this type of bird population indicates that insect food is abundant. A sparrow hawk is occasionally seen scattering the small birds in fright. There is a small area of bracken where roe deer can lie up, and there is evidence of other mammals like fox, stoat, hare and mole. From the point-of-view of wildlife which evolved in broad-leaved woodland, it is essential that some woods retain their ancient character and their privacy. Hogsbrook, and part of Mallocks Wood on the other side of the parish, are splendid examples of ones which do this.

A 16th century document[6] names Rockham Wood and Woodbury Wood; from the acreage given for the latter, it looks as though Rushmoor Wood was not then separated from it. However, by the 17th century all three woods have their separate acreages documented — Rockham 100, Rushmoor 30 and Woodbury 120 — and so they remained until the end of the 18th century.[7] Rushmoor and Woodbury are now largely coniferised but Rockham remains predominantly broad-leaf. In many ways, Rockham is similar to Hogsbrook except that it has been more obviously managed in recent times, with areas of oak thinned and some beech planted. Being a larger wood, there is scope for large birds of prey like buzzard and tawny owl, which regularly nest there. The roe deer can also make their "rings" — characteristic of their mating display — for which they need plenty of space! In the deep goyles, damp-loving species like golden saxifrage, shade forget-me-not, giant horsetail and many kinds of mosses, ferns and liverworts can be seen and woodcock often winter in these wet areas. Additionally interesting features are the decayed coppice stools, sometimes 5 feet or more in diameter, suggesting an age of at least 400 years.

At the end of the 18th century, the woodland in the parish probably totalled at least 300 acres, as compared with a Domesday *estimate* of 700 acres. The blockades of the Napoleonic War took a further toll of our woodlands. Timber was felled and not replanted; woodland hedges were not repaired and stock was able to get in, so much previous woodland was converted to scrub and furze. By the time the Tithe record was compiled in 1839, the parish woodland had dwindled to less than 100 acres. The effect, in terms of loss of habitat for woodland wildlife, is clear. Some, like robin and blackbird, foxglove and red campion, were able to adapt to the open conditions, but many of the large or shy species disappeared. Roe deer became extinct in southern Britain and it is only with increased afforestation that this species has made a come-back.

The Board of Agriculture and Internal Improvement was set up in 1793, as a result of fears of a French blockade. A survey of the whole country, both for agriculture and forestry, was undertaken and the report for Devon[8] was scathing about many aspects of our woodlands. Landowners were exhorted to grow more trees and several new plantations appeared in the parish. Some early ones, like Coombe, Redslow and The Brake were of broad-leaved (hardwood) trees and, when the demand for homegrown hardwood fell, they were retained as game cover. Coombe contains some very handsome sweet chestnut; The Brake contains box, a shrub not native to Devon, but often planted for pheasants. Game cover can provide a good habitat for wildlife in general, although the old-style keepering often produced an imbalance of predators, which led to an increase of small mammals like mice and voles. These depleted the woodland floor vegetation and prevented natural regeneration of the trees.

New woodland developed later at Tucker's Brake, near Heathfield. Here, several old strip fields, all arable in 1839, have become broad-leaf coppice which is now almost indistinguishable in appearance from the one strip which *was* coppice on the Tithe map. Good mature oaks have grown as "standards" but the underwood of some strips is still being coppiced. The early purple orchid does well with this sporadic disturbance. Unfortunately, where stock penetrates, the ground flora is very sparse.

Ironically, the First World War caused a similar destruction of woodland to that which had occurred a century previously. At Coombe Brake, some of the felled areas were never replanted but have regenerated naturally. This woodland is mainly of birch and hazel (similar to that which followed the Neolithic abandonments) although there are saplings of beech and oak, seeded from mature trees deliberately retained as a screen. The Forestry Commission, set up to remedy the deficit, advised the planting of conifers, being quicker-growing and more suited to modern timber needs. Castle Plantation dates from about this time and the mature conifers now provide a habitat for crossbill and siskin, the former often staying to breed. Most of Woodbury Wood, parts of Rockham Wood and Coombe Brake and, since 1980, the whole of Rushmoor Wood, are now coniferous, producing a much-needed timber crop in a similar way to the medieval woodlands. Some stages of a plantation provide excellent wildlife habitats — nightjars and blackcaps like the early "weedy" stages while goldcrests and redpolls prefer the tall, mature trees — and the evergreen cover provides shelter for many birds and mammals in hard winters.

THE COMMON

This dominating ridge reaches 580 feet above sea level near The Warren, drops to 430 feet at Four Firs and rises again to 550 feet at Black Hill. It takes the full force of the weather today, as it certainly did during the Celtic period. But the climate improved about 500 AD and, until about 1300 AD, southern Britain was much warmer and drier than now. As the Saxon population increased and more land was cleared for cereal growing, pasturage had to be sought ever further from the settlements.

Saxon farmers would have found the high ground much more suitable for grazing than it was for Celtic farmers. Much of the previous peat would have dried out and, except along the spring lines, turned into soil, and the climate was no longer ideal for heathers. Throughout the medieval period, "Woodbury Down" was the name used for this high pasture — it could never have looked like the chalk downs because the soil is so different, but the name correctly suggests its grassier nature. Its use intensified under the Normans and it became an integral part of the manorial system; common rights became established on it, giving rise to its present name.

Although the land actually belonged to the lord of the manor, the rights of tenants, for which they paid by the rent on their property, became well-defined. Those of pannage and estover have already been mentioned; the right to graze animals on the "waste" or uncultivated land was called "common of pasture", and all land-holders would have been entitled to use what is now the Common. A mid-13th century charter[9] describes the exact boundaries of that available to the Greendale tenant, although not for his exclusive use — the whole of the north of the Common as far as the Yettington road, comprising at least 400 acres. As no documentary evidence has yet been found, we must assume that the rest of the Common was divided between Woodbury and Nutwell manors. The southern area is called Coombe Common today and Coombe was part of Nutwell; Stony Lane was probably their drove road to the Common.

Up to about 1300 AD, the land-holders were not restricted in the number of their animals grazing the Common; this suggests that there was adequate "keep" for all. Only one case of "stinting" is known; this particular grazing right was a gift (see note 9) and the limitation on numbers may have been a precaution against possible future abuse. "400 ewes with lambs until weaned . . . 100 field beasts (draught oxen) . . . and 25 pigs annually" were allowed. A different picture emerges in a document of the early 16th century; by then, each tenant was limited to a fixed quota of beasts and some tenants had no grazing rights at all.[10] The number allowed came to 1090 sheep and 172 "animals" (draught oxen again), but this does *not* include the "stinted" tenant previously mentioned, nor the freeholders who now comprised half the parish — so these numbers may well have been more than doubled. At a conservative estimate, there were probably four sheep and one "animal" all the year round per acre of rough grazing — they could hardly have been prime specimens! Even with the fertilizing effect of that amount of manure, there cannot have been much surplus vegetation for wildlife of any sort. Moreover, as these animals were constantly shepherded, there would be little freedom from disturbance or trampling and no cover into which to escape. A barren prospect indeed!

Grazing was not the sole use of the Common. In Devon in the 13th and 14th centuries, it was customary for the lord of the manor to retain the right to cultivate part of the pasture common. Details of how this was carried out come from one of the Torre Abbey charters. "He and his heirs can till and enclose 10 acres of land . . . whether by spade or by team". When the corn crop had been taken, the enclosures were removed so the area could be grazed again and "every year, 10 acres afresh can be tilled". Gorse, a plant characteristic of disturbed soil, was likely to colonise these once-cultivated patches. The lord of the manor reserved to himself the right to cut this, as it was valuable for fuel and fodder. A Woodbury Manor record of 1289 details the profit from its sale.[11] Later, cultivation of the Common, along with cutting of furze, became extended to some of the tenants also, and "common of pasture and tillage upon Woodbury Down" was written into their leases well into the 19th century.

Eight centuries of favourable climate came to an end about 1300 AD., with a series of wet seasons, floods and poor harvests. The Common bore the brunt of this deterioration — peat re-formed in areas where it had not occurred since Celtic times and covered quite large areas. This makes the 16th century "grazing quota" system quite reasonable and the plight of the animals more certain. The weather was not only wetter but cooler, often with very cold winters and a short growing season. This general pattern lasted until about the middle of last century, although there were better spells from time to time. Events concerning the Common are set against this background.

Another common right became very important as a result of the increased growth of peat. The right of turbary — of cutting peat for fuel for one's own use (*not* for sale) — extended to all inhabitants of a parish, whether or not they lived in a cottage to which other common rights were attached. This was indeed a boon for the very poor but, unfortunately, as poverty increased,[12] this became much abused. By the 18th century, it was called by one writer on agriculture "the barbarous custom of turbary".[13] Common of turbary ceases when the peat is all worked out; it is not absolutely clear when this happened in Woodbury, but the poor of the parish, desperate for fuel, went on removing anything remotely combustible, including the vegetation and the topsoil itself. Charles Vancouver (see note 8) wrote of the Common in 1808 "Considerable injury has been done . . . by the paring off and carrying away the surface for fuel". He also described another habit which could not be other than damaging — the surface vegetation was completely pared off and burnt, and the resulting "beat-ashes" were scraped up and used as manure for arable crops, especially turnips.

After the break-up of the manorial system, there was no-one to check that common rights were not abused and the conditions on all commons went from bad to worse. All sorts of people, not necessarily living in the parish, made use of "common of pasture", and disease was rife among stock. Cultivation almost ceased after the Napoleonic wars and gorse took over, as it had done before. At the beginning of the 19th century, the right to cut gorse cost 50p - £1 per acre per annum and the traditional method was to cut on a 4-year cycle. But few were willing to pay for the right when "pirates" were likely to come in and make off with as much as they could hack; this was a common practice, as furze faggots sold for 66p per 100. By implication, there were no legitimate common rights exercised by 1839 —

the Tithe Map merely records that the Common covers 734 acres and, referring to another area altogether, shows "6 acres *used* as common land." By the mid-19th century, most of the Common was completely neglected and the wildlife, which had had such a "raw deal" during the centuries of over-exploitation, began to colonise. Today, there are some excellent habitats and the Common can boast many interesting and some rare species.

The dry heath

Gorse flowers can be found in almost every month of the year because there are two species and they flower at different times — common gorse (French furze) from December to May and western gorse (dwarf furze) from June to October. Sometimes it looks as though someone has been making a tangle of red threads among the gorse — this is a parasitic plant called dodder which obtains all its food from the gorse, produces hundreds of tiny pinkish flowers and dies back completely after seeding. Common gorse forms quite dense patches where wrens and stonechats find shelter and nesting sites. Meadow pipits and skylarks prefer the grassier areas, where small flowers may also be found — heath milkwort, heath bedstraw, lousewort and tormentil. Some years, there are also fine stands of heath spotted orchid among the grasses. On a warm day, common lizards may be sighted, darting after beetles and other insects. Ling (black heather) and bell heather make a blaze of colour in summer and, except where they are trodden, often grow quite tall. Their growth may conceal the mounds which heath ants make, where they store gorse seeds for the winter and raise their young, but the green woodpeckers seem to know just where they can be found. Ants form the main part of their diet, and they have a special long tongue for sucking up both the adults and the eggs. The great grey shrike is a regular winter visitor, recognisable by its undulating flight, rather similar to that of woodpeckers.

The wet heath

Along the spring line, where it is wet for much of the year, Sphagnum moss flourishes. It holds water like a sponge, and maintains the right conditions for deer sedge, cotton grass, purple moor grass, heath rush and cross-leaved heath. All these plants may form peat, because they cannot decay in waterlogged conditions. Two insectivorous plants occur here — the round-leaved sundew, often growing on a Sphagnum hummock, and the delicate, little pale butterwort, which prefers bare, wet peat. Creeping willow is very common and several species of lichen also occur. In winter, short-eared owls, snipe and curlew may be seen, and one or more pairs of curlew and lapwing used to breed. The nightjar, a summer visitor which nests in the wetter areas but tends to feed over the dry heath, is fascinating to watch after sunset. It flies back and forth, with its beak wide open, swallowing the night-flying moths as it goes. Curlews, lapwings and nightjars all nest on the ground and the increasing use of the wet heaths for military training is probably the cause of their reduction in numbers. They have their natural predators as well, such as adders, which may eat eggs and nestlings as well as beetles and young mice and voles.

The valley bog

Where minerals are washed down into shallow valleys, many additional plant species which need a richer peat in which to grow may be found. Patches of bog asphodel in flower make a splash of gold and flowers of meadow thistle and devil's bit scabious dot the ground with different shades of purple. Black bog rush and white beak sedge are less showy but quite common, whereas fragrant orchid, sneezewort, and saw-wort have to be searched for. Bog St. John's wort and bog bean may be found in the Colaton Raleigh brook, which rises on Woodbury Common. Bog pimpernel, with its beautiful pale pink flowers, may be found round the edges of small pools of standing water. The handsome golden-ring dragonfly may sometimes be seen laying its eggs in these pools, because the nymphs will live in the water for at least two years, feeding on the water beetles and bugs which can also be found there.

MARITIME HABITATS

The parish has an estuary shore just over two miles long, from Odam's Wharf to the Lympstone boundary, and the mouth of the Gillbrook is just about in the middle. Two interesting habitats result from the tidal nature of an estuary.

The mudflats

The ebb-tide reveals anything from 200-300 acres of mud (sandy or gravelly in places), sloping gently from the shore to the low-water channels of the Clyst and the Exe. Vast numbers of marine animals — worms, molluscs, crustaceans etc. are hidden just below the surface but only the occasional lugworm cast gives any clue to their presence. Wading birds, with bills specially adapted for probing the ooze, are very aware of this "hidden treasure" and winter in the estuary in large numbers. On a single day, 50 golden plover, 100 grey plover and 120 lapwing were counted from the railway embankment at Exton. A flock of black-tailed godwit, at the mouth of the Clyst, numbered well over 100, while dunlin and redshank numbers sometimes defy counting. An exciting winter visitor, slowly increasing in numbers, is the avocet and sometimes up to 20 can be seen. Eel-grass, the main food of the wintering flocks of brent geese, does not extend to our part of the estuary but the geese themselves often come as far as Nutwell on the flood-tide. Shelduck, oyster catchers, curlew and heron may be seen at most times of the year.

Saltmarsh

The sheltered upper reaches of the estuary provide ideal conditions for this habitat, noted for an interesting group of flowering plants actually able to tolerate salt water. This characteristic is particularly well shown by the cord-grass, Spartina, clumps of which grow right out in the soft mud, completely immersed at every high tide. At first glance, saltmarsh seems a rather uninteresting "grassy" expanse, because sea clubrush, sea rush, cord-grass, manna-grass, sea purslane, sea arrow-grass and sea plantain do not have showy flowers. But a closer look will reveal more colourful species — in spring, white masses of scurvy-grass; in summer, the pink of sea-spurrey and sea milkwort and the purple of sea lavender and sea aster. Shore crabs scuttle among the vegetation but the tiny Hydrobia snails remain firmly attached to stems until the next high tide enables them to become active again. Where rainwater washes out some of the salt, wild celery, parsley water dropwort, and an interesting rarity, buttonweed (from South Africa) may be found.

The railway embankment completed in 1861, now acts as a sea wall, cutting off the tide from low-lying areas where saltmarsh used to be. There were about 10 acres between the Clyst and the parish boundary at Ebford and, at Exton, the stream used to be tidal as far as the present main road and the saltmarshes occupied all the low ground on both sides of it. These "saltings" were traditionally used for sheep grazing and must have provided a welcome alternative to the long trek to the Common. The 1st edition Ordnance Survey map (1809) shows several lanes

(Hamslade is one) leading from Ebford and Exton to the saltmarshes.

FRESHWATER HABITATS

A glance at the map shows that the parish is well provided with streams. The Grindle Brook, which forms the parish boundary in two separate stretches of its course, has several "head-waters" on the Common. Gillbrook is fed, not only by Ford Water (which itself has several sources on the Common) but also by Polly Brook and the springs near Parsonage House and Cottles; when it becomes the Rydon or Exton Brook, it additionally receives the stream from the Bagmores valley. The Watton Brook rises in Coombe Plantation and flows for nearly a mile before reaching Lympstone parish and on to the estuary; short streams also flow to the estuary from Gulliford and Lower Nutwell. The Colaton Raleigh brook rises on the other side of the Common and flows east to the Otter.

The habitats in and along these streams vary according to whether the flow is fast or slow (preferred by roach and brook lamprey); the bottom is muddy (much loved by eels), sandy or gravelly; the banks are open or shaded by alders and willows; the water is clear (best for minnows and sticklebacks) or polluted, and so on; so only a few species can be mentioned. Hemlock water dropwort, great hairy willowherb, butterbur and kingcup are still common but snowdrops and daffodils have become quite rare, entirely due to picking. These are *not* garden escapes but our native wild plants, which need to multiply from seed; if they are picked, they never get the chance to do this. The only way to be sure that future generations will be able to enjoy them is not to pick any at all. Mallard and moorhen are often seen but rarer birds like water rail, dipper and kingfisher may sometimes be glimpsed. Water voles and sometimes water shrews can be seen during the day but mink, being mainly nocturnal, are rarely seen; their footprints may be found in damp mud in many places.

Some marls have a high lime content and were esteemed as a soil improver until well into last century. Disused marlpits became ponds and are a very common feature on old maps of the parish. Many have now been filled in, and the disappearance of these and other ponds has led to the relative rarity of frogs, toads and newts today, as compared with the quite recent past. Those which remain provide a most valuable still-water habitat, provided that they are not vandalised by being used as rubbish tips, and should be retained wherever possible. They form one of the few areas where that elegant swimmer, the grass snake, can still be seen. The disappearance of the marlpit pond has been somewhat counterbalanced by the increased popularity of the garden pond. These are much favoured by showy damsel flies and dragonflies, as well as the less conspicuous water snails and beetles. As the draining of wet areas has been part of agricultural progress over the centuries, any restoration of habitat for the species which need water is most valuable; ponds created for ornament, for sporting purposes, or for irrigation, satisfy this need.

HEDGES AND VERGES

Of all the habitats which have been mentioned, these probably provide the greatest contrast between past and present. Today they are often regarded as an expensive nuisance and their growth is disposed of as quickly as possible with the flail cutter; previously, they formed an integral part of the rural economy and were managed in such a way as to provide the maximum of large and small timber, fuel, and food for man and beast.[14]

First and foremost, hedges were boundaries, mainly to control stock, but they originated in one of two possible ways. A few are merely narrow strips of "relic" woodland, left when the clearings on either side of them did not quite meet! They are not always easy to identify,[15] but certain characteristics are helpful — the trees in them are typical of woodland (they would never have contained field elm), they are usually "flush" with the adjoining field or lane, and they contain plants which are not good "colonisers", like field maple, spindle and dog's mercury. The more common type of hedge is the Devon bank, standing 2-3 feet higher than the field and planted with hawthorn, oak, ash and field elm. But over the centuries, other shrubs have colonised the "made" hedge, so that very old ones are as rich in species as the woodland relic hedges.

The ancient drove road leading from Hogsbrook to the Common has a "relic" of Rockham Wood as the hedge on the left side; on the right side is a Devon bank, with remnants of field elm in it. However, the right bank is also very rich in species, including those poor colonisers listed above. The wording in one of the Torre Abbey charters[16] suggests that the hedge and road are contemporary. Many of the lanes known to be ancient, like Moor Lane, Watery Lane, Rydon Lane, Stony Lane, the lane past Coombe Park, Cottles Lane, Castle Lane and Ebford Lane are bounded by species-rich hedges. Their verges were grazed and seeds were dispersed by trampling. Some interesting verge plants to be found are grass vetchling and corky-fruited water dropwort.

The hedge, ditch and verge make a "unit" for many species. For example, dunnock (hedge sparrow) and goldfinch find nesting sites and song perches in the hedge, but feed mainly on the verge. Bank voles tunnel into the bank for nesting sites and shelter, but feed on the hedgerow fruits and verge seeds. Predators like stoats and weasels find the ditch a useful "corridor".

It is sad that the field, or English, elm, which was such a typical feature of so many hedges in the parish, has almost disappeared as a result of the virulent strain of Dutch elm disease which arrived in Britain about 1968. Change has been the keynote of this chapter and, except for this last-mentioned example, the changes described have been *gradual*. Most wildlife can adapt to new situations, given time and this is where the present differs from the past. Modern technology enables the destruction, in a few hours, of habitats which have lasted for centuries. Does "progress" sufficiently consider our often unseen neighbour? Perhaps it should do so more thoroughly, for most of them are our friends as well.

1998. Too many changes have occurred since the publication of the 1st edition for them to be included here. New information may be found in: Woodbury Parish 1894-1994 "Living a century of change" pp 76-87, and "A century of environmental change and its effects on wildlife", Transactions of the Devonshire Association Vol. 126 (1994) pp 123-144 "A Parish Wildlife Centenary 1894-1994".

Acknowledgements

This book has not been written without the help of many people and I am grateful to those who have advised and encouraged me. Firstly, I owe a debt to Professor W.G. Hoskins without whose initial encouragement the task might never have been undertaken.

Mrs. Margaret Parkinson has contributed an excellent chapter on her own subject and has provided me with useful criticism and stimulating argument. Mrs. Esmé Thomson has given steadfast support and accompanied me on countless expeditions to libraries, etc. Mr. G. Paley (Devon and Exeter Institution), Mrs. Margery Rowe (Devon Record Office) and Mrs. Audrey Erskine (Exeter Cathedral Library) and their staffs have been unfailingly patient and helpful, as have also my friends in the West Country Studies Library, Exeter. Cano J.A. Turner assisted with ecclesiastical references and Dr. David Keep with 'nonconformity'. Brig. C.R. Templer provided much military information and the Rev. J.G.M. Scott kindly contributed articles on the church bells and clock. Mr. Richard Osmond undertook researches in the Public Record Office, London, and Professor G.H. Harper sorted out the Rolle Estate catalogue for me at the Devon Record Office. Mrs. Sheila Smith's cheerful interest in the mountain of typing never flagged and Lady R.G. Taylor gallantly undertook the daunting task of correcting and proof-reading.

Much information has come from people here in the parish. The Rev. Alec Osmond and the Vestry Clerk have readily made available such church records as they have. The Wares and Summerfields have contributed information on their family businesses of tanning, milling and building, and Mr. Harry Jarman's long association with the Parish Council, Woodbury Charities and his great interest in "old Woodbury" have been most useful. The long and accurate memories of Mrs. Vera Stediford, Mrs. Mollie Skinner, Mr. Harry Stokes, Mr. Percy Sharland and the late Mr. Jack Hitchcock have brought the recent past very much alive. At Ebford I am indebted to Mrs. Esther Brimblecombe for help about Ebford Manor and the Lees. At Salterton I have received help from Mr. & Mrs. George Wilson, and also from Mr. Jeffrey Dagworthy, Mr. John Parker and Mr. Geoffrey Dearnley. To all these people, and to many others I take this opportunity to acknowledge my indebtedness and offer my thanks.

1998. I am grateful to John Allan, Curator of Antiquities, Royal Albert Museum, Exeter, for much help and encouragement in the revision of the first (prehistoric) chapter, and to Nigel Tucker of Woodbury who has made his collection of "finds" available for study and illustration, and has shared his infectious enthusiasm with me.

U.W.B. Woodbury 1998.

Notes

Abbreviations used in the Notes

DAS	Report of the Devon Archaeological Society.
DCNQ	Devon and Cornwall Notes and Queries.
DCRS	Devon and Cornwall Record Society.
DRO	Devon Record Office.
EFP	Trewman's Exeter Flying Post.
Ex Cath Lib	Exeter Cathedral Library.
FF	Devon Feet of Fines.
IPM	Inquisitions Post Mortem.
PRO	Public Record Office.
TDA	Transactions of the Devonshire Association.
TNHS	Transactions of the Torquay National History Society.
VC	Records of the College of Vicars Choral of Exeter Cathedral.
WCSL	West Country Studies Library, Castle Street, Exeter.

Chapter 1

The author is greatly indebted to Mrs. Margaret Parkinson for much of the contents of this chapter. Most of the artifacts found in the Woodbury area are excellently displayed in the Royal Albert Museum, Exeter.

1. *Roman Britain*. I.A. Richardson, Penguin Books 1955. pp. 145.
2. The axe head is in the possession of the Stokes family.
3. The excavation was carried out by Mrs. H. Miles (now Quinnell). See DAS 1975. pp 183-208.
4. *The Celtic World*. Barry Cunliffe. Constable 1992.
5. DAS No.45 (1987). pp. 59-73.
6. Aerial photo. RAF Film. County Hall, Exeter. No.106G/UK 1412 Ap.1946.
7. Torre Abbey Charter 96 (c.1240) mentions "milesteken" as a landmark at Greendale. See *Torre Abbey* by Deryk Seymour 1977 p.139.

Chapter 2

1. *The Westward Expansion of Wessex* – W.G. Hoskins. Leic. Univ. Press. 1960 p. 7.
2. Blackland is mentioned in 1434. VC/DD 3354.
3. Grindle Barton, Winkley, Hogsbrook, Wotton and Bridge all feature in the Greendale Charters. See *Torre Abbey* – Deryk Seymour 1977 pp. 133-146. Reginald de Wotton testified at Wm. Albemarle's death in 1361. PRO IPM Cl135 File 168 (3).
4. *Exeter Domesday Book*. O.J. Reichel pp. 388 and 407.
5. 'Virbecna' is mentioned as a landmark in Torre Abbey Charter 98 (c. 1250) See '*Torre Abbey*' p. 139. As fire-beacons were not used at the Norman Conquest, this must refer to an earlier use.

6. *Anglo-Saxon Chronicle* – (Everyman Edition 1962) p. 132.
7. *The Place-Names of Devon*. Vol. II p. 602.
8. VC/DD 3363 Ex Cath Lib.

Chapter 3

1. *The Beginnings of English Society*. Whitelock (Penguin). p. 46.
2. *Diplomatarium Anglicum Aevi Saxonici*. Benjamin Thorpe (MacMillan 1865) pp. 608/9.
3. I am grateful to Miss M. Dexter for help with these names.
4. Four 'Cotliffs'. See *Early Charters of Devon and Cornwall*. H.P.R. Finsberg (Leicester University Press) p. 9 Charter 19. Re: The King's Gift of a tenth of Royal Lands, "to the glory of God", see the *Anglo-Saxon Chronicle*. (Everyman edition) p. 67.
5. VC/DD 3360 Ex Cath Lib.

Chapter 4

1. *Two Thousand Years in Exeter*. W.G. Hoskins (Townsend 1960) p. 22.
2. *The Exeter Domesday Book*. Reichel p. 385.
3. *West Country Historical Studies*. H.P.R Finberg (David and Charles 1969) p. 135.
4. *The Domesday Geography of S.W. England*. Darby & Finn (C.U.P. 1967) p. 285.
5. PRO IPM C134, File 66 (21).
6. VC/3241 Ex Cath Lib.
7. Place-Names of Devon Pt. II p. 602.
8. *Ibid* p. 602. Michael de Exton testified in IPM c 133. File 54(4) PRO. 'Fishermen' seem to be well-established by 1407 – VC/DD 3351.

Chapter 5

There are numerous spellings of Albemarle – Alba Mara, Aumerle, Damerell etc. – but for clarity the modern spelling has been used throughout.

1. TDA Vol. 37 p. 414.
2. TDA Vol. 35 p. 299.
3. Cal. Close Rolls P. 341 WCSL.
4. FF p. 308 No. 606.
5. Deryk Seymour has dealt fully and readably with Greendale his his book *Torre Abbey*, to which readers are recommended. The Charter numbering is taken from his book, the translation from TNHS (1926-30) Vol. 5. p. 136.
6. FF p. 33. No. 54.
7. VC/3241 Ex Cath Lib.
8. PRO c 133/54.
9. *Devon*. W.G. Hoskins (1954) pp. 59/60.
10. *Devon Lay Subsidy of 1322*. Erskine DCRS 1969 pp. 103 & 119.
11. *Windmills of Devon*. W. Minchinton. Ex. Univ. 1977 p. 48.
12. PRO IPM File 54(4).
13. PRO IPM File 66 (21). Students are invited to reach their own conclusions on the family row, hinted at in IPM File 58 (5) and FF p. 11 no. 782.
14. Cal. Inq. Misc. Vol. 1 p. 507.

15. *Devon Place-Names*. Vol. II p. 602.
16. VC/DD 3359 (3).
17. Wm. Bonville's Will 1407 Moger Wills. DRO.
18. PRO IPM File 168 (5).
19. *Devon Lay Subsidy*. DCRS 1969 pp. 44 & 106.
20. PRO E 315/385 (folios 129-140).
21. John Hoppin's Will 1565. Moger Wills. DRO.
22. VC/3244.
23. *Complete Peerage*. G.E. Cokayne Vol. I. (1887) p. 55.

Chapter 6

1. VC/DD 3249 Ex Cath Lib.
2. When the Rev'd J.L. Fulford built the present vicarage in 1849 he made a note in the blank pages of the Burial Register (DRO) to the effect that he was the first Vicar of Woodbury to live at the Parsonage for 250 years.
3. VC/DD 3351.
4. VC/DD 3249.
5. VC/DD 3367.
6. VC/DD 3351 m.4.
7. Wm. Bonville's Will for 1407. Moger Wills. Vol. II.
8. VC/DD 3351 m.3.
9. Register of Bishop Stafford 1409. Ex Cath Lib.
10. VC/DD 3354.
11. G. Oliver. *Ecclesiastical Antiquities*. Exeter 1840 p. 34.
12. VC/DD 3366.
13. *Torre Abbey*. Seymour pp. 141-2.

Chapter 7

1. VC/DD 3247/8, 3358/9. Ex Cath Lib.
2. Reg. Ed. Lacy Bish. Ex. Vol. I p. 187.

Chapter 8

1. For local aspects of the Wars of the Roses see: R. Polwhele's *History of Devonshire*. Vol. I p. 250. *The Strife of the Roses & Days of the Tudors in the West*. Rogers TDA Vol. 18 p. 334.
2. *Devon* W.G. Hoskins. p. 82 and The Complete Peerage.
3. For general information on the Vestry & Tudor legislation see *The Parish Chest* by W.E. Tate (C.U.P. 1974).
4. Woodbury Malt Book DRO PX1.
5. VC/DD 3366 (5) Ex Cath Lib.
6. TDA 1950 p. 243.
7. TDA 1977 pp. 73-89.
8. PRO E 315/385.
9. *The Parish Chest*. Tate p. 190-1.
10. Report of the Charity Commissioners of Devon (Woodbury) 1823.

Chapter 9

1. For general background to the Reformation in England see Green's *A Short History of the English People*, Everyman Vol. I p. 328 onward.
2. *Devon* Hoskins p. 234.
3. For accounts of the Western Rebellion see Polwhele's *History of Devonshire* Vol. I, A.L. Rowse's *Tudor Cornwall*, and R.W. Dixon's *History of the Church of England* Vol. III pp. 51-79.
4. *The Devon Muster Rolls of 1569* ed. Howard & Stoate (1977).
5. General Information see *The Defeat of the Spanish Armada*, Garrett Mattingly.

Chapter 10

1. DRO Woodbury Charity Documents FT 8-9.
2. *Cadhay*. William-Powlett (handbook guide to the house).
3. *View of Devonshire in 1630*. Westcote (ed. 1845) p. 547.
4. PRO E 315/385.
5. DRO Z 15/42/4/3.
6. Oral tradition in the family called Woodbury, now living in Columbus, Ohio, U.S.A., who claim to be descended from the Goffes.
7. a) Walpole Society Vol. VII pp. 2-14. b) *Sculpture in Britain 1530-1830*, Whinney p. 24.

Chapter 11

1. *A Short History of the English People* J.R. Green, Everyman Vol. II pp. 444-458.
2. Woodbury Malt Book DRO PX1.
3. Wills (Moger). West Country Studies Library, Exeter.
4. *The Parish Chest.* W.E. Tate p. 242.
5. *The Custos and College of Vicars Choral in Exeter*. J.F. Chanter p. 21.
6. *A Short History of the English People*. Green p. 506.

Chapter 12

1. *The Book of Exmouth*. Robin Bush (Barracuda Books Ltd. 1977) p. 89.
2. *Devon*. W.G. Hoskins pp. 195-8.
3. *England's Recovery*. Spriggs (1854 edit.) pp. 170-1.
4. *Cadhay*. William-Powlett p. 6.
5. DRO Matthew Lee's Transcripts and Notes from the Parish Registers 2889Z F2.
6. *Custos and College of the Vicars Choral in Exeter*. Chanter pp. 25-6.
7. *Calamy Revised* (Edit. Matthews 1934) p. 204.
8. *Non-conformity in Woodbury & Lympstone*. David Keep. TDA 1977 p. 52.
9. *Devon*. Hoskins p. 252.
10. *Parish & Non-Parochial Registers of Devon & Cornwall*. Peskett. DCRS 1979 Intro. p. viii.
11. *The Parish Chest*. Tate p. 67.
12. *Education in the West of England*. Nicholas Orme. University of Exeter.
13. DCNQ Vol. I pt. 1. p. 225.
14. *A History of Presbyterian & General Baptist Churches in the West of England*. J. Murch 1835.

15. The original registers are on microfilm WCSL. Other papers relating to the Gulliford Meeting are held by the Trustees of George's Meeting, South Street, Exeter.

Chapter 13

1. Marriage settlement for George Venn's daughter. DRO 2694M.
2. Robert Venn's Will. DRO 2694M/F17.
3. Matthew Lee's Diary. DRO 2694M.
4. *Epidemics in Devon.* N.C. Oswald. TDA 1977 p. 97.

Chapter 14

1. DRO 96M/Box 49/3.
2. DRO 96M/Box 49/1.
3. *The Rolle Family.* Kaye. TDA 1977 p. 221.
4. Report of the Charity Commissioners for Devon 1823.
5. The Bishop's Questionnaire 1746. DRO No. 1287.
6. DRO 96M/Box 49/10.
7. DRO 1/17 Exeter Gaol Kalendar 1726-34.
8. DRO 96M/Box 49/18.
9. Notes made from documents belonging to Mrs. Esmé Thomson, Gilbrook House, now mislaid.
10. *A History of the Channel Islands* Raoul Lemprière. Hale 1974.
11. The purport of documents remembered, belonging to Mrs. Thomson, now mislaid.
12. DRO 2694M/LE 1 & 2.
13. Braddick, a subscriber and trustee of Gulliford Meeting was described *shipwright* in the Gulliford papers.
14. *General View of Agriculture in Devon.* Charles Vancouver 1808 p. 470.
15. DRO 96M/Box 50/2.

Chapter 15

1. For details of the Drakes of Nutwell see *The Family and Heirs of Sir Francis Drake* by Lady Elliot-Drake. (2 vols. London 1911).
2. The Bishop's Questionnaire 1746. DRO No. 1287.
3. DRO 2694M/LE1.
4. Vancouver's *General View of Agriculture in Devon,* 1808 p. 371.
5. *Railway Competition and Turnpike Rds in E. Devon.* Kanefsky TDA 1977 p. 59.
6. *A Turnpike Key.* Buckingham p. 12 WCSL.
7. *From Trackway to Turnpike.* Sheldon 1928 p. 98.
8. Minute Books of the Woodbury Bench DRO 1820P/M1-6.
9. The Vestry Minute Book from 1779 is still in use and kept by the Vestry Clerk.
10. The Teed and Rack Field references come from old deeds formerly in the possession of Mrs. Esmé Thomson, Gilbrook House, Woodbury but now mislaid.
11. "John Beal (fell-monger)" signed himself thus in a memorandum concerning the Yew Tree in the Churchyard in 1775, a copy of which belongs to the author. The Church Rate List for 1779 shows John Beal was at Beals.
12. *The Devon Cloth Industry in the 18th c.* Chapman. D & CRS 1978 p. 151.

13. a) Gulliford Register of Baptisms and Burials (microfilm WCSL). b) Account Book for Browns Farm from 1786 owned by Mr. J. Dagworthy, Browns Farm, Woodbury Salterton.

Chapter 16

1. EFP 7.12.1770 and 13.8.1779. WCSL.
2. Browns Farm Account Book. Property of Mr. Jeffrey Dagworthy.
3. *Devon.* Hoskins p. 74.
4. The Will of Mary Gregory in 1848 shows them to have been cottages since Langdon's time (Mrs. Langdon died in 1796).
5. EFP 7.5.1801.
6. Church Wardens' Accounts, current book in the keeping of the Vestry Clerk.
7. This and other references to 1808 come from Charles Vancouver's *General View of Agriculture in Devon* 1808.
8. EFP 12.8.1803.
9. Causes for the decline of Gulliford Meeting are put forward in Dr. David Keep's article TDA 1977 p. 55.
10. Tithe Apportionment Award for Woodbury DRO.
11. The property of Mr. J. Dagworthy, Browns Farm, Woodbury Salterton.
12. TDA 1950 p. 225.
13. *Woodbury News.* April 1965 p. 12.
14. From an inventory of the contents of Nutwell compiled in 1857, in the possession of the author.
15. Ware Family Tree — Mrs. E. Thomson, Gilbrook House, Woodbury.
16. *Epidemics in Devon 1538-1837.* Oswald. TDA 1977 p. 110.
17. Reports of Select Vestry. DRO Woodbury PV1. Details of Jarman family from Registers.
18. Mr. Furse's notes in the possession of the author.

Chapter 17

1. *Woodbury News.* July 1974.
2. TDA 1950, 47th Report on Folklore pp. 107-112.
3. DRO 382 add/E 1432.
4. *Notes on the Church of St. Swithin, Woodbury*, J.L. Fulford M.A., 1893. A copy of this address given to the Plymouth Institution is in the possession of the Vicar of Woodbury.
5. Medical Directory 1849-1853.
6. Pamphlet in the possession of Mr. Jeffrey Dagworthy.
7. A Talk on Old Woodbury given to the Woodbury W.I. in the 1930s by Robert Furse, Clerk to the Council. Possession of author.
8. The Diary of Isaac Critchard Wilson in the possession of George Wilson, Bidgoods Farm, Woodbury Salterton.
9. EFP 5.1.1860 (WCSL).
10. EFP 11.4.1860, 2.5.60, 27.4.64, 22.3.65.
11. EFP 22.7.1868.
12. Re Brent's directorship: DRO Rolle Estate Papers 96M/Box 27/1. Opening of Railway: *Book of Exmouth.* Bush p. 59.
13. DRO 96M/Box 39/15.

14. EFP 21.2.1872.
15. A collection of newspaper cuttings and other information kindly made available by the Brent Lodge of Freemasons, Topsham.
16. Sale Catalogue. Mr. H.G. Stokes, Woodbury.

Chapter 18

1. DRO 1077M/6/6.
2. Isaac Wilson's Diary, see note 8 Chapt. 17.
3. The story of Salterton in the 19th century is contained in a remarkable collection of letters and other memorabilia in an exercise book, in the custody of the Headmaster, Woodbury Salterton School.
4. Deeds in the possession of the owner of the present Bridge Farm.

Chapter 19

1. Unless otherwise stated the information in this chapter has been gleaned from the Tithe Apportionment Award 1839, the 1841, 51, 61 & 71 National Census Returns, newspaper reports from the Exeter Flying Post etc., the Church Vestry Minutes, 1848-1884 (privately owned by Mr. H.G. Stokes, Webbers Farm, Woodbury) the Church-wardens' Accounts 1779-1938 (Clerk to the Church Council), and White's, Billings & Kelly's Directories for the period.
2. Compare Benjamin Donn's Map 1765; O.S. 3-in. map 1809 and Tithe Map 1839.
3. a) *Alumi Oxoniensis 1715-1886* (Parker 1888) p. 461. b) Information kindly supplied by the Church-warden at Crundale.
4. Copy of Tax Return for Woodbury 1849 in the possession of Mr. Dagworthy.
5. History of Preston House (M.S.) by Ronald Heath – possession of author.
6. For full information about Honiton lace and "Woodbury Greek", see *The History of The Honiton Lace Industry*. H.J. Yallop. University of Exeter Press.
7. Exeter Turnpike Trust papers. Box 11, Bundle 2, pt. 4 DRO.
8. The Drainage Co's original working plan in the possession of Mr. Brian Glanvill, Bagmores Farm, Woodbury.

Chapter 20

1. Report of the Charity Commissioners for Devon. (Woodbury) 1823.
2. Broadmead School Log-Book. DRO 773 C/EFL1.
3. Woodbury Church Primary School Log-Book, in the custody of the Headmaster.
4. Vestry Minute Book. H.G. Stokes, Woodbury.
5. EFP 26.1.1792 WCSL.
6. Woodbury Parish Council's first Minute Book. DRO PX1 PR2.

Chapter 21

Most of the material for this chapter has come from the personal recollections of older residents and from their family documents, wills, letters etc.

1. History of Christ Church & The Brethren. E. Ware, *Woodbury News*, May & June 1965.
2. The Fulfords Pts 1 & 2, *Woodbury News*, July & August 1974.
3. Woodbury Fifty Years Ago. M.I. Turner. *Woodbury News*, Oct. 1964 p. 15.
4. Woodbury Looks Back. *Woodbury News*, Oct. 1979 pp. 15-17.
5. Home Guard Supplement. *Woodbury News*, Nov. 1980 pp. 11-14.

Part II
The Church

1. *Worthies of Devon*. John Prince (Exeter 1701).
2. a) Notes on work at the church written by J.L. Fulford in the empty pages of the Register of Deaths, DRO. b) Notes on the Church of St. Swithin, Woodbury 1893. Possession of the Vicar.
3. In the 1569 Muster Roll, Thomas Haydon, son of Richard, was assessed at £40 p.a. with 9 other "men of substance" in Woodbury.
4. See article *An Oak Bed at Montacute: a Study in Mannerist Decoration* by Anthony Wells-Cole. Furniture History XVII, 1981 p. 5.
5. *Ecclesiastical Antiquities of Devon*. G. Oliver (Exeter 1840-42) p. 23.
6. *The Visitations of the County of Devon*. J.L. Vivian (Exeter 1895) p. 624.
7. Condensed from an article by the Rev'd J.G.M. Scott in *The Ringing World* 26th July 1968 and used here by kind permission of the author and the Editor.
8. Vestry Minute Book. (Stokes).

Nutwell

Except where otherwise stated, the material for this chapter has come from *The Family and Heirs of Sir Francis Drake* by Lady Elliot-Drake.

1. *Feudal Aids* Vol. I p. 381.
2. *History of Devonshire*, Polwhele pp. 209-10 and footnote.
3. VC/DD 3352 & 3354 Ex Cath Lib.
4. EFP 10-1813 Report of Sale.
5. DRO 59/6/1/3(c).
6. DRO 96M/Box 27/1.
7. White's Directory 1878 p. 856.

The Great Field

1. a) *The Open Field in Devon*, W.G. Hoskins and H.P.R. Finberg (Devonshire Studies). b) *A Geographical Study of the Field Systems of Devon & Cornwall*, H.S.A. Fox. TDA 1972.
2. In the South-West, Braunton Great Field in N. Devon and The Lands at Portland in Dorset are well worth a visit.
3. a) General information from *The Open Fields*, C.S. & C.S. Orwin O.U.P. b) Local information on ploughing terms and customs from Mr. Geo. Wilson, Bidgoods Farm, Woodbury Salterton.
4. VC/DD 3354 Ex Cath Lib.
5. Domesday Book.
6. VC/3241.
7. IPM C 133, File 66 (21), 168 (5), PRO.
8. VC/DD 3351, 3354, 3359, 3366, 22234.
9. Common grazing rights at Heathfield are mentioned in the 1525 survey of Cecily Bonville's land in Woodbury. E 315/385 PRO.
10. *English Farming Past and Present*. Ernle (Heinemann 1961) p. 28.
11. *Place-Names of Devon*, p. 601.
12. R.A.F. Film at County Hall, Exeter. No.106G/UK, 1412, Ap. 1946.
13. VC/DD 22280.
14. *History of English Farming*, C.S. Orwin (Nelson 1949) pp. 22, 23.

Building Materials

1. Specification of Parsonage House DRO. 382 add/E 1432.
2. VC/DD 3367. Ex Cath Lib.
3. *The Story of Woodbury.* A.W. Leyland (1947) p. 34.
4. From verbatim account of Mr. James Hill.
5. *The Pattern of English Building.* A. Clifton-Taylor (Faber 1972) p. 220.
6. EFP 4.4.1860, 25.4.1860, 30.9.1863, 16.3.1864. My thanks are due to Mr. S.G. Spriggs for observations about the field excavations. His house, Conifers, is built on part of it.
7. *English Brickwork.* Brunskill and Clifton-Taylor (Ward Lock 1977) pp. 40-41.
8. Information from the late Mr. Jack Turbitt of Woolbrook, Sidmouth.
9. VC/DD 3351/2.
10. *Devon.* Hoskins p. 264.
11. *Devon Monastic Lands.* J. Youings, DCRS 1955 pp. 86-7.
12. Gilbrook Cottages were saved from demolition and by the author in 1965.
13. Account Book of Robert Phillips, possession of the author.
14. *The Pattern of English Building.* Clifton-Taylor pp. 390-3.
15. Description by Mr. Harry Jarman of Woodbury.
16. Report after an inspection by the S.P.A.B. 1970.
17. Information from Wm. Phillips' great-granddaughter, Mrs. V. Stediford.

Wildlife Neighbours and Friends?

1. VC/DD 3366 Ex Cath Lib. "Expenses in delivering wood to Henry Westcote for making a new hall." "Delivery of timber to Nicholas Bertelet for our new tenement." 1481 "Cost of houses . . . payments to Wm. Cortenaye and Wm. Worde for cutting down trees."
2. These three uses lasted until the end of the last century. From Isaac Wilson's diary:-
   1867 Ch. Skinner had a seam of ript oak wood 3/6. (The bark had been stripped off for the tannery.)
   1862 Mr. Jones had 10 seams of browse @ 1/- per seam 10/-
   1868 Fraith for staddling 2/6 (brushwood for the foundation of a corn stack.)
3. This was called agistment. Parts of Rockham Wood were traditionally used. a) VC/DD 3367 Agisters included "Richard Hoppyng for his part of the wood of Ruccombe . . ." b) PRO E 315/385. "Edward Hawle holds one close of pasture called Rotcombe Wood containing 60 acres."
4. One example is found in VC/DD 3352.
5. a) *Torre Abbey* — Seymour, pp. 139, 145. b) *The Possessions of Torre Abbey in Woodbury.* Hugh R. Watkin, TNHS, 1926-30. pp. 133, 137, 138.
6. See note 3b above, also:- "William Webber holds one close called Woodbury Wood containing 160 acres of woodland."
7. The manor of Woodbury passed to the Rolle family in 1633. Most of the Rolle papers are catalogued in DRO.
8. *General View of the Agriculture of Devon.* Vancouver, 1808.
9. See note 5.
10. The same source as note 3b.
11. *Field Systems of East and South Devon.* H.S.A. Fox. TDA 1972, p. 98.

12. Nearly 5% of the parish were paupers by 1793. *The History of Devonshire.* Richard Polwhele, Vol. 2, p. 209.
13. Middleton's *View of the Agriculture of the County of Middlesex.* 1798.
14. Vancouver (see note 8) describes the uses of hedge timber in several chapters. The Rolle records (see note 7) include details of the management of hedges in several of the lease documents, including landlord's and tenant's rights.
15. More information in *Hedges*, E. Pollard, M.D. Hooper and N.W. Moore, 1977.
16. See note 5a.

INDEX

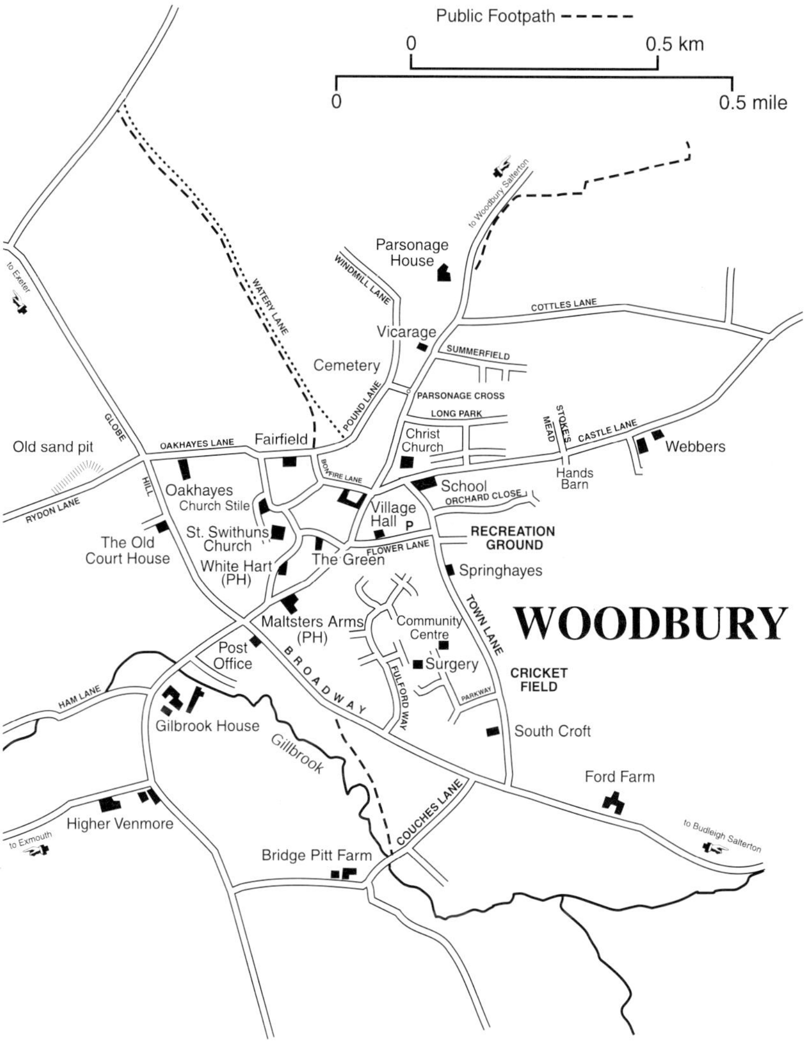
Public Footpath
0
0.5 km
0
0.5 mile
WOODBURY
to Exeter
to Woodbury Salterton
to Exmouth
to Budleigh Salterton
Parsonage House
WINDMILL LANE
WATERY LANE
Vicarage
COTTLES LANE
SUMMERFIELD
Cemetery
POUND LANE
PARSONAGE CROSS
LONG PARK
GLOBE
HILL
Old sand pit
OAKHAYES LANE
Fairfield
Christ Church
STOKE'S MEAD
CASTLE LANE
Webbers
Hands Barn
RYDON LANE
Oakhayes
Church Stile
BONFIRE LANE
School
ORCHARD CLOSE
Village Hall
P
RECREATION GROUND
St. Swithuns Church
The Old Court House
White Hart (PH)
The Green
FLOWER LANE
Springhayes
TOWN LANE
Maltsters Arms (PH)
Community Centre
Post Office
Surgery
CRICKET FIELD
BROADWAY
FULFORD WAY
PARKWAY
HAM LANE
Gilbrook House
Gillbrook
South Croft
Ford Farm
COUCHES LANE
Higher Venmore
Bridge Pitt Farm

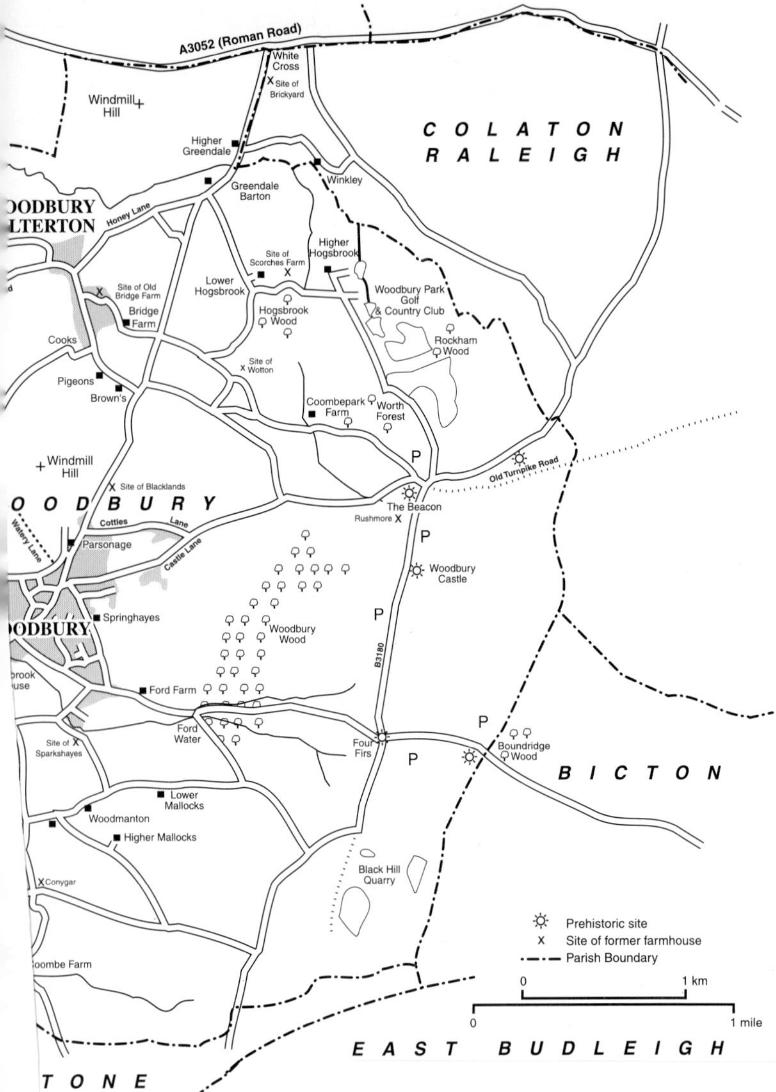

A3052 (Roman Road)
White Cross
Site of Brickyard
Windmill Hill
Higher Greendale
Greendale Barton
Winkley
COLATON RALEIGH
WOODBURY SALTERTON
Honey Lane
Higher Hogsbrook
Site of Scorches Farm
Lower Hogsbrook
Site of Old Bridge Farm
Bridge Farm
Hogsbrook Wood
Woodbury Park Golf & Country Club
Rockham Wood
Cooks
Site of Wotton
Pigeons
Brown's
Coombepark Farm
Worth Forest
Windmill Hill
Site of Blacklands
Old Turnpike Road
The Beacon
Rushmore
WOODBURY
Cottles Lane
Watery Lane
Parsonage
Castle Lane
Woodbury Castle
Springhayes
Woodbury Wood
B3180
Ford Farm
Ford Water
Four Firs
Site of Sparkshayes
Boundridge Wood
BICTON
Lower Mallocks
Woodmanton
Higher Mallocks
Black Hill Quarry
Conygar
Prehistoric site
Site of former farmhouse
Parish Boundary
0
1 km
0
1 mile
EAST BUDLEIGH

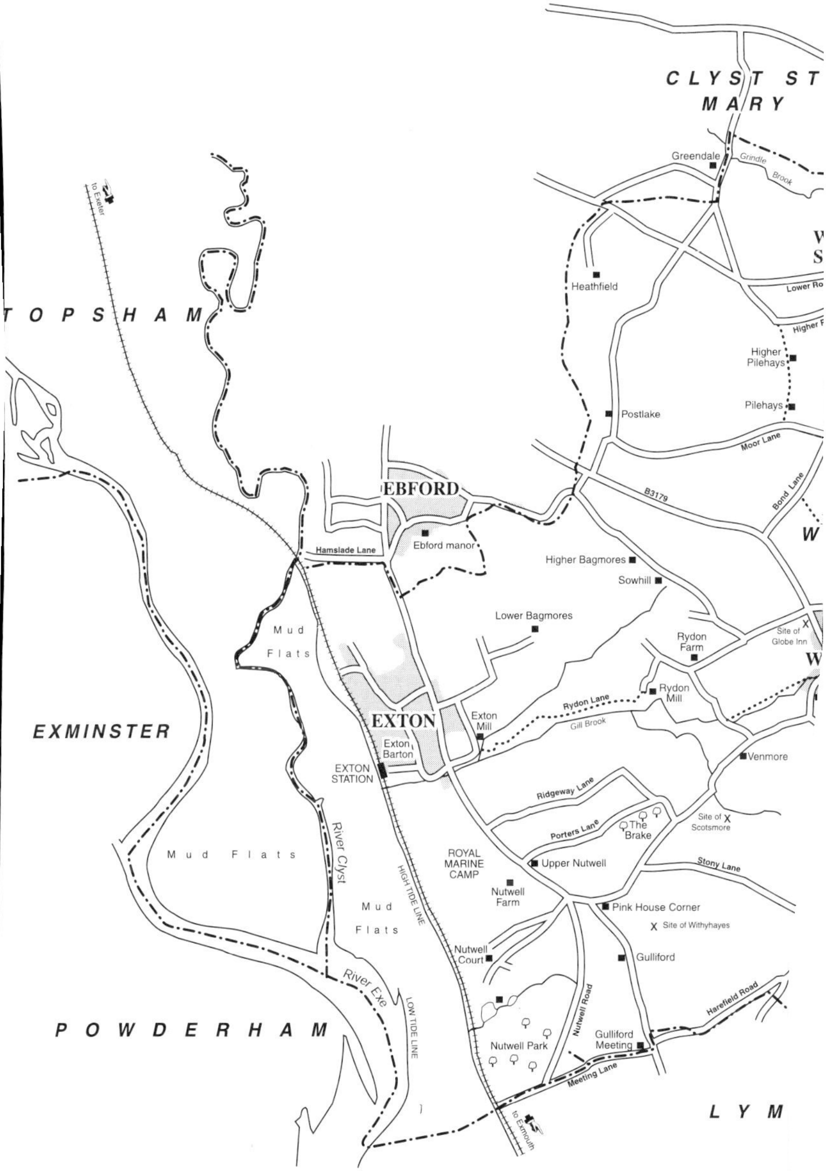

CLYST ST
MARY
Greendale
Grindle Brook
Heathfield
Lower Ro
Higher
Higher Pilehays
Pilehays
Postlake
Moor Lane
Bond Lane
B3179
to Exeter
TOPSHAM
EBFORD
Ebford manor
Hamslade Lane
Higher Bagmores
Sowhill
Lower Bagmores
Rydon Farm
Site of Globe Inn
Rydon Mill
Rydon Lane
Gill Brook
Mud Flats
EXMINSTER
EXTON
Exton Mill
Exton Barton
EXTON STATION
Venmore
Ridgeway Lane
Site of Scotsmore
The Brake
Porters Lane
Mud Flats
River Clyst
ROYAL MARINE CAMP
Upper Nutwell
Stony Lane
HIGH TIDE LINE
Nutwell Farm
Mud Flats
Pink House Corner
Site of Withyhayes
Nutwell Court
Gulliford
River Exe
LOW TIDE LINE
Harefield Road
POWDERHAM
Nutwell Road
Nutwell Park
Gulliford Meeting
Meeting Lane
to Exmouth
LYM